Approaches to Teaching Baudelaire's Prose Poems

Approaches to Teaching Baudelaire's Prose Poems

Edited by

Cheryl Krueger

The Modern Language Association of America
New York   2017

MLA and the MODERN LANGUAGE ASSOCIATION are trademarks
owned by the Modern Language Association of America.
For information about obtaining permission to reprint material from
MLA book publications, send your request by mail (see address below)
or e-mail (permissions@mla.org).

Library of Congress Cataloging-in-Publication Data
Names: Krueger, Cheryl L., editor.
Title: Approaches to teaching Baudelaire's prose poems / edited by Cheryl Krueger.
Description: New York : The Modern Language Association of America, 2017. |
Series: Approaches to teaching world literature |
Includes bibliographical references and index.
Identifiers: LCCN 2016054824 (print) |
LCCN 2017007434 (ebook) |
ISBN 9781603292719 (cloth : alk. paper) |
ISBN 9781603292726 (pbk. : alk. paper) |
ISBN 9781603292733 (EPUB) |
ISBN 9781603292740 (Kindle)
Subjects: LCSH: Baudelaire, Charles, 1821–1867 — Study and teaching. |
Prose poems, French — History and criticism.
Classification: LCC PQ2191.Z5 A666 2017 (print) | LCC PQ2191.Z5 (e-book) |
DDC 841/.8 — dc23
LC record available at https://lccn.loc.gov/2016054824

Approaches to Teaching World Literature 142
ISSN 1059-1133

Cover illustration of the paperback and electronic editions:
Carriages and Promenaders on the Avenue des Champs-Elysses,
watercolor on paper, by Constantin Guys (1802–92), Musée de la Ville
de Paris, Musée Carnavalet, Paris, France, Bridgeman Images

Published by The Modern Language Association of America
85 Broad Street, suite 500, New York, New York 10004-2434
www.mla.org

CONTENTS

ACKNOWLEDGMENTS

Respondents to the online survey provided helpful information on the relevance of the prose poems today. I am grateful to every participant. I thank all of the contributors to this volume for their patience and dedication, for providing a spectrum of perspectives on the prose poems, and for sharing the knowledge and insight that each essay offers. I am especially indebted to friends and colleagues who offered support at various stages of this book's composition. Some read my essay and introductory chapters along the way; others were available to answer questions or to dig up references at a moment's notice; still others offered advice and encouragement. Thank you, Aimée Boutin, Scott Carpenter, Ross Chambers, Françoise Lionnet, Claire Chi-ah Lyu, Steve Murphy, Catherine Nesci, Amy Ogden, Laurence M. Porter, David Powell, Maria Scott, Sonya Stephens, and John Urbach. I am also grateful to the knowledgeable, anonymous peer reviewers and to James Hatch, who offered expert guidance from proposal to prospectus to final manuscript.

PREFACE

One of France's best known and most influential poets, Charles Baudelaire (1821–67) has been called a Romantic, a realist, a symbolist, a decadent, a modern, and an antimodern. He did not belong to a movement or school, yet he knew, admired, and criticized contemporary Romantic poets. Best known for his volumes of verse (*Les Fleurs du Mal* [*Flowers of Evil*]; 1857) and prose poems (*Le Spleen de Paris* [*Paris Spleen*]; 1869), Baudelaire was also a prolific art critic, essayist, and translator. Though he published one short story early in his career (*La Fanfarlo* [1847]), his plans to complete more short fiction, plays, and novels never came to fruition. Drafts and notes for these works appear in the two-volume *Œuvres complètes*, edited by Claude Pichois. Baudelaire's deceptively titled *Journaux intimes* (which was not a daily journal but was always intended for publication) features both acerbic and poignant observations, usually with no commentary or elaboration, often delivered in shocking bursts that he called *fusées*, borrowing Edgar Allan Poe's term for rhetorical sky rocketing.

Baudelaire referred to the prose poems project as a *pendant*, a complement to his verse. The noun *pendant* (meaning "pendant" or "counterpart") captures the dynamic of temporal and spatial simultaneity that characterizes the relation of Baudelaire's two revolutionary works. *Le Spleen de Paris*, published posthumously as a single volume, may appear to have been written by Baudelaire later in life, as an afterthought or follow-up project to *Les Fleurs du Mal*, but, in fact, Baudelaire began drafting prose poems as early as 1855, eventually publishing six pieces in 1857 — the very year *Les Fleurs du Mal* was released, condemned, and censored. Nine more prose poems appeared in 1861; the following year *La Presse* printed twenty-six pieces. Finally, in 1869 — two years after Baudelaire's death — Charles Asselineau and Théodore de Banville compiled all Baudelaire's completed prose poems in volume 4 of *Œuvres complètes*, following the table of contents Baudelaire had left with his notes. Since that time, *Le Spleen de Paris* (also published today under the title *Petits Poèmes en prose*) has appeared in numerous editions and anthologies. The evasiveness of the volume's title (translated as *The Little Prose Poems*, *Short Prose Poems*, *Prose Poems*, *Paris Spleen*, *Paris Blues*, and *The Parisian Prowler*) and the nonconformity of the genre, style, and content contribute to the lasting appeal of this innovative work.

Baudelaire's writing reflects his time in distinctive ways. He was twenty-seven years old when the upheaval of 1848 brought down the July Monarchy, replacing it with the short-lived Second Republic (1848–51). By the time Baudelaire published his *Fleurs du Mal* (1857), Napoléon Bonaparte's nephew Louis-Napoléon Bonaparte had taken the throne as Napoléon III, leading France into a Second Empire (1852–70). Because several of Baudelaire's prose poems were drafted during these times of rapid change, his work has been read by many (most notably, Walter Benjamin) as a testament to the condition of the artist during a time of social upheaval, urban expansion, and an increasingly consumption-oriented culture.

If *Le Spleen de Paris* in particular has been considered an expression of modern urban life, this is due in no small part to Baudelaire's comments published in a dedicatory letter to Arsène Houssaye in *La Presse* in 1862, usually included in modern editions as a preface. Though his dubious homage to Houssaye has been the subject of much debate, Baudelaire's letter has been read as an ersatz manifesto of the prose poem genre. Inspired by the city streets, Baudelaire set out to depict modern life in a deliberately divergent form of Aloysius Bertrand's poetic prose. In the letter to Houssaye, Baudelaire claims that one of the most attractive features of the prose poems is their adaptability to readers:

> Mon cher ami, je vous envoie un petit ouvrage dont on ne pourrait pas dire, sans injustice, qu'il n'a ni tête ni queue, puisque tout, au contraire, y est à la fois tête et queue, alternativement et réciproquement. . . . Quel est celui de nous qui n'a pas, dans ses jours d'ambition, rêvé le miracle d'une prose poétique, musicale sans rythme et sans rime, assez souple et heurtée pour s'adapter aux mouvements lyriques de l'âme, aux ondulations de la rêverie, aux soubresauts de la conscience?   (*Spleen* [Pichois] 275–76)

> My dear friend, I send you this little work of which it cannot be said without injustice, that it has neither head nor tail, since, on the contrary, everything in it is both head and tail alternatively and reciprocally. . . . Which of us has not, in his ambitious days, dreamed of the miracle of a poetic prose, musical without rhythm and without rhyme, supple enough and choppy enough to fit the soul's lyrical movements, the undulations of reverie, the jolts of consciousness?   (*Parisian Prowler* 129)

Baudelaire was obviously not thinking of future students. Yet it is remarkable just how adaptable and influential the prose poems have proven to be for readers of all kinds, in different times and places.

Though not the first to write prose poetry, Baudelaire's work generated deep, lasting interest in this subversive, once surprising, literary practice. Some of the most prominent modern poetry, in France and beyond, owes at least its formal inspiration to *Le Spleen de Paris*, whose impact on poets such as Arthur Rimbaud, Stéphane Mallarmé, Lautréamont, Max Jacob, Henri Michaux, Francis Ponge, and Saint-John Perse is unmistakable. *Le Spleen de Paris* changed the course of poetry beyond France as well, paving the way for future writers of the prose poem genre: Jorge Luis Borges, T. S. Eliot, Franz Kafka, Rainer Maria Rilke, Walt Whitman, and Gertrude Stein, to name only a few. As Adrian Wanner remarks in a discussion of Ivan Turgenev and Baudelaire, "Interestingly enough, it was less Baudelaire's *Les Fleurs du Mal* than his *Petits poèmes en prose* that seemed to have had the greatest impact on Russian 'pre-decadence' of the 1880s" (61).

Despite (or perhaps because of) their initial readability (the language and syntax are not particularly difficult), the prose poems raise important questions about how to read both prose and poetic language. Though some of the pieces have lyric qualities, many tell stories, even at some length. For this reason, student readers (like many scholars) often find it challenging to discuss *Le Spleen de Paris* as poetry. At the same time, the often intrusive yet never identified narrative persona(e) and the shifting tone (from sentimental to ironic to abrasive) make the prose poems resistant to classification in terms of more traditional prose genres. An initial encounter with a piece such as "Le Vieux Saltimbanque" ("The Old Acrobat") still easily provokes initial consternation and dismay, as it did for one of the genre's first serious scholars, Suzanne Bernard (1959), who found the piece's everyday subject matter and journalistic tone antipoetic.

It is important, in any class setting, to encourage and respect students' first reactions before guiding them toward thinking objectively and critically and helping them formulate questions and carve out paths of inquiry suggested by those initial, subjective reactions. Just as generations of critics have turned to the prose poems to practice textual analysis, students who are properly guided will discover, through close reading of selected works, the power of rhetoric, figurative language, and narrative devices. Because so many of the pieces are brief, they lend themselves, unabridged, to a careful, detailed reading.

Le Spleen de Paris remains particularly engaging for students and scholars today because its form and content still challenge conventional boundaries. Owing perhaps to their transitional status, students understand duality, indecisiveness, the feeling of being pulled in two directions, and the urge to embrace contradictory convictions. Such emotions are implicit in the prose poem genre and are played out in the individual works. Students recognize that humor and irony can lead to sentimentality and earnestness and back again in the course of brief prose utterances. They are able to identify with the narrators' moods and dilemmas: the impulse to do what one should not in "Le Mauvais Vitrier" ("The Bad Glazer"); the desire to escape in "L'Invitation au voyage" ("Invitation to the Voyage") or "N'importe où hors du monde" ("Anywhere out of the world"); the writer's self-doubt in "À une heure du matin" ("At One O'Clock in the Morning"). The sense of chance encounter, of simultaneous observation and participation, of being at once an individual and part of a crowd ("Les Foules")—all these experiences draw students to the prose poems and, just as important, to nineteenth-century Paris.

With content, culture, and "authentic text" (readings composed by and for native speakers rather than scripted for pedagogical use) now a mainstay of second-language learning, the prose poems have a place in language courses as well. Because so many of the poems are succinct, it is not necessary to abridge them for use in lower-level classes. Students may explore just one or two poems in depth. Specialists in applied linguistics and researchers in second language acquisition have developed theoretically informed strategies for teaching reading skills: these strategies make the incorporation of literature in language courses more meaningful for students. Although we tend to speak of language and content courses separately, the gap between the two has narrowed significantly in the last two decades. Practically speaking, at many institutions the instructor who offers a course on nineteenth-century French poetry is also teaching fourth-semester French language. While some of the same prose poems can be read at both levels, pedagogical approaches should be tailored to the appropriate language level to keep students motivated and engaged.

The ambiguity of the genre, the unusual narrative and lyrical qualities of the individual poems, their historical and cultural resonance, and the richness and originality of the second volume have persuaded teachers to include it in their courses, both within and beyond French language and literature curricula. Survey respondents indicated that the prose poems play a significant role in the study of nineteenth-century French fiction and poetry, as well as in French language courses, translation studies, English and comparative literature, and a wide range of interdisciplinary topics. The prose poems appear in literary anthologies and on reading lists throughout North America and France and are included in the French literature portion of the 2015 *agrégation* (the competitive national examination necessary for high-ranking teaching posts in secondary-schools and universities).

Part One

MATERIALS

Editions and Translations

Most often used in scholarly citations of Baudelaire's work, the two-volume Pléiade edition of Baudelaire's complete works, *Œuvres complètes*, edited by Claude Pichois, remains a valuable resource for writers, though it is not the most practical for classroom use. Robert Kopp's much cited 1969 edition, *Petits Poëmes en prose*, is unfortunately out of print but can still be found at university libraries and in the personal collections of many Baudelaire scholars.

Instructors may select from countless affordable paperback editions in French, with various degrees of annotation (see the listing of editions of Baudelaire's prose poems in this volume's list of works cited). Designed for French high school students preparing for the *baccalauréat* exam, the Hatier edition (in the Classiques and CIE Lycée series), edited by Alain Couprie and Johan Faerber (2013), includes definitions in glosses on each page, along with study guides in the appendix. Kopp's 2006 Gallimard edition includes an introduction by Georges Blin (previously published in Blin's 1948 *Le Sadisme de Baudelaire*). The Flammarion edition, with an introduction, notes, and bibliography by David Scott and Barbara Wright (1987), was recommended by many survey respondents. Also highly recommended was *Baudelaire: Le Spleen de Paris: Petits poèmes en prose*, edited by Jean-Luc Steinmetz (2003), which was featured on the reading list for the 2105 *agrégation*.

Most contributors to this volume quote in English from Edward Kaplan's translation, *The Parisian Prowler: Le Spleen de Paris: Petits poèmes en prose* (1997). The translation takes its name from "Le Rôdeur parisien," a title Baudelaire considered but never used in publication. Survey respondents underscored the importance of comparing translations. In addition to Kaplan's *Parisian Prowler*, among the most often mentioned were Rosemary Lloyd's *The Prose Poems and* La Fanfarlo (1991), Louise Varèse's *Paris Spleen* (1947 and 1970), Keith Waldrop's *Paris Spleen: Little Prose Poems* (2009), Michael Hamburger's *Twenty Prose Poems* (a French/English edition; 1946 and 2001), Arthur Symons's 1905 *Poems in Prose from Charles Baudelaire* (includes eleven prose poems and the verse epilogue), Martin Sorrell's *Paris Spleen* (2010), and Francis Scarfe's side-by-side French-English edition, *Paris Blues* (2012). *Baudelaire in English* (in Penguin's Poets in Translation series [1997]) includes both *Les Fleurs du Mal* and *Le Spleen de Paris*, with contributions by more than sixty translators, many of them well-known writers and poets. It is also worth checking the ever-expanding selection of e-books for translated editions, such as Project Gutenberg's *Poems and Prose Poems of Charles Baudelaire*.

While some respondents say that they steer away from digital versions of Baudelaire's work, others report using only online resources, both for homework assignments and in-class textual analysis. Most advocate a blend of digital and print texts, from rare books to projected and highlighted digital copies of the prose poems, depending on the goals and logistics of the activity. Online databases like *Gallica* make it possible to bring to the classroom early versions of the prose poems in their original layout (see Catherine Nesci's essay in this volume for a detailed discussion of how to implement these sources). Several respondents report that the availability *of Le Spleen de Paris* and *Les Fleurs du Mal* at sites including athena.unige.ch/athena/baudelaire/spleen/baudelaire_petits _poemes_prose.html, *Charles Baudelaire's* Les Fleurs du Mal / Flowers of Evil (fleursdumal.org), and *Charles Baudelaire* (baudelaire.litteratura.com) has facilitated efforts to have students browse and select for themselves the works that they want to study in depth. Online access also allows instructors and students to consult poems as they come up naturally in the course of discussion, even if they were not on the syllabus for that day.

The Instructor's Library

Baudelaire's Life and Work

In entries from 1832 to 1866, Claude Pichois's two-volume collection of Baudelaire's letters, *Correspondance* (1973), tells a partial but intriguing story of the poet's constant financial hardships, publication plans, and the famously fraught relationship with his mother and stepfather. Rosemary Lloyd has translated a number of these letters in *Selected Letters of Charles Baudelaire* (2006). An illuminating companion piece to Baudelaire's letters, W. T. Bandy's *Baudelaire devant ses contemporains* ([1995] now in a third edition; also published in English as *Baudelaire Judged by His Contemporaries [1845–1867]*) presents commentary from friends and acquaintances, organized in chronological order from 1840, when Baudelaire was nineteen, to 1867, the year he died.

Baudelaire's enduring image as a pink-gloved dandy with a mordant wit was nurtured by contemporaries who wrote books on the poet's life and work, including Théophile Gautier (*Baudelaire* [1868]), Charles Asselineau (*Charles Baudelaire: Sa vie et son œuvre* [1869]), and Nadar (*Charles Baudelaire intime: Le Poète vierge* [1911]). Later, even Jean-Paul Sartre discussed Baudelaire's eccentricities, though with far less admiration (*Baudelaire* [1946]). Pichois and Jean Ziegler's detailed biography, *Baudelaire* (1987), focuses on the author's work, its reception, and its historical context. The abridged translation by Graham Robb (1989) as well Enid Starkie's *Baudelaire* (1958) are recommended by instructors, though Starkie's book is now out of print. Alex de Jonge's *Baudelaire, Prince of Clouds: A Biography* (1976), Joanna Richardson's *Baudelaire* (1994), and Rosemary Lloyd's *Charles Baudelaire* (2008) are especially recommended for reading in English. As the title suggests, Frank Hilton's *Baudelaire in Chains: Portrait of the Artist as a Drug Addict* (2004) examines Baudelaire's personality in relation to his commonly acknowledged, though not widely discussed, drug use.

Historical and Social Contexts

Walter Benjamin's essays on Baudelaire and Second Empire Paris were among the most cited secondary works in our survey. For advanced scholars, the incomplete *Passagenwerk* (written between 1927 and 1940 and published posthumously) is available in a 1,088-page English paperback edition (*Arcades Project*). The more manageable selections of essays in *The Writer of Modern Life: Essays on Charles Baudelaire* (2006) work well for class assignments, as does the French volume *Charles Baudelaire, un poète lyrique à l'apogée du capitalisme* (1980). The massive volume *Baudelaire* (2013), edited by Giorgio Agamben, Barbara Chitussi, and Clemens-Carl Härle, offers a fascinating reconstruction of Benjamin's planned but never written book on Baudelaire, painstakingly reconstructed from Benjamin's notes. Richard D. E. Burton's studies focus on Baudelaire's literary production in historical context: *Baudelaire in 1859: A Study in the Sources of Poetic Creativity* (2009), *Baudelaire and the Second Empire* (1991), and *The Flâneur and His City: Patterns of Daily Life in Paris, 1815–1851* (2010). *Baudelaire journaliste: Articles et chroniques*, edited by Alain Vaillant (2011), presents selected works of Baudelaire's (especially lesser-known texts) chronologically as they first appeared in the press.

The Prose Poem Genre in France

Suzanne Bernard's foundational *Le Poème en prose de Baudelaire jusqu'à nos jours* (1959) situates the shift from poetic prose to prose poetry in the late seventeenth century with the publication of Fénelon's *Télémaque*. Bernard traces the evolution of the genre through the works of Évariste de Parny, François-René de Chateaubriand, Aloysius Bertrand, Baudelaire, Stéphane Mallarmé, Lautréamont, Jean Cocteau, Max Jacob, Francis Ponge, and many more, ending with Saint-John Perse. In *The Prose Poem in France: Theory and Practice*, edited by Mary Ann Caws and Hermine Riffaterre (1983), eleven scholars and two poets present views on the genre's theory and practice. Nathalie Vincent-Munnia, Simone Bernard-Griffiths, and Robert Pickering's *Aux origines du poème en prose français (1750–1850)* offers forty essays on the pre-Baudelairean prose poem, emphasizing the development of the genre and individual works, many by less-well-known writers. Another work centered on the genre, *La Poésie en prose française du XIIᵉ siècle à nos jours: Histoire d'un genre*, by Christian Leroy (2001), situates Baudelaire's prose poems in the larger context of lyricism expressed in forms other than verse (meditations, descriptions, etc.). More recently, Fabienne Moore's *Prose Poems of the French Enlightenment:*

Delimiting Genre (2009) provides a focused study of prose poems written before the nineteenth century. Luc Bonenfant devotes *Les Avatars romantiques du genre: Transferts génériques dans l'œuvre d'Aloysius Bertrand* (2002) to the study of Baudelaire's often overlooked precursor, Aloysius Bertrand and his *Gaspard de la nuit* (1842). Steve Murphy has edited a collection of twenty-four essays on Bertand's work in *Lectures de* Gaspard de la Nuit *de Louis ("Aloysius") Bertand* (2010).

Reception and Influence outside France

Baudelaire's reception and impact on literature beyond French and francophone studies is a topic of increasing interest in books and articles. William F. Aggeler has compiled the work of Spanish critics in *Baudelaire Judged by Spanish Critics, 1857–1957* (1971). Hans-George Ruprecht analyzes Baudelaire's poetics and an "Epidemia Baudelairiana" in relation to Mexican modernist poetry in "Aspects du baudelairisme mexicain" (1974). Noting that Baudelaire was translated into Russian before any other language, Adrian Wanner analyzes Baudelaire's influence on Russian poetry from 1852 to the end of the Soviet era (1996). The 2004 volume of *L'Année Baudelaire* is devoted to the topic of Baudelaire and Germany.

Studies of Baudelaire's Prose Poems

Since 1979, Baudelaire's prose poems have attracted considerable, ongoing critical attention (see the introduction to this volume for further discussion of critical reception). Among the works most often mentioned by survey respondents and contributors are Barbara Johnson's groundbreaking *Défigurations du langage poétique: La Seconde Révolution baudelairienne* (1979) and Steve Murphy's *Logiques du dernier Baudelaire: Lectures du* Spleen de Paris (2003). Murphy's study of selected prose poems written after 1860 provides perceptive close readings informed by publication history, as well as by a comprehensive range of secondary sources in French and English. Also frequently cited as useful resources for teachers were Patrick Labarthe's book of commentary on *Le Spleen de Paris* (2000) and Patrick Wright and David Scott's critical guide to *La Fanfarlo* and *Le Spleen de Paris* (1984).

J. A. Hiddleston's *Baudelaire and* Le Spleen de Paris (1987), Edward Kaplan's *Baudelaire's Prose Poems: The Esthetic, the Ethical, and the Religious in* The Parisian Prowler (1990), and Sonya Stephens's *Baudelaire's Prose Poems: The Practice and Politics of Irony* (1999) are cornerstones to any library on the topic. Instructors may build on these works and their bibliographies according to their needs and interests. Murphy has edited a new collection of essays by some of the best-known scholars in the field, *Lectures du* Spleen de Paris (2014). For recent literary criticism that treats *Les Fleurs du Mal* and the prose poems together, see

Randolph Paul Runyon's *Intratextual Baudelaire: The Sequential Fabric of the* Fleurs du Mal *and* Spleen de Paris (2010) and Françoise Meltzer's *Seeing Double: Baudelaire's Modernity* (2011).

Teaching Literature in Foreign Language Programs

In departments of French language, literature, and culture, students deal with the double challenge of confronting new material while learning to master the language in which that material is written. Articles by both literature and second language acquisition scholars have addressed the need to bridge the gap between language and literature study in university programs (see, e.g., Krueger, "Form"). Likewise, instructors may benefit from essays on specific pedagogical approaches designed to promote the study of literature in a foreign language. In "Breaking the Sounds of Silence" (1993), Laurey K. Martin offers strategies for formulating discussion questions that will promote participation. *SLA and the Literature Classroom: Fostering Dialogues*, edited by Virginia Scott and Holly Tucker (2001), includes eight essays on topics ranging from the development of literary competence to the integration of literature in language courses.

Literature and the Humanities

Reading literature is most likely second nature to anyone perusing this volume, yet it can be helpful for instructors to consider why they value works of fiction and to convey their reasons to their students. Many of the contributors to this volume address both the importance of students' emotional connection to course materials and their motivation to learn (a factor more crucial to learning than methodology per se, according to recent research). For instructors who want to open discussion and debate among colleagues and administrators or to fine-tune their own thinking about literary studies, Mark Edmundson's *Why Read* (2004), Rita Felski's *Uses of Literature* (2008), and Martha Nussbaum's *Not for Profit*: *Why Democracy Needs the Humanities* (2012) are good places to start. Laurence M. Porter's preface to *Approaches to Teaching Baudelaire's* Flowers of Evil (2000) offers an eloquent statement on the relevance of poetry to twenty-first-century students (4).

Courses

Respondents teach Baudelaire's prose poems in French and English, primarily in French studies, comparative literature, and creative writing curricula. The prose poems appear on syllabi at all levels, from basic French language courses to highly specialized graduate seminars. Most respondents incorporate at least some of the prose poems in several different courses. The course topics mentioned include (but are hardly limited to) modernism and the avant-garde, postmodernism, postcolonialism, world poetry, poetry and gastronomy, the art of brevity, European identities, representations of Paris, poetry and the invention of experience, the modern city, intellectual history, and Romanticism. Some respondents treat all the prose poems in certain courses. More often, instructors select individual prose poems according to the course topic. Among the many types of assignments mentioned, close reading and textual analysis — in in-class presentations, papers, or discussion — stand out. Creative writing, comparative translation, and analytical writing are practiced both at home and in classroom workshops. Most respondents emphasized the increasingly active role students play in discussion, presentation, and even the selection of texts.

Part Two

APPROACHES

Introduction

Cheryl Krueger

A burst of scholarly attention to the hybridity of prose poetry in the late 1970s assured the broad, continuing importance of this genre for literary and cultural studies. It was the prose poems' innovative poetics and textual dynamics that drew in a first generation of structuralist and poststructuralist critics. Since the 1980s, critical interest in Baudelaire has converged on his prose poetry, particularly for its stylistic, thematic, and cultural relation to modernity. While *Le Spleen de Paris* remains an invaluable text for the study of reader response, literary genre, poetics, and narrative theory, its current appeal derives largely from its depiction of life in Paris during the Second Empire, whether in literal or heavily figurative ways. The reader encounters the rich and the poor, poets, painters, friends, lovers, strangers, glaziers, acrobats, prostitutes, *flâneurs*, cats, and a good number of dogs on the pages of *Le Spleen de Paris*. Images such as muddy gutters ("Perte d'auréole" ["Loss of Halo"]), carriage traffic ("Un Plaisant" ["A Joker"]), and the rubble of demolition and new construction ("Les Yeux des pauvres" ["The Eyes of the Poor"]) remind us that the city—itself a work in progress under Georges-Eugène Haussmann's supervision—serves as an ever-shifting backdrop to the anecdotes and varying modes of contemplation related in many of the pieces. Yet in the more urban poems, Baudelaire goes beyond illustrating city life; he also evokes, through style and structure, the pace, discontinuity, and spatiotemporal distortions of an era that often caught the poet in a tug of war between progress and nostalgia.

Thus the fifty prose poems in Baudelaire's *Le Spleen de Paris* have emerged as works central to the study of developing literary genres, the shifting social and political terrain of nineteenth-century France, the evolution of French poetry and narrative, the history of literary publishing, and the relation of artistic production and modernity. Pieces from this collection remain important to undergraduate and graduate programs in French and comparative literature, in part because they complement the verse poems in *Les Fleurs du Mal*, treating similar, often identical themes in a more realistic, ironic mode.

Critical reaction of *Le Spleen de Paris* could be sorted into three general chronological categories, eventually intersecting in later scholarly studies. A first wave of reactions casts *Le Spleen de Paris* as an accessory to *Les Fleurs du Mal*. A second celebrates the thematic, formal, and textual complexity of the individual prose poems and their genre, and a third, stemming from studies of modernity, focuses on the historical, social, cultural, and postcolonial contexts. Each approach connects to the others by a strong thread of interest in the strangeness (newness, otherness) of Baudelaire's prose poems and by concern for how they represent reactions to the literary, social, or cultural other.

Suzanne Bernard's encyclopedic *Le Poème en prose de Baudelaire jusqu'à nos jours* (1959) furnishes a thorough, colorful summary of the earliest critical responses to *Le Spleen de Paris*, most of which persistently measure the prose poems against verse. From this perspective, the value of each prose poem depends entirely on how closely it re-creates the rhythm, musicality, sonority, and "harmony of representation" of traditional poetry (9). In this contest for "most poetic genre," the prose poems are destined to lose: the most journalistic, didactic, novelistic, and lengthy pieces provoke not just disappointment but consternation and even resentment. Bernard's struggle to find worth in Baudelaire's least poetic prose poems is palpable throughout her analysis of individual works, her comparisons of verse and prose pairings (she considers the prose versions *remaniements* ["reworkings"] of the verse poems), and her meditations on commentary gleaned from Baudelaire's lifetime to the date of her book. What finally drives Bernard from academic objectivity to a passionate lament is Baudelaire's seemingly willful mixing of tones and his voluntary use of platitudes, which Bernard asserts he venerates "étrangement" ("strangely"). Bernard chides Baudelaire in no uncertain terms ("J'en veux à Baudelaire") for having opened the door to scores of future insipid scribblers of "journalisme pseudo-poétique" ("pseudo-poetic journalism") who will inundate the public with clichéd, greeting-card prose on the subject of organ-grinders and found objects (127).

Despite her apparent frustration with Baudelaire's prose poem project, Bernard touches on several features of *Le Spleen de Paris* that eventually became the prime focus of scholarship on it. The unusual subject matter and mixing of tones and the difficulty of defining the genre (or Baudelaire's iteration of it) test the formal limits, as well as the essence and thus our comprehension, of what we call poetry. This travesty of genre, rhetoric, and content is enough to bring Bernard's chapter on Baudelaire to a close, but it is precisely what propelled *Le Spleen de Paris* into the critical spotlight twenty years later. Likewise, her observation that the prose poems constitute "une poésie *urbaine*" ("*urban* poetry") and an expression of "son intention *moderniste* ("his *modernist* aims") is not the focus of her study but does reappear at the core of future scholarship on Baudelaire (106, 109).

As phenomenology and the Geneva school flourished in the 1950s, scholarship on Baudelaire continued to focus primarily on *Les Fleurs du Mal* (see, e.g., Poulet). It took a convergence of new interests in literary criticism during the 1960s and 1970s to provoke the seismic shift that led to the rediscovery of *Le Spleen de Paris* in the late 1970s then to unprecedented scholarly attention throughout the next two decades. Growing interest in analysis (including psychoanalysis) and in text (now broadly defined) released the genre of the *poème en prose* from the shadow of *Les Fleurs du Mal*, obviated the need for its literary justification, and caused readers to embrace, rather than resent, prose poetry's strange, slippery resistance to genre classification. Even the name—*Le Spleen de Paris* or *Petits Poèmes en prose*—remains undecided.

Perusing the scholarship on *Le Spleen de Paris* is like tracking the trajectory of literary theory in French studies over recent time. Fernande M. De George brings structuralism's methodological attention to "The Structure of Baudelaire's *Petits Poèmes en prose*" (1973), mapping various features of the individual poems to show that their arrangement in the volume forms serpentine curves on a series of charts (147). Because the prose poems (both the genre and the individual texts) are so resistant to taxonomy, criticism on *Le Spleen de Paris* begins to thrive in tandem with the emergence of poststructuralist approaches. Sima Godfrey's "Baudelaire's Windows" (1982) reads windows and frames in terms of Jacques Derrida's center and frame, as discussed in the "Parergon" section of *La Vérité en peinture* (1978). In 1983, Mary Ann Caws and Hermine Riffaterre compiled the volume *The Prose Poem in France: Theory and Practice*. The list of contributors, including Michel Deguy, Michael Riffaterre, Roger Shattuck, and Tzvetan Todorov, attests to the convergence of interest, energy, and approaches bestowed on the genre at the time.

This explosion of interest in *Le Spleen de Paris* led to new examinations of the form and textual features of the prose poems, as well as of their strange and strangely *narrative* features. Richard Terdiman advocates reading the prose poems "from the side of prose" in his 1985 *Discourse: Counter-discourse* (261), and indeed a great deal of scholarship thereafter focuses less on the poetic qualities of *Le Spleen de Paris* than on rhetorical and linguistic features (rather than prosody) and narratology and storytelling. In *Repetition and Semiotics: Interpreting Prose Poems* (1986), Stamos Metzidakis argues for the importance of repetition in literary creation and interpretation. Marie Maclean's 1988 *Narrative as Performance: The Baudelairean Experiment* casts the prose poems as textual subjects on which to practice speech act theory. Edward Kaplan treats the prose poems as fables of modern life in *Baudelaire's Prose Poems: The Esthetic, the Ethical, and the Religious in* The Parisian Prowler (1990), and Scott Carpenter reads "Le Mauvais Vitrier" as an allegory of artistic censorship in *Acts of Fiction: Resistance and Revolution from Sade to Baudelaire* (1996). Sonya Stephens studies literary caricature in *Baudelaire's Prose Poems: The Practice and Politics of Irony* (1999). Steve Murphy's 2003 *Logiques du dernier Baudelaire* (the title recalls Charles Mauron's 1966 *Le Dernier Baudelaire*) focuses especially on the less lyric prose poems of the 1860s. Cheryl Krueger studies poetic struggle with human time and progress, played out in narrative time keeping, in *The Art of Procrastination: Baudelaire's Poetry in Prose* (2007).

There are two works to which nearly all studies of *Le Spleen de Paris* are indebted. Drawing on semiotics, psychoanalysis, and deconstruction, Barbara Johnson's *Défigurations du langage poétique: La Seconde Révolution baudelairienne* (1979) was in itself a revolution. The first book to examine Baudelaire's prose poems in such depth, so playfully, carefully, and caringly, it celebrates the displacement, difference, and *différance* of the self-negating term *poème en prose* and examines the "literalization" of figurative language within the individual prose poems. Johnson's work confirmed definitively the literary status of *Le Spleen de Paris* and inspired hosts of scholars to investigate Baudelaire's new poetics.

Though Walter Benjamin wrote little about the prose poems, his collected essays on Baudelaire, *Illuminations* (published in German in 1969; in French in 1979), generated interest in the urban and modernist aspects of Baudelaire's work: the experience of living in a city undergoing daily transformation according to Haussmann's design, the sensation of being alone in the crowd, a new sense of time, and the shock of modernity. Of course, Benjamin's work resonates well beyond nineteenth-century French studies. His reading of Baudelaire in the context of a rapidly expanding capitalist culture has influenced scholarship from the perspective of social history as well as poetics. Ross Chambers, arguing that poetry should not be excluded from cultural studies, expands Benjamin's notion of modernity shock to articulate what he calls the "shock of knowing," recognizing the ordinary and thus making it noteworthy, discovering its "uncanny duality of familiarity and strangeness" in the *flâneur* tradition and in Baudelaire's poetry ("Modern Beauty" 250, 251). In his 2015 *An Atmospherics of the City* Chambers compares the prose poems to a construction site (*un chantier*), comparable to the *New York Times* Metropolitan Diary section: "the noisy, *chantier*-like properties of each successive moment, as time passes and passes us by" (159).

Recent developments in scholarship on nineteenth-century France, on *Le Spleen de Paris*, and on Baudelaire's work in general inspire fresh approaches to teaching the prose poems, particularly from the perspective of cultural and social history. In *Baudelaire's* Le Spleen de Paris*: Shifting Perspectives* (2005), Maria Scott reveals the ironic social commentary present throughout the prose poems, a dimension that can only be treated in courses where students explore class structure and the values and attitudes of the Second Empire bourgeoisie. In her 2008 article "'The Indies': Baudelaire's Colonial World," Françoise Lionnet introduces the question of geographic perspective in the study of Baudelaire's poems about the world beyond France. She underscores "worldness" (a translation of *mondialité*, the term Édouard Glissant offers as an alternative to *globalization* to distinguish global dialogue from global homogenization) "with the goal not of regrounding representation in reference but of claiming Baudelaire for a redefined French and francophone literature that includes the colonial literary and travel influences on his poetry as well as his legacy in European modernist traditions" (733). *Le Spleen de Paris* provides rich terrain for examining Baudelaire's work from this expanded perspective on travel, exoticism, and colonialism.

Reading Baudelaire's Prose Poems Today

Though hardly exhaustive, the survey of books and articles mentioned here gives a sense of scope and shifting emphasis in the study of Baudelaire's prose poems. The challenges *Le Spleen de Paris* has posed to the most seasoned literary scholars echo the difficulties and rewards, for both instructors and students, of reading these works. The three waves of criticism mentioned in the preface could be transposed to define three general modes of framing the prose poems in high school and university courses: approaching them along with *Les Fleurs du Mal*; performing close reading of individual texts with an emphasis on textual strategies, poetic and narrative language, thematics, and the convergence of form and meaning; and reading the prose poems in the context of social history and cultural studies (e.g., modernity, gender studies, the visual arts). These categories are permeable and overlapping, but they provide a helpful, if somewhat arbitrary, starting point for the selection of poems to be read in any course, at any level, in any language. Likewise, the kinds of questions that fueled decades of scholarship serve as a logical starting point for creating course materials and guiding interaction with Baudelaire's prose poems. What do students make of the initial surprise or shock they may experience when they first encounter them? What is the relation of *Le Spleen de Paris* to *Les Fleurs du Mal*? How does *Spleen* relate to aesthetic currents and literary movements of Baudelaire's time? What is prose poetry? What does close reading reveal about the lyrical qualities or narrative interest of individual pieces? Who speaks in the prose poems? Is there just one narrative persona? What other characters and character types appear? Who are the outsiders? How do people relate to one another? How are women represented? How do the prose poems evoke the city, the crowd, and the experience of modern, urban life? What is the role of the everyday in these texts? How do they engage with exoticism, orientalism, and alterity? What is their relevance today? Since there are fifty poems and a verse epilogue in the collection, the first step for most instructors is to make a selection of poems based on the scope and sequence of the course. In language courses, where students are still developing reading skills, important criteria might include brevity and accessible language and content. In literature courses, where students spend time on interpretation and critical analysis, it is often helpful to start (or end) with Baudelaire's would-be preface, the letter to Arsène Houssaye.

The Essays in This Volume

The essays in this volume reveal a great deal about the changing landscape of courses in modern languages, literatures, and cultures, in terms of both how and what we teach. They suggest that narrow, hierarchical curricular tracks have been broadened to promote inclusive, comprehensive, complementary approaches to learning. Even essays sharply focused on textual analysis inevitably reveal interdisciplinary connections. Regardless of theoretical perspective, disciplinary context, or course level, each essay deals in some way with both form and content, with both language and context, with both receptive and productive learning skills. Each essay acknowledges students as active learners and presents ways to promote a deep engagement with texts and contexts. Even those essays not centered on the classroom experience and learner needs are valuable for instructors, particularly nonspecialists, those who have not read Baudelaire for some time, or those who have been teaching the prose poems from a given perspective for some time. Instructors may consult those essays to enrich their knowledge, enhance their approach to the course content, and come up with discussion questions and paper topics.

The organizational plan of this part of the volume, "Approaches," by no means suggests that certain questions, topics, and perspectives belong to one section exclusively. Like the prose poem genre, these categories remain permeable and interconnected. The first part opens with the section "Reading Strategies," in which essays bring students closer to the prose poems through textual analysis, deciphering, interpretation, reader response, and attention to the prose poems' often evasive narrative persona(e). All the essays in this section take as a point of departure students' initial reactions—from bafflement, consternation, and surprise to appreciation and identification. Arguing that Baudelaire's prose poems offer outstanding examples of empathy, Laurence M. Porter focuses on what the lyric poet and student readers have in common, their shared emotions and experiences. Claire Chi-ah Lyu's essay links the selfishness and egotism detected in some of the prose poems to a reexamination of the meaning of *mal* (an allegory of pain, evil) in the light of the verse poems in *Les Fleurs du Mal*. Lyu encourages students to develop an awareness of words and to engage in a transformative connection to *le mal* in both text and life. Scott M. Powers guides students from personal reaction to critical perspectives by having them question the identity and function of the first-person narrator in *Le Spleen de Paris* while they consider the role of other voices or viewpoints in the poems. Noting that several prose poems build toward unexpected moral pronouncements, Scott Carpenter shows how dissonance in the prose poems leads to allegorical interpretations. Edward K. Kaplan emphasizes that the prose poems do not teach an ethical point of view; instead, their tonal and narratorial ambiguities provoke self-examination by challenging complacently held norms.

The next section, "Literary and Aesthetic Currents," presents courses that situate the prose poems in the aesthetic and literary movements of their time, examined from new perspectives. Stamos Metzidakis rethinks *Le Spleen de Paris* in terms of Romanticism, stressing a typographical visuality of composition that links Baudelaire's efforts to that of later nineteenth-century poets. Beryl Schlossman's essay continues the discussion of modernity, showing that modern experience is analyzed through an interpretation of "Loss of a Halo" and its central role in Benjamin's theory. Joseph Acquisto explores the coexistence of modernity and resistance to it (antimodernity) in the prose poems and related European works.

The four essays in the next section, "Social and Cultural Intersections," purposefully broaden the reach of Baudelaire studies—although discussion of such intersections also certainly appears elsewhere in the volume. Maria Scott discusses prose poems in which women are associated with disappointing travesties of inaccessible ideals. She outlines an approach to teaching the prose poems that complicates their apparent misogyny. Debarati Sanyal sees connections between the post-1848 generation's disillusionment and Baudelaire's violence as reactions to conditions of postmodern global capitalism and resistance to commodity culture. Presented in cultural context, the prose poems enhance the study of urban change and Second Empire Paris, and for Aimée Boutin they make possible an examination of street vendors and noise, echoed in the cry of the glazier in poems by Baudelaire and Houssaye. Boutin studies the poetic cry in relation to literary guidebooks, picturesque figures, and sound recordings that situate the glazier in his historical context. Françoise Lionnet expands the geographic scope of Baudelaire's prose poems in her consideration of Baudelaire as a global poet, influenced by colonial discourse and Creole poetry.

In "The Prose Poems across the Curriculum," contributors examine courses focused on translation theory, comparative literature, and the development of French language skills. Responding to goals for both linguistic and literacy skills when teaching in a foreign language, Heather Willis Allen and Kate Paesani delineate a sequence of activities for reading "L'Invitation au voyage" informed by a multiliteracies approach. Larson Powell uses "L'Invitation au voyage" as a starting point for both the theory and practice of translation in his interdisciplinary course. Drawing on a wide range of translation theory and historical context, Peter Connor navigates the intertextual complexity of the prose poems.

In the final section, "Print and Digital Culture," Catherine Nesci sees a bridge between digital reading today and the encounter with poetry in Baudelaire's time, when literary texts were included in the pages of newspapers and magazines. Cheryl Krueger reads the prose poems in relation to Baudelaire's theories of flânerie and posits that the sidetracked Second Empire street-stroller and the peripatetic twenty-first-century net surfer may blaze trails to contemplation and critical inquiry in similar ways.

Note about Editions in This Volume

The individual prose poems are indicated by title, not number, except in essays that deal with the order and placement of the poems within the volume or the history of their publication in the press. Because there is no definitive title, both *Le Spleen de Paris* and *Petits Poèmes en prose* are used in this volume.

The Lyric Self and Its Others in Baudelaire's *Petits Poèmes en prose*: Teaching Strategies

Laurence M. Porter

Teaching creates bridges between students and areas of knowledge and experience initially unfamiliar to them. As students become familiar with new people and practices, they enter a world with broadened possibilities for relatedness, socialization, and creativity. The study of literature can help students who plan to pursue careers in business or politics learn to identify the stakeholders in a particular situation, understand their individual interests and motives, persuade them, and work with various parties to achieve consensus, as well as identify issues where cooperation and progress are impossible. Students who learn from example how to express their views more articulately, and how to better understand expressions of the views of others will benefit in any situation that allows or requires them to take initiatives.

In courses in which I have taught Baudelaire—whether in general humanities courses, courses for French majors, comparative literature courses, or even specialized graduate courses—many of the students read for pleasure but are not primarily interested in critical theory. To engage such students, I begin by recognizing who they are; showing them that there are many common bonds between their personal experience and the representation of human experience in literary works of art; and getting them accustomed, from the beginning, to reflect on those works for themselves. Many of the essays in this volume—for example, those by Cheryl Krueger, Claire Chi-ah Lyu, Scott Carpenter, Edward K. Kaplan, Maria Scott, and Françoise Lionnet—can show us how to do just that. And Krueger's recent book on the prose poems does a compelling job of bringing them down to earth:

> Many of Baudelaire's *Fleurs du Mal* achieve poetic transport through their uncanny amalgam of desire and disgust. Through what often amounts to a complete formal and aesthetic reversal, the prose poems resist elevation, not only by replacing elegant verse with protracted storytelling and dialogue, but also by diluting potentially resonant references to death through humor, irony, and platitude.   (*Art* 13)

Even professional teachers of literature live most of the time in the everyday, and that is where we can find many commonalities with our students. We all inhabit a sensorium (a world of sense impressions); we all bathe in an individual emotional world of feelings, moods, and desires; we all make plans; we all experience altered states of consciousness such as reverie, sleep, and dreams; memory and recollection connect our consciousness to earlier moments in time; we all recognize occasional differences between perceptions and physical reality (the "witch water" we may see on the highway on hot days is not real water; our environment disappears visually at night, although sounds, smells, tastes, and kinesthetic sensations remain); we all recognize how a fiction (such as a lie, a theatrical performance, a film, a wish) can exist side by side with the real world. And we all must live with other people, with or without effective communication and with or without mutual understanding. To build on this social basis of the everyday, before lecturing, contextualizing, and theorizing—before sending our objects of study off into the realm of abstraction or nostalgia—we must acquaint our students with the inner world of the literary text, with its feelings and attitudes. We need to give them immediate, vivid reasons for caring about what they will study: we need a "hook."

As it happens, Baudelaire wanted desperately to share his emotional world with us in his prose poems. Including the epilogue, there are fifty-one poems in the *Petits Poèmes en prose* (also known as *Le Spleen de Paris*). Thirteen of them focus on expressing empathy with widows, children, the poor, and other unfortunates. In fourteen of them, he presents general allegorical insights on the human condition; in ten of these, the poet dramatizes himself as a spectator. In another ten, he shares the ecstatic experience of a privileged moment of delight with his readers (in five others, these moments are disrupted). In five, he contemplates the crowds on city streets. These motifs overlap extensively, but the point is that in at least thirty-one of the prose poems the poet communes with the rest of humanity. In "Les Foules," Baudelaire defines the poet as having the special endowment of identifying simultaneously with himself and another person: "Il entre, quand il veut, dans le personnage de chacun" ("He can identify, at will, with the personality of anyone"[1] (*Petits Poèmes* [Lemaître] 59). Eleven of the thirty prose poems in the middle of the volume claim that the poet can read other people's thoughts and character in their eyes. In contrast, the poet of *Les Fleurs du Mal*, although he frequently gazes into others' eyes, is bewitched, subjugated, and enslaved by them. Otherwise, he is alone.

So the poems in *Petit Poèmes en prose*, short, accessible, and with a pervasive intersubjective element, offer an ideal opportunity to involve students, especially those trying to navigate the storms of late adolescence, even if the teacher chooses only a few. David Scott emphasizes the down-to-earth topics of several of Baudelaire's prose poems, such as eating and fighting (7–8). Sonya Stephens has made a persuasive case for using prose poems as a gateway to verse poetry: "Verse and prose versions of the same poem provide a ready-made translation, which is itself poetic, though in the more familiar language of prose" ("Unfamiliarity" 94). Critical studies of these "doublets," which are frequent in Baudelaire's work, present a manageable corpus of excellent models, by Barbara Johnson (*Défigurations*) and Graham Chesters. Scott further emphasizes the importance of self-examination in Baudelaire's prose poems, a topic congenial to college students preoccupied with the crucial task of self-definition as they transition to adult life. And Kaplan proposes a more profound, ethical dimension of this task ("Poetry" 20–23).

I usually discuss only about ten of the poems from *Petits Poèmes en prose* over a two-week period. One can lay the essential groundwork for successful class participation by distributing brief lists of discussion questions—*all of which should be explored in class*—at least a week ahead of time and preferably at the beginning of the term. Ideally, the instructor creates and maintains the expectation that students will discuss what they have read. I divide the class into small groups (whose membership, if possible, changes every time) and ask each group to choose a spokesperson (a different person every time). That spokesperson shares her reactions to the assigned issue; then others in her group can speak ad lib; then the whole class has an opportunity to react. Periodically, I interject a word of appreciation, express doubt or disagreement about some remarks, provide some information about French culture, correct critical errors in French, and summarize. With the committed, gifted, articulate students at Oberlin College, I can get through three to eight questions in a fifty-minute class period and have time to make announcements and general observations.

Rather than begin with Baudelaire's dedication to Arsène Houssaye, I start with "L'Étranger," the first prose poem in the collection. One could ask students what the title "L'Étranger" makes them expect. It sets the mood for the entire collection, and that mood is alienation. Is "Foreigner" a misleading translation of the title? Is the eponymous character's estrangement circumstantial (the Stranger would just happen to be traveling in France), or existential (like that of Camus's Stranger)? Students can be invited to discuss why Baudelaire's anonymous stranger feels no connection with the society and values of the first speaker, who interrogates him. He says that he has no family or friends, no homeland, no attachment to imperfect terrestrial beauty and that he detests money. The instructor might explain that Baudelaire was strongly influenced by the great Christian preachers of the late-seventeenth and early-eighteenth centuries and ask students whether they hear any New Testament resonances in this last statement and whether they see connections between the Stranger's statements and other philosophical or religious writing or to today's popular culture. (What does the Stranger mean when he says that his questioner hates God? Why does he himself claim to love, above all else, the remote, transient, ever-changing clouds?)

At this point, the instructor could invite the class to discuss why the poet speaks through the Stranger instead of speaking in his own voice. I help focus the discussion by explaining the basic concept of the poet persona (*le persona* [mask] *du poète*) or lyric self (*le moi lyrique*), terms used to distinguish the historical author from the role that the author chooses to play in the text and to inhibit the reader from assuming that the text is composed of fragments of the biography of the historical author. For the *Petits Poèmes en prose*, the concept of the lyric self as an instrument for role-playing and pretending is particularly important, because it allows one to understand "Le Mauvais Vitrier" or "Assommons les pauvres" (for example) as fantasies, used to create Romantic irony (witty authorial self-deprecation) in the first text and to present a sardonic satire of visionary socialism in the second. It also helps us understand that Baudelaire initially presents "himself" as a naive observer so as not to distance himself, at the outset, from readers who are experiencing the same puzzlement at the Stranger's attitudes. It might be useful to compare how he associates "himself" with his readers in "Au Lecteur" of *Les Fleurs du Mal*. At this point, students could be referred to the prose poem "La Soupe et les nuages," where the lyric self assumes the Stranger's role. There, the motif of *l'incommunicabilité* (the impossibility of communicating with others), the major element of symbolist poetry, recurs (see Porter, *Crisis*). The poet's companion tragically misunderstands him: as he contemplates the sky without noticing the soup she had served him, he was thinking of the beauty of her hair, finding it superior even to the splendor of the clouds. Her coarse, materialistic reaction promptly destroys the ideal image of her that the poet had been cherishing.

For each of the poems we read closely in class, I assign closely related prose poems to provide students with a sense of context. Baudelaire has designed the prose poems to illuminate each other as they gradually form a recognizable worldview for their reader. For instance, adjacent pairs often emphasize differences in perspective (e.g., "Le Vieux Saltimbanque" and "Le Gâteau"; "L'Horloge" and "Un Hémisphère dans une chevelure"; "Portraits de maîtresses" and "Le Galant Tireur"; "Anywhere out of the world," "Les Bons Chiens," and "Épilogue"; see Runyon). Just as we can often identify a particular musical composition we hear as being the work of a particular composer, we can recognize an author's individual vision in constellations of motifs, preoccupations, and themes (properly speaking, motifs with an added evaluation) in a literary text.

Immediately after a detailed discussion of one key text or passage by Baudelaire is an ideal time to sensitize students to the author persona revealed through a series of texts. One might select two of the most frequent characterizations of Baudelaire: as a Parisian poet or as a decadent poet. (For graduate courses, I sometimes add a discussion of how Walter Benjamin used Baudelaire as a pretext for diving into Marxist theorizing and brilliant excursuses about Paris, in ways that quickly move far from Baudelaire's texts [see Porter, "Baudelaire"]).

I encourage students to think about whether, where, why, and how they have felt excited and exhilarated by being in a large city. Baudelaire's dedication to Arsène Houssaye expresses the desire to celebrate "vast cities" and crowds. Baudelaire often writes as an urban poet, and contemplating the activity of a large city is a popular spectator sport — witness the High Line park above the lower West Side of Manhattan, where bleachers have been arranged to allow strollers to sit and look down over two of the busiest streets. But how often in the *Petits Poèmes en prose* does Baudelaire specifically mention Paris or any identifiable place-names, streets, businesses, residences, or monuments in Paris? The Abbé Prévost, Denis Diderot (in *Le Neveu de Rameau*), Honoré de Balzac, Victor Hugo (in *Les Misérables*), Lautréamont, or Guillaume Apollinaire (to name only a few) clearly outdo him in this category. He happens to go or be outdoors in six of the fifty-one poems (including the verse epilogue): the only deliberate strolling he does occurs in "Les Foules," where he tries to achieve "a holy prostitution of the soul" 'une sainte prostitution de l'âme' among crowds; he recommends that the reader stroll about at Christmastide, distributing toys to poor children, but does not depict himself doing so in "Le Joujou du pauvre"; a woman with a fetish for surgeons picks him up in the street in "Mademoiselle Bistouri"; he rejects the academic muse to celebrate stray dogs in "Les Bons Chiens"; and, finally, in the epilogue he climbs an allegorical mountain to contemplate Paris from a great height, as Dante might have contemplated Florence in *The Divine Comedy* ("Épilogue"). One could find ten city scenes among the prose poems: "Les Foules," "Le Joujou du pauvre," and "Les Bons Chiens" relate a pleasurable experience; "Un Plaisant" and "Les Yeux des pauvres" are marred by the lyric self's acute distaste for the complacency of the privileged; "Le Mauvais Vitrier," "Perte d'auréole," "Assommons les pauvres," and the epilogue are allegorical; in "Mademoiselle Bistouri," a neurotic woman accosts him. Five of these scenes are concentrated among the six concluding texts, so that one could more properly speak of a Parisian section of the *Petits Poèmes en prose* than of a Parisian collection of poems. Could certain general moods or attitudes in these poems be considered urban or Parisian even though specific places in the city are rarely mentioned?

Time permitting, the instructor can clarify that allegory, also prominent in *Les Fleurs du Mal*, typically has both a general significance regarding the human condition and a specific historical referent, subject to moralizing judgments. "Assommons les pauvres" invents a violent encounter with a beggar to illustrate the general foolishness of egalitarian visionary socialism. After selecting promising texts, the instructor can ask students to identify and comment on places where Baudelaire explicitly or implicitly condemns various human behaviors and whether he appears to condone behaviors conventionally considered immoral in 1857. Such a discussion can put to the test the hoary cliché that Baudelaire was a decadent writer. (And, using the modern-day examples of same-sex marriage and the legalization of marijuana, the instructor might point out that attitudes toward sexual behavior and drug use can evolve rapidly.)

In *Les Paradis artificiels*, Baudelaire says or implies that he used opiates and hashish, but he also condemns their use from a moralistic viewpoint as well as from a practical one: an artificial paradise doesn't last (*Œuvres complètes* [Pichois] 1: 377–537). In the *Petits Poèmes en prose*, however, the moments of exhilaration and ecstasy he describes are innocent. One should guide the students toward identifying and understanding them by characterizing the experiences of hyperesthesia (an unusually keen sensory response to the external world, as in the passage where Goethe's young Werther lies on the ground and can feel the tiny worms stirring in the soil beneath him) and synesthesia (the experience of multiple, simultaneous sense impressions). I prepare the discussion by reviewing the French names for the five senses (*la vue, l'ouïe, le goût, le toucher, l'odorat*), which undergraduates usually don't know, and by reading a few verses out loud to create a sense of rhythm and movement (*le rythme, la dimension cinétique*) in one's environment, as opposed to proprioception. ("La Chambre double," "Un Hémisphère dans une chevelure," "L'Invitation au voyage," "La Belle Dorothée," "Le Thyrse," "Déjà!" and "Le Port" are good examples here.) I then ask students to identify sensory elements in these poems and to comment on what their effects are in combination. Among the fifteen instances of heightened awareness and second states of consciousness in the *Petits Poèmes en prose*, five are brought about by a loved woman's eyes ("L'Horloge") or hair ("Un Hémisphère dans une chevelure"), by daydreams ("Les Projets") or memories ("La Belle Dorothée") of the woman, or by a global impression of her as a world ("L'Invitation au voyage"). In eleven other poems, transcendence arises from allegorical visions ("Chacun sa chimère" and "Le Fou et la Vénus"), dreams ("La Chambre double"), the sky ("L'Étranger," "Le *Confiteor* de l'artiste," and "Les Projets"), the sea ("Le *Confiteor* de l'artiste" "Déjà!"), intoxication (literal or figurative; "Enivrez-vous), a seaport ("Le Port"), and music ("Le Thyrse").

To provide a concluding overview, for which I recommend at least two class periods, I generally return to the intersubjective dimension of Baudelaire's more than two hundred prose and verse poems. What is his poet persona doing with himself during them? Occasionally, Baudelaire is hearing voices (prosopopoeia) or talking to entities that can't talk back (apostrophe, addressed to nonhuman creatures; inanimate objects; abstract ideas; absent or dead people), all of which one could characterize as imaginary playmates. He invents these voices and chooses what he wants them to say, often relating to real others in one of three distinct ways. To provide students with convenient guidelines for identifying these ways, I summarize the neo-Freudian psychoanalyst Karen Horney's characterization of three predominant strategies for relating to others: literally or figuratively moving away from others (withdrawal), moving toward others (compliance), or moving against others (aggression). The mentally healthy person, she says, selects from among them flexibly, depending on the particular situation of the moment. The neurotic person often favors one to excess over the other two, sometimes choosing behaviors that are self-defeating or badly adapted to a particular situation. I ask students, sometimes in groups, to identify and comment on individual poems that predominantly illustrate each of these interpersonal strategies. One can assign a few pages either from Horney's simplified popularization of her theories in *Our Inner Conflicts* or from her more fully developed analysis in *Neurosis and Human Growth*. For the course instructor, the comparatist Bernard J. Paris has written a theoretical overview of Horney's thought. Horney omits a fourth behavior that is found in higher vertebrates, such as birds: altruism or nurturance, involving movement toward the other to bring aid and comfort rather than to ask for those.

Is Horney's scheme simplistic and reductive? Of course it is—as are all critical schemes. Obviously, in real life one's attitudes toward others are often far more complex than three or four simple rubrics can convey. Having initially warned students to keep this fact in mind, the instructor can then ask them to develop richer, more complex views of interaction for themselves. But to begin with a simple model is to conform to a sound basic practice of teaching and coaching: successive approximation. One begins by setting a manageable task and then progressively refines it as the learners' capabilities increase. In a second stage of intellectual development, one can provide students with the exhilarating experience of questioning and refining explanatory models by themselves. Ideally, students will leave a course with an inquiring, open-ended attitude. To illustrate the importance of maintaining such an attitude in the real world, one can point to the radical way that recent fossil finds have transformed our understanding of human origins and development.

One promising strategy for refining the Horneyan grid is to point out that any strategy may be pursued from a position of dominance, equality, or subordination. The instructor might begin by asking students to reflect on how they might introduce this complication into the initial model. They might decide—for example—that withdrawal could involve the dominant stance of scorning or expelling the other party in a relationship, the egalitarian stance of inwardly dissenting while remaining silent, or the submissive stance of hiding from that person. Compliance, instead of being seen as a symptom of neurotic dependency, could result from respect and trust or involve benevolently nurturing, educating, and mentoring another, mutually cherishing and being cherished. Aggression could involve literally or figuratively attacking the other; contending with another in a consensual, rule-governed competition; or, without acting overtly hostile, employing secretive, underhanded strategies such as lying, sabotage, or passive aggression that deliberately avoid warning or assisting the other. Relations with others can also have a sadistic or masochistic tinge. Baudelaire's poet persona sometimes plays the confessional role of acknowledging his sins while implicating others in similar moral failings, seen as an inevitable fact of the human condition (e.g., "Au Lecteur" in *Les Fleurs du Mal*). The only sort of statement conspicuously absent from his poetry would be an explicit exhortation to partake in fellowship and collective action.

Whatever attitudes Baudelaire expresses in his poems, however, are often markedly ambivalent. Love and hate, submission and aggression, exaltation and despair frequently alternate or mingle. Students can benefit by being introduced to the concept of tone (the emotional climate of a particular work or passage, which may be enriched by an expression of the speakers' attitudes toward situations and events). Tone may involve a complex mixture of contrasting attitudes, such as nostalgia or Romantic irony. In that mode, the self-deprecating poet plays two roles at once, the *alazon* ("braggart") and the *eiron* ("deflator"), who mocks and disparages the *alazon*; good examples from Baudelaire's century appear in Byron, Stendhal, Heinrich Heine, and Alfred de Musset. Cervantes's Sancho Panza is a naive but effective *eiron*.

In Baudelaire's prose poems, the dominant mode of withdrawal is to express scorn. At such moments, his poet persona speaks as an elitist. This attitude blends with that of the satirist in the epilogue of the *Petits Poèmes en prose*, in which Baudelaire as impenitent elitist alludes to the Roman poet Horace's *odi profanum vulgus et arceo* ("I loathe the common herd and shun them") and as a satirist, writing in Dante's terza rima, echoes the Italian outcast's fierce moral condemnation of society, situating himself on an imaginary mountaintop overlooking the Great Whore, Paris.

To tune students in to their inner elitist, I ask them to identify instances of bad taste or immoral behavior in the prose poems. Baudelaire particularly condemns a lack of sympathy for others, based on a fatuous sense of entitlement ("Un Plaisant," "Les Yeux des pauvres," "La Femme sauvage et la petite-maîtresse," and "La Fausse Monnaie") or on blind, brutal abuse of the helpless other. The most striking feature of such abuse is either that horrific mistreatment by a third party is reported dispassionately ("La Femme sauvage et la petite-maîtresse," "Une Mort héroïque," and "La Corde") or that physical assaults ascribed to the lyric self are reported in a humorous tone and treat incidents that probably existed only in the poet's imagination ("Le Mauvais Vitrier" and "Assommons les pauvres"). Students can be invited to share their reactions to such incongruous disparities between the disastrous reported event and the lyric self's complacent reaction. Typically—"Le Gâteau" is a prime example—the lyric self plays two social roles at once: more sensitive and less indifferent to suffering than are most of his contemporaries, he calls it to our attention as a pervasive symptom of social dysfunction. At the same time, his matter-of-fact tone mimics the flat affect of the average person vis-à-vis others, condemning such callousness by implication. In a word, Baudelaire dramatized himself not as a stroller hoping to encounter unexpected curiosities (a prominent mode of much twentieth-century poetry) but as a social critic who implicitly but strongly disapproves of our neglect of the unfortunate.

To withdraw from his unsympathetic milieu, his squalid poverty, an establishment that condemned him (the government censorship bureau put him and his publisher on trial for offenses against public morality and religion, levied a fine, and banned the publication of seven poems from *Les Fleurs du Mal* in 1857), and a publishing industry that failed to find enough capital to publish the prose poems as a complete volume until two years after Baudelaire's death, the poet often took refuge in the ideal world of beauty that inspired his writing. Fifteen of the prose poems evoke that world: the poet's idyllic dream is brutally interrupted by reality in "La Chambre double," "Déjà!," and "La Soupe et les nuages"; he directly or indirectly represents himself as unable to attain the ideal on which he is fixated in "Le *Confiteor* de l'artiste," "Chacun sa chimère," and "Le Fou et la Vénus"; he finds an ideal world in the beauty of a woman he loves in "Un Hémisphère dans une chevelure," "L'Invitation au voyage," and "Les Projets," but in "L'Horloge" he mocks himself for presuming to do so and his compliments for that woman (the allegorical "Féline") as being merely "cette prétentieuse galanterie" 'this pretentious gallantry'; another such woman remains only a faraway, inaccessible memory in "La Belle Dorothée"; and additional ideal worlds include the music of his friend Franz Liszt in "Le Thyrse" and the evocative escapist setting of a seaport in "Le Port."

In less ecstatic moments, Baudelaire moves toward unfortunate others: the downtrodden and unprivileged, the bereaved and the lonely, such as widows ("Le Désespoir de la vieille," "Les Veuves," and "Les Fenêtres"), children ("Le Gâteau," "Le Joujou du pauvre," "La Corde," and "Les Vocations"), and circus performers and court jesters ("Le Vieux Saltimbanque" and "Une Mort héroïque"), attempting to empathize with them and often claiming to be able to read their thoughts and dispositions in their eyes. His sympathy never transforms itself into effective help, perhaps because Baudelaire believes that France's social problems far surpass one person's ability to solve them. Once, however, he relates the speciously factual (but historically unattested) episode when his friend Édouard Manet took in a boy unwanted by his parents, to serve as an assistant and model, only to become the innocent immediate cause of the boy's suicide ("La Corde"). Of course it has been easy to explain the lyric self's predilection for sympathizing with elderly widows as a symptom of the historical author's supposedly unresolved Oedipus complex. But we are dealing with lyric selves in this course, and they have no unconscious other than what the text explicitly attributes to them or what we readers project onto them from our own psyche. It can be helpful to students to point out that Baudelaire's persona enjoys the further moral superiority of higher self-knowledge, because he denounces himself along with the rest of us as being hypocritical—as being Good Samaritans only in our fantasies.

At the same time, with Romantic irony (authorial self-deprecation: compare Heine, Musset, Byron, and others), Baudelaire's poet persona calls into question his passionate efforts at self-transcendence through empathy with others. From this perspective, one can recognize his fellow feeling with dirty, mangy, starving stray dogs in the concluding prose poem as the ultimate, outrageous paroxysm of Romantic irony—one that we find centuries earlier in the self-conscious tradition, for example, in Cervantes's "El coloquio de los perros" ("Colloquium of the Dogs") in his *Novelas ejemplares* ("Exemplary Tales"). The pervasive movements in two opposite directions, toward the haughty superiority of detachment (as in the epilogue) and toward self-abasement, stamp Baudelaire's entire prose poem corpus with Romantic irony, preempting the others' rejection. Loser wins moral independence. To better understand Baudelaire's profound ambivalence, which approaches the intensity of a bipolar disorder, the instructor (and graduate students) might find it helpful to read Françoise Meltzer's *Seeing Double: Baudelaire's Modernity* and trace it back to the Jansenists and *moralistes* of seventeenth-century France: they had a profound influence on Baudelaire, as did the reactionary Catholic Joseph de Maistre.

A necessary corrective to speculation about the lyric self's relation to others is to examine how many of these others actually exist in the virtual worlds of the prose poems and how many appear only as a second tier of fantasy. In how many of the poems does the dramatized other (described as being present) actually respond? In fourteen poems, the lyric self is an onlooker, who does not engage in dialogue. Many others are anecdotal or allegorical and do not place a personified lyric self on stage at all. In a number of poems, the lyric self claims to be able to read thoughts and feelings in the eyes of a person or persons he observes. Of course he can always do so, because he has just verbally created them, but his intuitions are never tested in reported, direct, two-way, verbal communication with them. ("À une passante" in *Les Fleurs du Mal* reports a significant two-way glance exchanged with the anonymous woman in the street, but she says nothing.) Occasionally, the poet persona will lose himself in contemplation of a loved or admired woman—present or remembered ("La Chambre double," "L'Horloge," "L'Invitation au voyage," "Les Projets," "La Belle Dorothée," "Le Désir de peindre," and "Les Bienfaits de la lune")—but either unwelcome intruders disrupt his reverie, or, on the rare occasions when the woman speaks, her words betray her complete lack of understanding what emotions the poet hopes to find in her. Only a few prostitutes may play the role of a devoted partner to ensure the poet's sexual satisfaction ("Un Cheval de race," "Perte d'auréole," and "Épilogue"), but they could not appreciate his flights of aesthetic enthusiasm. The instructor might choose a poem for discussion from each of these types of interactions and prompt students to identify others like it.

Students might also be invited to find the temptations of self-abasement and moments of self-loathing that multiply at the end of the *Petits Poèmes en prose* ("Les Foules," "Perte d'auréole," and from "Anywhere out of the world" to "Épilogue." These poems blend a prideful sense of superiority and freely assumed social disgrace into a paradoxical elitism, neatly encapsulated by the prayer that ends "À une heure du matin": "Mécontent de tous et mécontent de moi, je voudrais bien me racheter et m'enorgueillir. . . . Seigneur mon Dieu! accordez-moi la grâce de produire quelques beaux vers qui me prouvent à moi-même que je ne suis pas le dernier des hommes, que je ne suis pas inférieur à ceux que je méprise" 'Dissatisfied with everyone and with myself, I would like to redeem myself and recover my self-esteem. . . . Oh, my Lord God ! Grant me the grace of producing a few lines of fine poetry to prove to myself that I am not the last of all men, that I am not inferior to those whom I despise' (*Petits Poèmes* [Lemaître] 51).

At the conclusion of the classes devoted to the *Petits Poèmes en prose*, I find it enlightening to discuss how the epilogue closes the frame created by the dedication and the first poem. In the epilogue, the poet switches for the first time to rhymed verse. Here Baudelaire's poet persona distances himself further from the reader than anywhere else in the collection: he reintroduces the artifice of verse as opposed to prose; he situates himself on an allegorical mountaintop, looking down at Paris from a great height; and his choice of a verse form (terza rima) associates him with the great satirist Dante, whose *Divine Comedy* created a custom-made hell and purgatory to imprison and punish the political enemies who had forced him into exile. To provoke an appropriate concluding class discussion, one could pose this oversimplified question: Should we despise Baudelaire's lyric self for his self-absorption, weaknesses, and immaturity or admire him for his unsparing insight and his sympathy for the elderly, the poor, children, and social outcasts?

NOTE

[1] All unattributed translations are mine.

A Renewed Relationship with Words: Reacting to Evil through "Le Mauvais Vitrier"

Claire Chi-ah Lyu

Ross Chambers offers two valuable insights among many in his contribution to *Approaches to Teaching Baudelaire's* Flowers of Evil ("Classroom"). The first is that we face "a categorical paradox" when teaching literature (170). The "genres and contexts of pedagogy" do not "correspond to the discursive modes we classify as literary," and when we bring pedagogy and literature together, the former tends to eclipse the latter: literary texts we study aren't literature "so much as they're classroom exercises," and "they're not so much classroom exercises as mere supports and pretexts for the real business of the classroom: Q and A, analysis, commentary" (171). The second is "[w]hat Baudelaire has taught [him]": "that teaching poetry can be an educational enterprise when it becomes a way of teaching also about living in the world" (181). I cite Chambers not only for these thoughts but also because his work has taught me so much and continues to do so, about poetry and reading poetry. As I reflect on teaching Baudelaire's prose poems, Chambers comes to mind first and foremost as the teacher to whom I feel deeply indebted and grateful.

In another illuminating moment, while standing in line at a buffet dinner organized by the dean of students, the colleague in front me, who, I later learned, teaches in the school of education, turned around and asked, "What do you teach?" I answered, "French literature," and asked in turn, "And you?" She replied, "I teach students," emphasizing that "it isn't about teaching math, music, or history but teaching *students* about math, music, or history. We teach people, not subject matters."

The remarks by Chambers and my colleague—pedagogy over literature; subject matter over students—reveal what happens when we teach literature: in the classroom, literature and students tend to become invisible. Given that my goal as an instructor is to become invisible so as not to interfere too much with students as they encounter the texts, teaching students French literature (I adopt my colleague's syntax) seems to present not only a "categorical paradox" but also a categorical *impossibility*: an invisible instructor teaching invisible students about invisible literature. Were my classroom to be video recorded for teaching evaluation purposes, might it resemble a pantomime of ghosts?

Recently, however, something happened that pulled the class out of this triple invisibility. It felt almost like a chemical precipitation that occurs when the invisible elements that are dissolved in the liquid react with one another to form a solid and newly visible entity. Suddenly the text, the students, and I interacted with one another as if coalescing into a new state: we all showed up. And it was Baudelaire's "Le Mauvais Vitrier" ("The Bad Glazier") that precipitated the event: the text provoked the students to condemn the narrator severely for abusing the glazier.

The narrator's final pronouncement shocked the students the most: "Ces plai-santeries nerveuses ne sont pas sans périls, et on peut souvent les payer cher. Mais qu'importe l'éternité de la damnation à qui a trouvé dans une seconde l'infini de la jouissance?" 'Such neurotic pranks are not without peril, and one can often pay dearly for them. But what does an eternity of damnation matter to someone who has experienced for one second the infinity of delight?' (*Spleen* [Pichois] 287; *Parisian Prowler* 15). They accused the narrator of generating selfish pleasure at the expense of another person. Some referred back to "Les Fenêtres" ("Windows"), which we had read earlier, saying that something simi-lar was going on: there too the narrator has no respect for the woman or her story: "Peut-être me diriez-vous: 'Es-tu sûr que cette légende soit la vraie?' Qu'importe ce que peut être la réalité placée hors de moi, si elle m'a aidé à vivre, à sentir que je suis et ce que je suis?" 'Perhaps you will ask, "Are you sure that legend is the true one?" Does it matter what the reality located outside of me might be, if it has helped me live, to feel that I am and *what* I am?' (339; 93). A few others thought that the disregard in "Les Fenêtres" was more or less in line with Baudelaire's poetics expressed in "Les Foules" ("Crowds"), where the poet takes pleasure at the expense of humanity ("jouir de la foule . . . faire, aux dépends du genre humain, une ribote de vitalité" 'enjoying crowds . . . go on a binge of vitality, at the expense of the human species' [291; 21]), because for him, self and others are interchangeable ("[m]ultitude, solitude: termes égaux et convertibles pour le poète actif et fécond" '[m]ultitude, solitude: equal and interchangeable terms for the active and fertile poet'). The disregard in "Les Fenêtres" was not as bad as the abuse in "Le Mauvais Vitrier," but the slide from interchangeability ("Les Foules") to disregard ("Les Fenêtres") to abuse ("Le Mauvais Vitrier") brought to light the potentially dubious side of literary creation, which students hadn't fully seized until reading "Le Mauvais Vitrier." "But we thought," a few of them said, "that Baudelaire was the defender of the underprivileged, marginalized people in *Les Fleurs du Mal*. Why is the narrator so mean here?"

When prompted to be more precise, students identified as problematic the phrase "qu'importe" 'what does it matter?' at the end of both prose poems: it conveyed dismissive indifference and was unacceptable. Soon the class became polarized, with one camp accusing and the other defending Baudelaire with equal energy and conviction. When students turned to me hoping that I would resolve the matter (thereby forcing me out of my invisibility in which I was hoping to remain, since I didn't have an answer), I could only acknowledge the validity of both views. What follows is a response to this failed opportunity and some thoughts on how I might proceed the next time.

I say failed for three reasons. First, because I let a golden opportunity, when we were no longer pantomiming ghosts but fully engaged and present, slide by. Second, because the situation arose about two-thirds of the way into the se-mester in an advanced seminar devoted entirely to Baudelaire. We had already discussed poetry's relation to moral judgments, especially when reading about

Baudelaire's trial. We had spent seven weeks on *Les Fleurs du Mal* and its trial and one week on "Le Poème du hashich" ("The Poem of Hashish") before we began *Petits Poèmes en prose*, on which we were spending four weeks. If there was one thing I had hoped students would have seen by mid-semester, it was the problematic status of too quick a condemnation, not only in the context of poetic writing and critical thinking but also in life in general. But contrary to my hope and as if collective amnesia had struck, our session felt like a replay of the trial of 1857, in which the students, as modern-day versions of the prosecutor Ernest Pinard, were judging Baudelaire's text through the categories of good and evil, right and wrong, and through slippage, accusing Baudelaire himself of evil. Third, because I realized after class that we had discussed the phrase "qu'importe" when reading *Les Fleurs du Mal*: in the last stanzas of "Hymne à la Beauté" ("Hymn to Beauty") and "Le Voyage" ("The Voyage"). "Hymne à la Beauté" ends with "De Satan ou de Dieu, qu'importe? Ange ou Sirène, / Qu'importe, si tu rends . . . / L'univers moins hideux et les instants moins lourds?" 'From Satan or from God, what does it matter? Angel or Siren / What does it matter, if you make . . . / The universe less hideous and the instants less heavy?' ([Pichois] 1: 25; my trans.); "Le Voyage" ends with "Plonger au fond du gouffre, Enfer ou Ciel, qu'importe? / Au fond de l'Inconnu pour trouver du *nouveau*!" 'To plunge into the depths of the abyss, Hell or Heaven, what does it matter? / To the depths of the Unknown to find something *new*!' (134; my trans.). In both poems the phrase "qu'importe" was key to students' understanding Baudelaire's poetics for the new ways in which it aligns the experience of beauty and the unknown with an unconventional approach to binary opposition. (The titles *Les Fleurs du Mal* and *Petits Poèmes en prose* exemplify this.) The contrast between the two reactions we have to the same phrase—we find "qu'importe" aesthetically praiseworthy in the verse poems but ethically questionable in the prose poems—would have provided ample material for reflections had I brought our awareness to focus on this paradox.

How do these instances of "qu'importe" differ, and what makes us react to them differently? By parsing out the types of indifference, offensive or otherwise, that "qu'importe" denotes in each text as well as our reactions to them, we would practice the art of making distinctions as a way into the nondifferentiating "qu'importe." This exercise in distinction could open three lines of inquiry, all addressing the process of shift: What if we shifted our attention from the phrase "qu'importe" to the effect it has on us? We would be making a similar move as the poet-narrator in "Hymne à la Beauté," who changes his focus from Beauty to the effect Beauty has on him. Could the change in our reaction to "qu'importe" inform us about the formal divide between poetry and prose poetry? How is evil treated in prose poetry and in verse poetry? Does the treatment of evil relate to the concern for form in Baudelaire's experimental prose poetry?

It would be fruitful to read "Le Voyage" in the light of what Baudelaire states in the first draft of his dedication of *Les Fleurs du Mal* to Théophile Gautier: "Je sais que dans les régions éthérées de la véritable Poésie, le Mal n'est pas, non plus que le Bien" 'I know that in the ethereal regions of true Poetry, Evil is not, nor Good' (1: 187; my trans.). Once we understand that nondifferentiation governs the space of poetry for Baudelaire, we would appreciate more fully what "qu'importe" accomplishes in "Le Voyage": it opens a passage toward what lies beyond the founding binary opposition between Good and Evil. This could shed light on how "qu'importe" introduces a change of perspective in "Hymne à la Beauté": Beauty is an object of knowledge in the beginning but becomes a source of life at the end. The poet realizes that what matters is not figuring out Beauty's origin through the opposition between Good and Evil but receiving its life-giving effect that makes a true difference. In both verse poems "qu'importe" marks the dawn of lucidity: there is realization that the difference that has served as our guiding principle (Good and Evil, right and wrong) and to which we have been attached so far is no longer relevant and that something else now makes a difference. This lucidity liberates.

It is helpful to clarify for ourselves that letting go of one type, or level, of difference, albeit as fundamental as the one between Good and Evil, does not mean getting rid of distinctions altogether or that anything goes. (A student once asked, "Does that mean murder is okay?") Gilles Deleuze's statement regarding Friedrich Nietzsche's *On the Genealogy of Morals* and Benedict de Spinoza's *Ethics* can be enlightening: "There is no Good or Evil, but there is good and bad. 'Beyond Good and Evil, at least this *does not* mean: beyond good and bad'"; "The opposition of values (Good-Evil) is supplanted by the qualitative difference of modes of existence (good-bad)" (22, 23). We could explore how the nominal couple "Good-Evil" ("*le Bien–le Mal*") relates to the adjectival couple "good-bad." We might discern how nuanced, qualitative distinctions ("good-bad") can sometimes lead to separation and opposition and result in rigid hierarchy, value judgments, and condemnation ("Good-Evil"). We might also ask how often we ourselves slide down the slope of distinction-separation-opposition-hierarchy-judgment-condemnation and, without knowing it, confuse the act of making distinctions with the act of condemning. This exercise might help us realize that the more unaware we are the more we run the risk of condemning what seems distinct or different. Would it be possible not to slide down this slope, not to subject distinct entities to hierarchy, judgment, and condemnation, and to let them be simply as they are?

From the "qu'importe" of the verse poems we can turn to that of the prose poems and think about why only the latter offends us. We can reflect on our own act of judging the narrator of "Le Mauvais Vitrier" and by extension Baudelaire. How have we come to condemn? On closer inspection, we would discover that the abusive narrator whom we took as the poet persona could also be the complacent and ennui-laden public who demands that literature and poetry offer an embellished picture of reality. If so, the glazier, not the narrator, would be the poet, and the absence of colored glasses would be consonant with the poetics of *Les Fleurs du Mal* in its refusal to deliver hypocritical accounts of life "qui fassent voir la vie en beau" 'which make life beautiful' or 'that make life seem beautiful' (*Spleen* [Pichois] 1: 287; *Parisian Prowler* 15; my trans.). Would our attitude change once we see that the narrator can take the place of both the poet and the public? Why or why not? What does this tell us about the way we judge? A discussion of how the same phrase can function and be read differently in different texts and contexts can lead us to think about how we receive and react to words.

We could reflect on the impact words have on us through the sound of the shattered glasses in the context of homonymy of "verre" or "verres" ("glass," "glasses"), "vers" ("verse"), and "ver" ("worm"). As a homonym of "vers" and as the "vitres qui fassent voir la vie en beau," could "verres" stand for the convention of verse poetry? If so, the broken "verres"-"vers" would thematize the act of breaking the convention of verse poetry and be emblematic of the project of prose poetry as Baudelaire envisions it in his *lettre-dédicace* ("dedication letter") to Arsène Houssaye. All the more so, since the shattered "verres," also a homonym of "ver," evoke the truncated serpent of the *lettre-dédicace*. We could explore how the serpent in the *lettre-dédicace* denotes verse as well as Evil and thereby links the prose poem collection to the verse collection. We could then ask how both texts deal with breaking the verse as well as breaking evil. Might "Le Mauvais Vitrier" break the "verres"-"vers," just as the *lettre-dédicace* cuts the serpent-"ver"? Could we say that breaking evil occurs through breaking the verse? It might be useful for students to know that Baudelaire wished to, but never did, publish a frontispiece for the second edition of *Les Fleurs du Mal* in the style of a Renaissance wood engraving he found in a book that depicts the tree of knowledge of Good and Evil, Adam and Eve, and the serpent (Pichois, *Album* 200–05). Could the serpent of the verse poems have reincarnated into the prose poems? If so, prose poetry would inherit directly the verse poetry's project to reveal the logic of evil as announced in the opening poem, "Au Lecteur" ("To the Reader"). In fact it seems to carry the project even further by subjecting the serpent's body—"le Mal" as Evil, pain, and ennui—to explicit and systematic formal treatment that is akin to a surgical intervention.

Here we could step back for a moment and ask how "le Mal" as ennui might manifest itself in the realm of language. Could we think of the process of banalization that significant words and genres inevitably undergo over time as a kind of ennui spreading across language? Italo Calvino speaks of "a plague afflicting language, revealing itself as a loss of cognition and immediacy, an automatism that tends to level out all expression into the most generic, anonymous, abstract formulas, to dilute meanings, to blunt the edge of expressiveness, extinguishing the spark that shoots out from the collision of words and new circumstances" (56). The present-day use of the word *awesome* illustrates perfectly the phenomenon Calvino describes: our students say *awesome* when they want to say "okay," "nice," or "thank you," but do they know that its original meaning is "awe inspiring"? And speaking of "a plague afflicting language" that "dilutes meanings," do they know that the word *ennui*, which we translate habitually as "boredom," goes back etymologically to "hatefulness" (*ennuyer* derives from the Latin *inodiare*, which comes from *odium*, "hatefulness") and anger (melancholia is related to the French *colère*, "anger")? An active state of strong emotion (hatefulness, anger) has come to stand for a passive inertia of emotional indifference (boredom). Just as Calvino says, "the spark that shoots out" from the words *awesome* and *ennui* seems to have been "extinguish[ed]"; their "edge of expressiveness"—verve, tonicity (or anger?)—has been "blunt[ed]"; our sensibility has "level[ed] out." We live and speak under anesthesia. Students may now see how Baudelaire's prose poetry counteracts the phenomenon of automatism and banalization in language by modifying, or even infringing on, existing conventions of lyric poetry in such a way that suddenly they become questionable and worthy of attention. Words and sentences lose their conventional meanings and become strange, revivified, and newly readable, just as the fragments of the severed serpent of the *lettre-dédicace* take on new life.

It is worth noting the ways in which what happens in language mirrors what happens in life: the mechanism of ennui—the outward expressive energy turned inward in mute repression and depression—permeates both language and life. This brings us back to Chambers's second insight, that "teaching poetry can be an educational enterprise when it becomes a way of teaching also about living in the world" ("Classroom" 181). Poetic synesthesia, in the sense both of Baudelairean *correspondance* and Rimbaldien *dérèglement*, operates against anesthesia in language and in life. So how do the issues of prose poetry we have been exploring through "Le Mauvais Vitrier" teach us about living in the world, and how do they address our life? When Baudelaire names ennui at the end of "Au Lecteur," he discloses what had remained invisible by liberating through expression the tonic anger that has been kept down and banalized into boredom. In "Le Mauvais Vitrier" too Baudelaire shakes language out of boredom and convention by shattering the "verres"-"vers"-"ver": he delivers an impact that reverberates through mind and body, opening the possibility of liberating the tonicity and verve of life that might be buried deep down within ourselves and lived merely as boredom. In hindsight I see that our failed class session has accomplished something: we were shaken out of our complacent boredom of triple invisibility and propelled into a state of engaged and engaging anger. We were no longer pantomiming, bored ghosts but expressive, angry human beings. And it was the phrase "qu'importe," which moves between indifferent boredom and liberating anger, that pulled us out of our complacency. Could we venture to say that in Baudelaire poetic disclosure turns inward repression to outer expression and that it does so through the practice of measured anger that liberates rather than deadens?

Our class session allowed me to see better how we react to evil. And the experience continuously invites me to reflect on our own act of condemning the narrator of "Le Mauvais Vitrier"—or any person or thing, for that matter. I find helpful the contemporary philosopher Jean-Luc Marion's statements in *Prolegomena to Charity*: "Before all else, evil hurts ['le mal fait mal']" (1). "[I]f evil's first effect is suffering, its second is the demand that the suffering cease. . . .

How?": "by arousing in me, who is suffering, the desire . . . to return to the evil its hurt," "to attack the attack" (2), and to "kindle a counter-evil . . . of the accusation" (5). Except that "[c]ounter-evil remains an evil, just as a backfire is still a fire—destructive, first and always" (5). Marion calls it "the logic of evil": the instinctive and legitimate attempt to eliminate evil only perpetuates further the evil it seeks to suppress. Suffering and pain, vengeance in hatred and anger, endless perpetuation of evil, death by ennui: *Les Fleurs du Mal* and *Le Spleen de Paris* expose in an exemplary manner the immutable logic of evil Marion describes.

In one of the drafts for the preface to the second edition of *Les Fleurs du Mal*, Baudelaire writes:

> Quelques-uns m'ont dit que ces poésies pouvaient faire du mal. Je ne m'en suis pas réjoui. D'autres, de bonnes âmes, qu'elles pouvaient faire du bien; cela ne m'a pas affligé. La crainte des uns et l'espérance des autres m'ont également étonné, et n'ont servi qu'à me prouver une fois de plus que ce siècle avait désappris toutes les notions classiques relatives à la littérature. ("Projets de préface" 181)

> Some have said that these poems could do harm. That didn't make me rejoice. Others, good souls, that they could do good; that didn't afflict me. Both the fear of some and the hope of others have astonished me and served only to prove to me once more that this century has unlearned all the classical notions regarding literature. (my trans.)

As Marion says, "evil hurts": this is undeniable. What else is there to say except that *Les Fleurs du Mal* "pouvaient faire du mal" 'could do harm [evil]'? And how else can *Les Fleurs du Mal* be defended except through a compensatory counterargument that asserts that *Les Fleurs du Mal* "pouvaient faire du bien" 'could be beneficial [do good]'? Marion's thoughts illuminate how thoroughly both the prosecution and the defense parties at the trial enacted and confirmed the eternal logic of evil, since whatever is launched as counterevil, even good, cannot fight but only reinforces the logic of evil. Simone Weil gives a similar view: "Good as the opposite of evil is, in a sense, equivalent to it, as is the way with all opposites. . . . Good considered on the level of evil and measured against it as one opposite against another is good of the penal code order" (70–71). These insights prompt us to ask how much our own condemnation of the narrator of "Le Mauvais Vitrier" might be participating in the logic of evil. Weil and Marion concur: we must break out of the circle (self-enclosure) and spell (self-perpetuation) of the logic of evil. So too does Baudelaire: we must free ourselves from the serpent's circle and go from the logic of evil to the flowers of evil. True to his words, Baudelaire proceeds in *Le Spleen de Paris* to treat evil formally, cutting open systematically and methodically in content and form the eternal circle of the serpent.

That day in the classroom, our experience spanned the whole spectrum from boredom (repressed energy) to anger (outward energy) to poetry (measured expressive energy). And for me such attending to and countering the law of entropy (which is a turning of energy) is one way in which we pass from the logic of evil to the flowers of evil. To read Baudelaire's work is to engage in a transformative relationship with the inexorable law of entropy and evil in both text and life. And we learn that this transformation begins with a renewed awareness of form that comes with a renewed relationship with words, since being attentive to texts enables us to be attentive to our own acts of judgment when we read carefully. What I hope my students would ultimately take away from reading "Le Mauvais Vitrier" is this: to be able to pause the next time they say "what does it matter?" or "so what?" or "whatever" and to be aware of the energy with which they imbue their words and, if they so choose, to turn it around or leave it as is.

NOTE

I wish to dedicate this essay to Ross Chambers.

Who Is the "Je" of Baudelaire's *Le Spleen de Paris*? Engaging Undergraduate Students in the Study of Narrative Voice and Polyphony

Scott M. Powers

The political and religious instability of late-eighteenth- and nineteenth-century Europe increasingly inspired writers such as Denis Diderot, Pierre Choderlos de Laclos, George Sand, Gustave Flaubert, and Baudelaire to adopt equivocal and unreliable narrative voices. The self-protective and self-parodying lyricism of *Les Fleurs du Mal*, responsible for the collection's complex attitudes toward women, art, the divine, and modernity, presents such a case. In *Le Spleen de Paris*, the element of self-parody intensifies, thereby rendering interpretation especially difficult. The collection's various narrators become more ostensibly unreliable as the prose poems become increasingly dialogical in foregrounding opposing worldviews. Recent criticism has often concluded that these equivocal texts resist definitive interpretation. For this very reason, *Le Spleen de Paris* provides ideal opportunities for generating class discussion and for creating critical readers.

Scholars have warned that any reading of *Le Spleen de Paris* is a precarious endeavor. Sonya Stephens has noted that the pieces of the collection offer "conflicting perspectives as mobile and as unstable as the clouds" (*Baudelaire's Prose Poems* 21). Maria Scott similarly asserts that the Baudelairean text "allows for no absolute certainty as to the direction of its irony" (80). In wrapping up his seven-hundred-page study of the collection, Steve Murphy proposes a type of anticonclusion by stating that all we can take away from *Le Spleen de Paris* is a "complexité pragmatique de l'interprétation" 'pragmatic complexity of interpreting' (*Logiques* 679; my trans). For Murphy, *Le Spleen de Paris* possesses not a logical continuity but rather a deliberate polyphony of contradictory voices and ideologies aimed at manipulating reader reception and triggering diverse ideological reactions (15–32).[1]

Because *Le Spleen de Paris* resists traditional forms of interpretation, instructors may need to consider ways to modify their approach to teaching the prose poems to undergraduate students who have just begun developing their skills in literary analysis. The purpose of this essay is to encourage instructors to embrace the collection's elusiveness as an opportunity to engage students in a discussion of reader reception and in the cultivation of interpretive skills. I envision the approach to teaching *Le Spleen de Paris* delineated here for use in various types of undergraduate courses that study the texts either in the original French (e.g., a survey course of French literature) or in translation (e.g., a course in world literatures) and that can devote two or three class sessions to the collection.

Students in introductory literature courses often conflate the first-person narrator with the text's author. It could be argued that even literary scholars have hastily attributed the apparent misogyny of "La Femme sauvage et la petite-maîtresse" and "Les Yeux des pauvres" to Baudelaire rather than to the narrative personae. I propose here that an effective way to lead students in adopting a critical perspective is to provide them with opportunities to question the identity and function of the first-person narrator in *Le Spleen de Paris* and to consider the importance of other voices or points of view in the poems.

To sensitize students to how they receive the narrator's thoughts and actions, instructors might point out that the narrative voice varies considerably from piece to piece. For instance, "Le Mauvais Vitrier," "Les Yeux des pauvres," and "Mademoiselle Bistouri" contain a first-person narrator directly involved in the action. "La Corde" features two narrators: a frame narrator relays to us a tragic tale that his painter friend first recounted to him. The narrator of "Les Vocations" remains a simple observer of a conversation among four children. In "La Femme sauvage et la petite-maîtresse," the *je* would appear to be fully implicated in the story, intent on teaching his mistress a lesson. And yet the poem is entirely framed in quotation marks. Finally, "L'Étranger" features not a narrator but a dialogue among two (perhaps more) interlocutors.

I propose as the first day's reading assignment four or five prose poems containing various types of narrative voices and personae, accompanied by a series of questions that solicit observations regarding the narrators. An overarching question could be, How do students position themselves toward the speaker and the other characters in the various pieces? For example, students often express moral disgust on a first reading of "La Femme sauvage et la petite-maîtresse." In class, they should feel free to share the conclusions that they drew regarding the intent of the story and any judgment that they may have passed on the collection or even the author. A crucial follow-up question would be whether their reactions took into account the fact that the poem is sealed within quotation marks. What about texts such as "Les Yeux des pauvres" and "Mademoiselle Bistouri," which dramatize conflicts in point of view? Did students take sides with one character of the altercation? If so, can they explain which attributes of the narratives influenced their identification with a specific character? For instance, what function might the titles have played in orienting reader reception? And finally, how did students position their reading of "L'Étranger"? Did they identify one of the interlocutors with the narrator of other pieces? During this discussion, the instructor should allow students the time to come to an awareness of what, during their first reading of the poems, may have constituted an uncritical, preconscious response.

To formalize (and facilitate) the identification of different types of narrator, the instructor may wish to introduce Gérard Genette's terminology. In acquiring the concepts of heterodiegetic narrator (who remains absent from the world of the story), homodiegetic narrator (who takes part in the narrated action), and autodiegetic narrator (a homodiegetic narrator who is the main character of the story), as well as the terms denoting levels of narrative—namely diegetic (the description of characters' thoughts and actions), extradiegetic (elements of the narrative that do not occur in the story), and metadiegetic (a story embedded within another)—students are already encouraged to adopt a critical distance that aims to categorize (see Genette 238–46, 251–59). In "Mademoiselle Bistouri," for instance, we can make reference to a classic example of the homodiegetic narrator who recounts his own story of an encounter with an enigmatic woman. In "La Corde," it would be more appropriate to speak of two narrators as well as of two levels of text. In the diegetic text, a conversation between a homodiegetic narrator and an artist friend serves as a pretext for another story. In the metadiegetic story, the artist friend discusses a tragic event that has befallen him. It might also prove useful to distinguish between a homodiegetic narrator who plays a secondary role or even that of simple observer (*narrateur-témoin*) of events, as in "Les Vocations," and the autodiegetic narrator who stars in his own show, as in "Le Mauvais Vitrier."

In defense of their association of the *je* with Baudelaire, students will likely point out that the various narrators are categorically male and that they often identify themselves as poets. Although these attributes suggest some biographical overlap between the narrators and the author, evidence exists to problematize this association: the atypical framing quotation marks of "La Femme sauvage et la petite-maîtresse" are a strong indication that the homodiegetic poet-narrator is not the author, as is the fact that the identity of first-person narrators varies from piece to piece. Moreover, a detailed discussion of the narrator's attributes in other pieces, especially indicators of his financial security in "Les Yeux des pauvres" and "Le Gâteau" among other poems, contrasts with Baudelaire's chronic penury throughout most of his adult life. The point here is not to dismiss associations that the students make between Baudelaire and his narrators but rather to instill in them the habit of questioning such associations. It could be argued that in offering varying textual framings of narrative voice the prose poems solicit an active monitoring of the narrator's identity and subject position in each story. In the end, even if we conclude that some of the narrators are the fictitious doubles of Baudelaire, we still need to determine how the text might condition us to react to the views that the poet's doubles express. After all, a given poem could present in an ironic mode a psychological attribute of the author that he wishes to reject. Rather than attempt to determine whether the narrators are Baudelaire's fictitious doubles, we might consider whether the text casts the narrator's and others' subject positions in a positive or negative light.

During the second day, the class may pursue the discussion of the reader's reaction to the narrator through an in-depth analysis of one or two assigned texts. I have found that "Le Mauvais Vitrier" lends itself especially well to such a discussion. The instructor can guide a collaborative analysis of the poem by inviting students to explore elements of the narrative that might manipulate the reader's reception of the concluding violent act. Students readily pick up on the opposition between artifice and the real as dramatized in the narrator's destruction of the "bad" glazier's colorless panes of glass. Up for discussion are the ostensible moments of irony, including the two paradoxes of the final paragraph: "Ces plaisanteries nerveuses ne sont pas sans péril, et on peut souvent les payer cher. Mais qu'importe l'éternité de la damnation à qui a trouvé dans une seconde l'infini de la jouissance?" 'Some neurotic pranks are not without peril, and one can often pay dearly for them. But what does an eternity of damnation matter to someone who has experienced for one second the infinity of delight?' (*Spleen* [Pichois] 287; *Parisian Prowler* 15). Here, students can discuss how such a conclusion might serve to condition the reader's response. Does it frame the narrator's destructive act in such a way that we readily identify with or dismiss the speaking subject? When asked to compare eternal damnation with a moment's pleasure, is the reader in fact led to side with or against the aesthete narrator? And what about the narrator's repetitive pronouncement of the cliché "voir la vie en beau," which students may recognize as the French equivalent of "to see the world through rose-colored glasses"? Can we consider its repetition, often accompanied by exclamation points, indicative of parody? Students will likely agree that the abundance of stylistic devices evidences the manipulation of reader reception, but instructors should encourage multiple interpretations of possible overarching messages. Whereas some students will interpret the violent act as absurd and regard the poem as pronouncing judgment against idealist art, others may sympathize with the narrator, who falls victim to the irrational dimension of human behavior. A discussion of "Le Mauvais Vitrier" forces students to mull over the evidence to choose their angle of interpretation. They must decide whether the poem pokes fun at idealism or assaults the ideology of realism. Is the narrator the target of irony, or does he solicit our empathy? Does the poem present a case of a realist author ridiculing an idealist narrator, or does the narrative candidly depict the irrationality of the subconscious?[22]

Likewise "La Chambre double" raises the question of whether the text sides with the narrator in favoring the dreamy world invoked by hallucinogens over the daily stress and discomforts of the real world. This poem provides the opportunity to discuss the use of italics as a stylistic device to oppose conventional language. In underscoring the words *spirituelle* and *mirettes*, does the text attempt to create a cognitive distance between the reader and the idealist tableau? Another topic of discussion is the juxtaposition of conflicting registers. The pejorative qualifiers *bleuâtre*, *rosâtre*, and *stagnante*, used to describe an otherwise ethereal scene, incite us to draw conclusions regarding the message behind the description. Does this narrative provide a subtle critique of the drug user and his desperate attachment to an artificial paradise (and therefore prove consonant with Baudelaire's moral stance against the consumption of hallucinogens in *Les Paradis artificiels* [*Œuvres complètes* 1: 377–537]), or does it represent a sincere (and autobiographical) depiction of the anguish that afflicts the poet in his struggle to combat the tyranny of the real?[23] Similar questions can be asked regarding the portraits of the two Bénédictas juxtaposed in "Laquelle est la vraie?," as well as the contrasting depictions of sea and land in "Déjà!"

Many poems of *Le Spleen de Paris* exacerbate the obstacles of interpretation in featuring a conflict between opposing subject positions. To prepare students for the critical analysis of poems containing multiple points of view, the instructor might next discuss polyphony as a defining attribute of prose. A discussion of points of divergence between poetry and prose seems especially suitable in a survey course in which it is likely that professors have already analyzed defining characteristics of lyric poetry. The important distinctions that Mikhail Bakhtin makes in *The Dialogic Imagination* between lyric poetry and prose may prove especially useful and can be concisely summarized. To recall, Bakhtin discusses the premise of poetry as rooted in the idea of a "unitary and singular language"—the poem itself constituting "a unitary, monologically sealed-off utterance" (296). In stark contrast, in the "heteroglossia" of prose the novelist weaves into the text's very fabric countless "words of intentions and tones that are alien to him" (296, 298). The prose writer communicates to the reader his worldview through the careful orchestration of multiple languages, discourses, and ideologies. A text's message is not directly communicated in an unmediated utterance from narrator to narratee; rather it is "refracted" as the author, through humor, irony, parody, juxtaposition, and other stylistic effects, integrates multiple voices into the text (299).

This is not to say that verse does not manifest heteroglossia. Quite to the contrary, many pieces of *Les Fleurs du Mal* (such as "Bénédiction") feature multiple voices. However, following Bakhtin, we can say that the irruption of dialogism in verse is not what makes the text poetic. In fact, it calls the foundational premise of lyricism into question. For Bakhtin, "the poet is a poet insofar as he accepts the idea of a unitary singular language" (296). That is, "each word must express the poet's *meaning* directly and without mediation; there must be no distance between the poet and his word. The meaning must emerge from language as a single intentional whole: none of its stratification, its speech diversity, to say nothing of its language diversity, may be reflected in any fundamental way in his poetic work" (297). In this light, we may regard Baudelaire's turn to prose as a logical outcome of a sustained movement in his verse poetry to question the lyric self's assumption of a "complete single-personed hegemony over his own language" (297).

To be sure, in his elaboration of heteroglossia Bakhtin has in mind the prose of novels, whereas the genre in question here is the prose poem. But as Jonathan Monroe has noted, the prose poem's turn to prose aims precisely to undermine "the sublime pretentions of the lyric" (24; see also 27, 29). Barbara Johnson specifically describes Baudelaire's prose poems as effecting "une amputation de tout ce qui, dans la poésie, s'érige comme unité, totalité" 'an amputation of everything in poetry that presents itself as unity or totality' (*Défigurations* 154; my trans). We can say that much of the prose poem's dialogism owes to its hosting the interplay of poetry and prose. As Monroe describes it, the prose poem constitutes "a dialogical struggle . . . between and among various literary discourses" (17), predicated on opposing philosophical systems. Moreover, as a collection of fifty prose poems, *Le Spleen de Paris* compounds the dialogical struggle as the characters, ideas, and circumstances of any given story inevitably resonate with others that precede or follow it. Overall, Bakhtin's important observations on the novel can aid in delineating for the reader the task of discerning a possible overarching worldview through the analysis of ways the prose poem interrelates multiple voices, discourses, and ideologies.

The instructor may choose to assign poems that feature two or more voices, such as "L'Étranger," "Les Dons des fées," "Les Yeux des pauvres," "Portraits de maîtresses," "La Soupe et les nuages," and "Mademoiselle Bistouri." To facilitate discussion, it is helpful to provide accompanying questions that prompt students to identify the different characters' subject positions as well as the oppositions established between objects or spaces placed in dialogue with each other and to explain the manner in which the poems conclude. For instance, did one worldview appear to gain dominance? Instructors can also urge students to consider elements of narrative stylization including the modes of irony, parody, or humor that, as indicators of authorial orchestration, would appear to cast characters, ideas, and spaces in a particular (often negative or disturbing) light.

A collaborative analysis of "Les Yeux des pauvres," for example, can serve to highlight multiple interpretations of the story. Some may side with the narrator, who, while enjoying a sumptuous dinner at a café, begins to empathize with the suffering of others. When he catches sight of a famished family gazing at his table from the street, the narrator would appear to adopt an ethical stance: "Non seulement j'étais attendri par cette famille d'yeux, mais je me sentais un peu honteux de nos verres et de nos carafes, plus grands que notre soif" 'Not only was I moved by that family of eyes, but I felt a little ashamed of our decanters, larger than our thirst' (*Spleen* [Pichois] 319; *Parisian Prowler* 61). Such a response sharply contrasts with the lady's expression of disgust: "Ces gens-là me sont insupportables avec leurs yeux ouverts comme des portes cochères! Ne pourriez-vous pas prier le maître du café de les éloigner d'ici?" 'I can't stand those people with their eyes wide open like entrance gates! Can't you ask the headwaiter to send them away?' Other students may side with the woman rather than the narrator, who could appear to be constructing a self-serving, misogynist argument. After all, in the poem's first paragraph, he proposes to offer his female companion a lesson in "imperméabilité féminine" 'feminine impermeability.' The instructor might encourage the class to consider whether the narrative features the narrator's thoughts and actions in a positive light. What conclusions can be drawn regarding the use of italics when the narrator seeks out the reflection of *his* empathy in his companion's eyes? Does such underscoring further value the narrator's perspective as distinct from the lady's? Or does italicization ironically convey the narrator's viewpoint by drawing attention to the narcissism at play here? Many other points of contention among students may include the narrator's qualification that he "[se] sentai[t] un peu honteux" 'felt *a little* ashamed' and that he has no difficulty in turning his gaze from the starving family to his *bien-aimée*. How might the reader's apprehension of the narrator's seemingly lukewarm reaction be conditioned by the preceding description of the café's garish interiors and decorative images of gluttony? In contrast, the woman's intolerance may in fact suggest a hyperempathetic reaction; her request to have the family removed from the premises could be interpreted as the symptom of the inability to distance herself emotionally from their spectacle.[4] Another possibility is that neither the narrator's nor the woman's viewpoint is privileged. Could textual framing equally ridicule both? A similar exploration might be made of "Mademoiselle Bistouri" and "Le Gâteau," in which the narrator appears to adopt an ethical position toward poor children and a prostitute.

After a few sessions devoted to the discussion of authorial orchestration and reader reception in *Le Spleen de Paris*, I suggest asking students to draft a composition in which they justify their interpretation of a prose poem not covered in class but which contains many of the same stylistic markers, namely the use of irony, italics, and the commingling of discursive registers such as lofty, didactic, material, colloquial, and pejorative language (e.g., as in "Le Galant Tireur" and "Le Joujou du pauvre"). Whereas the traditional assignment of an individual essay can certainly serve this purpose, I have found that the study of narrative voice and polyphony in Baudelaire's prose poems lends itself especially well to student collaboration on a coauthored project. In my classes, I prompt students to pair up, discuss their reactions to a given text, and envision ways in which they could feature two interpretations in a single essay in order to illustrate polyphony and reader reception. I encourage the pairs of students to consider two distinct ways of interpreting the piece that take into account contrasting angles of interpreting the narrator's persona as well as the roles played by other characters. In a planning session, students discuss at length with their partners ways to present contrasting readings of the poem. Then they draft an outline together and decide who is responsible for each section. Oftentimes, students opt to work separately on the construction of an individual interpretation, but they must read and give feedback on a draft of their partners' interpretations and work together to meld the two parts through effective transitions and the elimination of repetition. Jointly, they compose an introduction and conclusion that present the two readings in a larger discussion of polyphony and textual framing in the prose poems. Collaboration on the articulation of a prose poem's contrasting interpretations offers students a valuable opportunity to develop skills in critical reading and analytic writing. Not unlike the polyphony of Baudelaire's *Le Spleen de Paris*, collaborative writing presents the important task of orchestrating opposing views in the service of a broader argument.

NOTES

[1] For a similar assessment of *Le Spleen de Paris*, see Stephens, *Baudelaire's Prose Poems* 19–20.

[2] For a helpful commentary on other elements of irony in "Le Mauvais Vitrier," see Kaplan, *Baudelaire's Prose Poems* 42–48; Stephens, *Baudelaire's Prose Poems* 64–71; and McLees 102–05.

[3] For a more detailed description of polyphony in "La Chambre double," see Stephens's analysis of the poem as "a vehicle capable of containing other texts and discourses" that "stages a self-questioning mirroring of the lyric persona" (*Baudelaire's Prose Poems* 30–36).

[4] For helpful commentaries on "Les Yeux des pauvres," see Stephens, *Baudelaire's Prose Poems* 92–96; Murphy, *Logiques* 243–76; and M. Scott 93–98.

What's the Point?
Allegory and the Prose Poems

Scott Carpenter

Un train peut en cacher un autre ("One train may conceal another"). In rural France such warnings used to be commonplace at level crossings. The danger was that inattentive drivers might start forward after one train had passed, only to collide with a different locomotive rocketing by on a second set of tracks.

For many students, Baudelaire's prose poems are reminiscent of this dynamic, resulting in false starts, double takes, and a panicked application of brakes. They also generate a good deal of readerly anxiety. After all, if one train can hide another, why couldn't the second hide a third, or the third a fourth? Crossing the railbed becomes a fraught affair.

When I teach Baudelaire to advanced undergraduates (usually in French, usually in classes focused on poetry, and always with only two or three days to dedicate to a sampling of his work), the prose poems are a problem. On the one hand, students find them easier to read than verse: the syntax is somewhat simpler, and these anecdotal pieces offer an Ariadne's thread of narrative. On the other hand, students are left flummoxed by the apparent contradictions and provocations of many of the pieces. *What*, they ask, *is the point*?

What is the point? A naive query, on the face of it, but I'd suggest that this is actually the question that matters the most. And the answer is far from obvious: as with trains, one point may conceal another. It's tricky going.

Unlike certain of Baudelaire's verse pieces, which may lull readers with a lie of wholeness (most famously in "Correspondances"), the prose poems gape; they are rife with gaps, omissions, and puzzles. How, for instance, could the poet advocate beating up the poor ("Assommons les pauvres!")? Why does he celebrate the physical assault of street vendors ("Le Mauvais Vitrier")? In what sense is capital punishment a *"faveur"* ("Une Mort héroïque")? Can one seriously assert that stupidity is worse than vice ("La Fausse Monnaie")? Many of the poems build toward a kind or moral pronouncement—but the lessons they proclaim jar with readerly expectations, producing more dissonance than resolution. Something feels incomplete, off, wrong. It's often helpful to put students in groups to discuss the problems they have detected in a poem; they participate more confidently after discovering that others share their perplexity. Nevertheless, they often feel they've missed the real point, whose presence they can almost sense, like the distant hum of another train coming down the rails, still out of sight.

After we read a couple of the pieces in class (it almost doesn't matter which—and I often accept Baudelaire's invitation to jumble the order), I focus on our discomfort with the poems' endings. Once I reassure students that their impressions are (usually) not due to weak language skills, we can turn our attention to the effects of nonconclusions. Perhaps, I suggest, the point of the tale is partly to dissolve the notion of clear points and simple resolutions and thus to force the reader to loop back into the narrative. What do we find if we do so? My idea in such a class is to investigate gaps, ironic and otherwise: between the text and our expectations, between what a poem says and what it does, between the story that is told and others that are merely hinted at.

This last idea—that a text may allude to other stories—paves the way for a discussion of allegory that invariably enriches our readings of the poems. Critics have long associated this complex rhetorical figure with Baudelaire, and the prose poems offer a laboratory for experimenting with it. A pedagogical advantage when discussing allegory is that students are more familiar with this term than they are with many other tropes. The obstacle is that they often have a naive understanding of it. For instance, they may be familiar with moral or philosophical allegories (say, Plato's allegory of the cave or Aesop's fables), but these models suggest a simplicity one rarely finds in Baudelaire. Without dedicating long sessions to the formulations of Paul de Man (*Blindness* 187–208) and other theorists, I find it helpful to draw on the images that Walter Benjamin—a deep reader of Baudelaire—used in his 1923 essay "The Task of the Translator." (Benjamin's essay does not deal explicitly with allegory, but the link between *allogoria*—"speaking otherwise"—and translation should not be underestimated.) For Benjamin the translator's mission is to remain so close to the original that the reader will hear the other language whispering between the lines (82; see also Spivak 400). In another passage, he refers to translations and originals fitting together like two shards of a larger (broken) vessel (Benjamin, "Task" 79). There may be many such shards, of course, and the edges of each will hint at the presence of the others. So, too, for allegory.

Armed with this concept, one can now return to Baudelaire. I like to begin with a poem that appeared between the publication of the censored edition of *Les Fleurs du Mal* (*Flowers of Evil* [1857]) and *Le Spleen de Paris*: "Le Masque" ("The Mask"). Looking at this piece helps students understand the overlap between verse and prose—a distinction with fuzzier borders than students expect. Appearing in the 1861 edition of *Les Fleurs du Mal*, "Le Masque" is a narrative piece in verse, arguably representing an intermediate step between Baudelaire's earlier work and the prose poems. It is especially useful for our purposes because it reproduces the experience readers have when puzzling through *Le Spleen de Paris*. In "Le Masque," the narrator depicts the sculpture of a flawless, beautiful woman—only to reveal belatedly that his description is incomplete. As he steps to the left or the right, the illusion of perfection disintegrates, yielding to an image of monstrosity. The edge of a mask appears, behind which the grief-stricken woman has hidden her grimace. As Baudelaire describes elsewhere, it is behind the mask that the viewer can discover "le secret de l'allégorie, la morale de la fable, je veux dire la véritable tête révulsée, se pâmant dans les larmes et l'agonie" 'the secret of the allegory, the moral of the fable—I mean the real, contorted face, stricken with tears and agony' (*Salon de 1859* 678).[1]

Because a later version of this sculpture (by Ernest Christophe [1876]) is prominently displayed at the Musée d'Orsay, it's easy for students to view pictures of it and see how it works. The sculpture is already an allegory about the human condition—about what we show and what we hide—but Baudelaire adds another level, turning the act of his narrator's initial misperception (leading to surprise and reassessment) into a model for modern aesthetic experience. Baudelairean allegory has to do with the discovery of a gap that produces a sudden, new understanding.

In "Le Masque" the reader's discovery of otherness is experienced as shock, as the kind of jolt that's associated with change and chance encounters. These are key elements of Baudelaire's modernity, whether expressed in his own reflections on art (*"Le Beau est toujours bizarre"* 'Beauty is always bizarre' [*Exposition Universelle* 2: 578]; "Le Beau est *toujours* étonnant" 'Beauty is *always* surprising' [*Salon de 1859* 616]) or brought to our attention by other readers (see M. Scott 119–21; Newmark). Add to this a creeping uncertainty about how many levels may exist in the sculpture (are we sure the second face is not a mask, too?), and we find a compelling illustration of the allegorical operation.

In "Le Masque," Baudelaire refers explicitly to allegory, as he does in three other poems in *Les Fleurs du Mal*. However, the word all but disappears from the prose collection—as if the "warning signs" for the reader had been removed. If one story may conceal another, we are left to fend for ourselves.

A useful next step in the discussion comes in the brief poem "Le Chien et le flacon" ("The Dog and the Scent Bottle"). In this piece, the narrator offers his pet a whiff of a fine perfume, only to see the dog recoil and bark in protest. "Ah!" he responds with disdain, "si je vous avais offert un paquet d'excréments, vous l'auriez flairé avec délices et peut-être dévoré" 'Had I offered you a package of excrement you would have sniffed at it with delight—and perhaps even lapped it up' (*Spleen* [Pichois] 284). The commentary on the vagaries of canine taste leads the narrator to pronounce his unambiguous comparison: "Ainsi . . . vous ressemblez au public, à qui il ne faut jamais présenter des parfums délicats qui l'exaspèrent, mais des ordures soigneusement choisies" 'In this way . . . you resemble the public, to whom we should never offer delicate perfumes that will infuriate, but only carefully selected filth.'

"Le Chien et le flacon" operates in a simple mode of allegory that becomes nearly explicit: the general public, like dogs, is drawn to crap. Because the narrator turns the appreciation of fragrances into an aesthetic judgment, it's a small step to see the scented offerings as a stand-in for poetry—either fine verse (perfume) or doggerel (excrement). Even harried undergraduates with only a few semesters of French behind them can understand this level of the poem and its lesson, and the portrait of Baudelaire as resentful and underappreciated contributes to their vision of the *poète maudit*.

But class discussion typically generates a series of questions that complicate the apparent simplicity of the text. For instance, if students enjoy "Le Chien et le flacon," what exactly does that mean in the poem's own logic? Are they admiring one of the finest fragrances, or is the piece an example of "carefully selected filth"? That is, are we the idealized readers of whom Baudelaire dreams, or are we instead dogs? And how is one to tell the difference?

If the point of "Le Chien et le flacon" has to do with the evaluation of poetry, does this short piece bear any relation to Baudelaire's other poetic production? One might signal that *Les Fleurs du Mal* includes a poem entitled "Le Flacon"—in which poetry and fragrance are also linked. In this light, "Le Chien et le flacon" appears as a bitter commentary on the public reception of art in general and of the censorship of *Les Fleurs du Mal* in particular. One story appears to conceal another, and we see the mechanics of allegory at work.

The connection between *Les Fleurs du Mal* and *Le Spleen de Paris* becomes evident in a glance at the tables of contents of the works, where similarities abound, including some exact duplicates (e.g., "Une Chevelure," "Le Voyage à Cythère"). A small number of poems have been "translated" from verse to prose, and others bear more subtle connections. In any case, when reading the prose poems it's hard not to hear *Les Fleurs du Mal* in the background, the way Benjamin's ideal translation retains echoes of the original.

Many of the poems appear to contain allegorical elements at the same time that they bear allegorical links to other pieces or even other collections. Ross Chambers has described such chains of representation as "open" allegories (*Mélancolie* 174–76), which have no clear stopping point. While a text like "Le Chien et le flacon" is relatively accessible (at least at the first level), others, such as "Le Mauvais Vitrier," "La Fausse Monnaie," or "Laquelle est la vraie?," lead readers into mazes of logical and representational difficulty that defy the possibility of a definitive exit.[2] The extraordinary open-endedness of the poems can leave one ill at ease, but it also helps explain the enduring power of these intriguing narratives.

"Le Mauvais Vitrier" is a useful step in this study because it complements "Le Chien et le flacon," and its physical proximity in the collection (it comes next in the sequence) suggests a thematic connection too. In addition, Baudelaire singles this poem out in his letter to Arsène Houssaye that serves as a preface to the collection: "Vous-même, mon cher ami, n'avez-vous pas tenté de traduire en une *chanson* le cri strident du *Vitrier*, et d'exprimer dans une prose lyrique toutes les désolantes suggestions que ce cri envoie jusqu'aux mansardes, à travers les plus hautes brumes de la rue?" 'You yourself, my dear friend, haven't you attempted to translate into *song* the strident cry of the *Glazier* and to express in lyric prose all the sorrow that this cry sends echoing up to the rooftops?' (*Spleen* [Pichois] 276).

At the center of this narrative poem lies a nasty trick. After forcing a street-going vendor to mount the six stories leading to his garret, the narrator expresses indignation at the fact that he carries only clear glass—no panes in pink, red, or blue, no *vitres de paradis* ("panes of paradise") that might make life beautiful. He shoves the man back down the stairs, and when the glazier reappears at street level, the poet drops a flowerpot from the window, landing it squarely on the poor fellow's back and destroying the entire "palais de cristal" 'crystal palace' of his wares. The poem concludes with the most paradoxical of morals: "Ces plaisanteries nerveuses ne sont pas sans péril, et on peut souvent les payer cher. Mais qu'importe l'éternité de la damnation à qui a trouvé dans une seconde l'infini de la jouissance?" 'These spirited jokes are not without their dangers, and one often pays dearly for them. But who cares about eternal damnation when you've found within an instant the boundlessness of pleasure?' (287).

We have mentioned above the importance of shock in Baudelaire's aesthetics, and no one would dispute that the glazier has weathered a significant jolt. However, so has the reader, stunned by a display of cruelty that is subsequently touted as an aesthetic triumph. Ordinarily one might reach for a figurative (allegorical) reading in hopes of making sense of an otherwise problematic text, but that endeavor is only partly successful here. Certainly "Le Mauvais Vitrier" reminds us of "Le Chien et le flacon," where the poet's job is to shock the general public. But the dropping of a pot of flowers onto sheets of glass creates additional echoes. First, it allegorizes an idiom—*casser les vitres* ("to break window panes")—that in everyday parlance means "to create scandal." Moreover, the tool of this wreckage—a flower pot—is startlingly close to an *anthology* (the Greek term for a "collection of flowers"), such as the one that had earlier caused such an uproar that it led to censorship: *Les Fleurs du Mal*.

This emphasis on shock is a key component of the aesthetic experience. After all, in 1861 Baudelaire announced the completion of his revised collection in these terms: "Nouvelles *Fleurs du Mal* faites. A tout casser, comme une explosion de gaz chez un vitrier" 'New *Flowers of Evil* done. Enough to shatter everything, like a gas explosion at a glazier's' (*Correspondance* 1: 568). But "Le Mauvais Vitrier" is not just a diatribe about the scandal surrounding *Les Fleurs du Mal*. One might ask students to ponder what the poem also has to say about language—about clear glass and colored glass and about the force and fragility of expression. A starting point might be the representation of the glazier, whose wares supposedly carry no poetic or transformative value—at least until they are shattered. The complexity of "Le Mauvais Vitrier," which points to many different allegorical levels (among them *Les Fleurs du Mal*, poetic language, bourgeois morals, and more) should suffice to demonstrate that there is no single key for unlocking the poem. Instead, we find ourselves in a text that is haunted by others, like Benjamin's model of the interlinear translation.

A more complex example—which also challenges the transparency of representation—occurs in "La Fausse Monnaie" ("The Counterfeit Coin"). As the narrator and his companion leave a tobacconist's shop, the friend offers a beggar a surprisingly generous handout. The poet approves: "Vous avez raison," he says; "après le plaisir d'être étonné, il n'en est pas de plus grand que celui de causer une surprise" 'You're right. After the pleasure of being astonished one-self, there's none greater than surprising others' (*Spleen* [Pichois] 323).

Then the friend explains that the coin he just gave away was counterfeit.

The narrator's head swims as he reflects on the possible outcomes. Financially the beggar has been set on a course that may lead to riches or ruin: if the coin is recognized as a fake, he will likely end up in jail; otherwise, this small capital may lead to increased wealth. Aside from the jab at the speculative economy of the Second Empire, where high finance relied on machinations no more authentic than the beggar's coin, Baudelaire links this distribution of counter-feit currency to an act that is less economic than aesthetic: it is the creation of surprise.

I ask students to reflect on the central action of "La Fausse Monnaie" in the context of hoaxes (which are a seriously playful pastime on our campus). What is the pleasure of mystifying someone—or of being mystified? And what are the dangers? Is it still a mystification if the victim of the prank never understands he has been tricked? These questions help them discuss an issue that is both moral and aesthetic, after which we can return to the poem. When the beggar receives a handout that greatly exceeds his hopes, it triggers a surprise that is, at least initially, pleasurable. Yet the gift is hardly innocent, especially for a pen-niless person clinging to the fringe of society. The donation will propel the man into the economic system, with unpredictable and potentially dangerous results. As Jacques Derrida has said, the coin (and, indeed, the poem itself) becomes a "machine à provoquer des événements" 'machine for creating events' (*Donner le temps* 125), a fact demonstrated by the surprises already experienced by the narrator and reader.

Like so many of the prose poems, "La Fausse Monnaie" closes with a coda that blurs morality and aesthetics: "On n'est jamais excusable d'être méchant, mais il y a quelque mérite à savoir qu'on l'est; et le plus irréparable des vices est de faire le mal par bêtise" 'It is never justifiable to be mean, but there's some merit in knowing that you are; and the most irreparable of vices is to perform evil through stupidity' (324).

"La Fausse Monnaie" introduces a topic that often comes up in discussions of allegory: if one story is employed to tell another, which is the real one? In "Le Masque" we see a covering that conceals (and yet reveals) a "véritable tête" 'true head'; in "Le Chien et le flacon," we wonder about the difference between real poetry and "carefully selected filth"; in "La Fausse Monnaie," pleasurable anxiety comes from a counterfeit. Given all this, what is the relation between allegory and lying?

This question lies at the heart of a bizarre little poem entitled "Laquelle est la vraie?" ("Which Is the Real One?"), whose very title evokes the problems of duality and authenticity. Here the narrator recounts his relationship with a woman whose idealized description recalls not just the beautiful "lying face" of "Le Masque" but also the perfection associated with "Correspondances" (from *Les Fleurs du Mal*). After evoking her immortal beauty, the narrator reports that Bénédicta—"trop belle pour vivre longtemps" 'too beautiful to live for long'—expires (342). Stricken with grief, the poet will undertake to inter his beloved himself, and as he completes this grim task, a small creature appears on the grave. Bizarre and hysterical, she bears a strange resemblance to the dead woman, and this duplication of Bénédicta, where perfect beauty and absolute hideousness blend together, recalls many other allegorical doublings in Baudelaire, where the gap between reality and illusion startles us. The duplicate Bénédicta tramples the grave, crying out: "*C'est moi*, la vraie Bénédicta! C'est moi, une fameuse canaille! Et pour punition de ta folie et de ton aveuglement, tu m'aimeras telle que je suis!" *'I'm the real Bénédicta! It's me, a real scoundrel! And to punish you for your folly and your blindness, you will love me as I really am!'* The poet, sure of himself, shouts back at this intruder while stomping on the ground:

> Mais moi, furieux, j'ai répondu: "Non! non! non!" et, pour mieux accentuer mon refus, j'ai frappé si violemment la terre, que ma jambe s'est enfoncée jusqu'au genou dans la sépulture récente, et que, comme un loup pris au piège, je reste attaché, pour toujours peut-être, à la fosse de l'idéal.

> But furious, I replied: "No! No! No!" And the better to emphasize my refusal, I stomped so hard on the ground that I sank my leg up to the knee in the fresh grave. So, like a wolf caught in a trap, I remain bound, perhaps forever, to the grave of the ideal.

How ironic that the poet should lose his footing precisely at the moment of his greatest certainty, when firm ground gives way. In this single moment we find the conjunction of shock, stumbling, surprise, allegory, and fakes. Suddenly confronted with a creature purporting to be the real Bénédicta, the poet has to wonder about the one he has just buried, the supposedly fake one. Representation has lost all its currency here. There are two Bénédictas, similar but opposite (like the two faces of "Le Masque"), and one of them is presumably a counterfeit. But as with the coin of "La Fausse Monnaie," it's impossible to tell for sure which one is which, for the very presence of a fake casts all authenticity into doubt.

In "Laquelle est la vraie?" the narrator has buried his ideal and mourned the loss of perfection. But does that mean that the creature dancing on *la fosse* ("the grave"—which in French is a perfect homophone for *la fausse* ["the false one"]) is somehow the real one? The poet leaves us in the lurch, indefinitely suspended between two answers, one foot on the solid earth, the other sunken into an abyss. As so often happens, Baudelaire's allegory leaves us oscillating between two (or more) incompatible readings.

The old question returns: What is the point of such an oscillation? Partly it's to stop asking questions about the point—as if the function of a text were a final and univocal thing, a kind of period or full stop that might at long last arrest the shifting sands of representation.

Benjamin has provided an enticing model for this kind of open-ended and ongoing representation. In his *Arcades Project*, he describes Baudelaire as a brooding allegorist who feels a jolt of recognition when two puzzle pieces (like the shards of a translation) suddenly match without the aid of "natural mediation":

> The brooder's memory ranges over the indiscriminate mass of dead lore. Human knowledge, within this memory, is something piecemeal—in an especially pregnant sense: it is like the jumble of arbitrarily cut pieces from which a puzzle is assembled. An epoch fundamentally averse to brooding has nonetheless preserved its outward gesture in the puzzle. It is the gesture, in particular, of the allegorist. Through the disorderly fund which his knowledge places at his disposal, the allegorist rummages here and there for a particular piece, holds it next to some other piece, and tests to see if they fit together—that meaning with this image or this image with that meaning. The result can never be known beforehand, for there is no natural mediation between the two.   (368)

These pieces may be assembled (disassembled, reassembled) in many ways, some of which will produce surprising combinations without ever producing a stable whole. Once students are freed from the notion that a text is a lock for which they seek a magic key, they can practice (in groups, for example) juxtaposing images and ideas within the poems to see what that process reveals. It's especially effective with poems that play explicitly on the allegorical register: "Une Mort héroïque," "La Chambre double," "Le Don des fées," "Le Galant Tireur," among others. This process—consisting of privileging fragments—comes up in Baudelaire's image of the textual serpent, described in his preface to the collection:

> Nous pouvons couper où nous voulons, moi ma rêverie, vous le manuscrit, le lecteur sa lecture; car je ne suspends pas la volonté rétive de celui-ci au fil interminable d'une intrigue superflue. Enlevez une vertèbre, et les deux morceaux de cette tortueuse fantaisie se rejoindront sans peine. Hachez-la en nombreux fragments, et vous verrez que chacun peut exister à part.   (*Spleen* [Pichois] 275)

> We may cut wherever we wish—I my daydream, you the manuscript, the reader his reading. For I do not dangle the unruly will of the reader at the end of some thread of superfluous plot. Pluck out a vertebra, and the two pieces of this twisted fantasy rejoin effortlessly. Chop it into fragments, and you'll see that each can survive on its own.

This passage describes a way of reading the collection, but the process also applies to each of the poems in it. The Baudelairean experience of reading is based on pieces that join provisionally in unintended and unceasing ways, creating connections and illuminations that we experience as necessary accidents.

That is the point.

NOTES

[1] All translations from French texts are my own.

[2] Some portions of the following analyses draw on work I have published elsewhere, in *Acts of Fiction* (ch. 5) and *Aesthetics of Fraudulence* (ch. 8.)

An Ethical Reading of Baudelaire's Prose Poems

Edward K. Kaplan

Le Spleen de Paris is a heterogeneous collection, unified by a shifting, self-critical narrative persona I call the Parisian prowler (*le rôdeur parisien*). Since my emphasis is on textual interpretation, I begin by informing students that most of the so-called prose poems are not poems as often understood—that is, verse or lyrical excursions in melodic prose, or parallels to *Les Fleurs du Mal*—although some are. I call them fables of modern life or fables of modern consciousness.[1] Baudelaire's dedicatory letter to his editor, Arsène Houssaye, asserts that these works depict *"une vie moderne et abstraite"* 'one modern and abstract life' (*Spleen* [Pichois] 275; *Parisian Prowler* 129), the consciousness of an alienated, hypersensitive *flâneur*, a stroller, as Walter Benjamin famously pointed out, a modern city dweller of artistic temperament (*Charles Baudelaire*; *Writer*).

Ethical Irony

I have taught *Le Spleen de Paris* in French or in English translation at all levels, from first-year humanities students to a graduate seminar on Baudelaire and Søren Kierkegaard. My ethical approach is pragmatic and pedagogical, a thematic foundation for multiple readings. My principle of the collection's foundational coherence emphasizes conflicts between the aesthetic, the ethical, and the religious dimensions of human experience. Adapting Kierkegaard's terminology, the aesthetic in Baudelaire refers to plastic beauty, reverie, idealized memories, and other modes of imaginative freedom; the ethical recognizes the preciousness of other human beings and seeks communication or dialogue; whereas the religious, ultimate meaning or absolute truth, transcends human understanding.

My ethical approach emphasizes conflicts between aesthetic goals, such as intense stimulation or *volupté*, versus truth and common human decency. The class becomes involved in a dialogue with the narrator. This dynamic has been defined by Gary J. Handwerk: *"ethical irony* focuses on how verbal incompatibilities set up and provoke a deeper interrogation of self-consciousness" (2).[2]

Irony is a prime locus for shared insight as well as ambiguity and misunderstanding. Baudelaire's ethical irony can become a salutary instrument of self-knowledge. The narrator's often outrageous attitudes can force readers to reexamine their assumptions. As would a Second Empire Socrates, the prowler challenges us to question complacently held norms such as family, faith, and loyalty to the status quo. All of us are hypocritical, or prone to self-deception.

Students can become fascinated by this indirect communication of values. Through the indirect power of irony, Baudelaire avoids "l'hérésie de l'enseignement" 'the heresy of didacticism' ("Études sur Poe," *Oeuvres complètes* [Pichois] 1: 333; my trans.), explicit moral judgments and edifying lessons, such as those of Victor Hugo. As a historical backdrop, we can explain to the class how non-ironic, conventional readings of the 1857 *Les Fleurs du Mal* (and of Flaubert's *Madame Bovary*) had outraged French government prosecutors seeking to safeguard public morality.

Learning to Interpret

Baudelaire sets his ironic mode in the dedicatory letter to Arsène Houssaye, a writer with democratic pretensions. His playful tone camouflages a harsh judgment of the conventional author and journalist, whom Baudelaire nevertheless needed to please. He masks his repudiation of propaganda with this ironic compliment: "Vous-même, mon cher ami, n'avez-vous pas tenté de traduire en une *chanson* le cri strident du *Vitrier* et d'exprimer dans une prose lyrique toutes les désolantes suggestions que ce cri envoie jusqu'aux mansardes" 'You yourself, my dear friend, did you not try to translate the *Glazier's* strident cry into a *song*, and to express in lyrical prose the woeful associations that cry sends all the way up to the attics?' (*Spleen* [Pichois] 276; *Parisian Prowler* 129). Students can compare "Le Mauvais Vitrier" ("The Bad Glazier"—one of Baudelaire's most infamous mystifications) with Houssaye's "La Chanson du vitrier" ("The Song of the Glazier"), which trivializes decent popular sentiments: "La fraternité avait trinqué avec lui" 'Fraternity had a drink with him' (*Spleen* [Pichois] 311; my trans.).

Still another irony in this putative preface is Baudelaire's "humble" confession, at the very end, of failing to imitate Aloysius Bertrand's *Gaspard de la nuit*. Baudelaire's claim to be "un esprit qui regarde comme le plus grand honneur du poète d'accomplir *juste* ce qu'il a projeté de faire" 'a mind that considers as the poet's greatest honor to execute *exactly* what he planned to do' appears to deny the value of originality while proclaiming his emulation of a talented but secondary writer (*Spleen* [Pichois] 276; *Parisian Prowler* 130).

My heuristic unity hypothesis helps students confirm irony within individual pieces, across analogous texts, and in groupings. Our model is the first sequence of fables, originally published on 26 August 1862 in *La Presse* as *Petits Poëmes en prose* ("Short Prose Poems") and retained in the same order in Baudelaire's memorandum used to organize the 1869 posthumous edition.[3]

The first two fables, which I interpret as a diptych, constitute an implicit table of contents of the collection of fifty pieces: "L'Étranger" ("The Stranger") depicts a radical aesthetic position, whereas "Le Désespoir de la vieille" ("The Old Woman's Despair") overtly expresses the narrator's compassion, his ethical foundation. Both fables question the possibility of love. The narrator who interviews the dreamer of the initial fable cannot make him admit to loving anything but mobile fantasy. This aesthetic stranger literally spaces out: "J'aime les nuages . . . les nuages qui passent . . . là-bas . . . là-bas . . . les merveilleux nuages!" 'I love clouds . . . drifting clouds . . . there . . . over there . . . marvelous clouds!' (277; 1). By contrast, the ethical stranger of the second fable is an old woman whose wrinkled face terrifies an "innocent" baby. As she withdraws into her "solitude éternelle" 'eternal solitude,' the compassionate narrator deplores her loneliness as an aged female who has lost her conventional charms (277; 1). An ideal of compassionate community joins these models of the narrator's own aspirations and defeats.

The next two pieces, "Le *Confiteor* de l'artiste" and "Un Plaisant" ("The Artist's *Confiteor*" and "A Joker"), depict radically aesthetic views, the first one directly, the second one ironically. "Le *Confiteor*" celebrates the perilous sensations of intense reverie and acknowledges its limits: "L'énergie dans la volupté crée un malaise et une souffrance positive" 'The force of voluptuous pleasure creates uneasiness and concrete suffering' (278; 4). The heroic artist concludes, nevertheless, that he will not abandon his tragic vocation: "L'étude du beau est un duel où l'artiste crie de frayeur avant d'être vaincu" 'Studying the beautiful is a duel in which the artist shrieks with fright before being defeated' (279; 4). Students can debate the meaning of the ambiguous "shriek [of] fright" that accompanies Nature's inevitable victory: tragic self-affirmation or surrender to despair?

As a contrast, "Un Plaisant" parodies this Romantic pursuit and then explicitly denounces the amoral aesthetic position. The fable is set in a Parisian New Year's Eve celebration during which a pretentious rich young man plays a prank on a donkey, symbol of a worker: "un beau monsieur ganté, verni, cruellement cravaté et emprisonné dans des habits tout neufs, s'inclina cérémonieusement devant l'humble bête, et lui dit, en ôtant son chapeau: 'Je vous la souhaite bonne et heureuse!'" 'a handsome gloved gentleman, polished, cruelly cravated and imprisoned in brand-new clothes, bowed obsequiously to the humble beast, and said to him, as he raised his hat, "I wish you a good and happy one!"' (279; 5). The joker, an aspiring dandy who displays new clothes, is a caricature of an artist who ignores the feelings of others, human or beast. The narrator's sarcasm (a lower form of irony) is signal enough of his disapproval: "puis [il] se retourna vers je ne sais quels camarades avec un air de fatuité, comme pour les prier d'ajouter leur approbation à son contentement. L'âne ne vit pas ce beau plaisant, et continua de courir avec zèle où l'appelait son devoir" 'then [the joker] turned with a fatuous look toward some companions or other, as if requesting them to add their approval to his conceit. The donkey did not see that fine joker, and continued zealously to rush along where his duty called him' (279; 5). The sarcastic play on *beau* ("beautiful") would suffice to denounce the fellow's stupidity and conceit, his fatuity, a major sin in Baudelaire's system of values. The joker is, after all, "un beau monsieur," which could mean both handsome and "a fine sort." The donkey, for his part, is "zealously" fulfilling its "duty" (*le devoir* is a major principle of the French bourgeois power structure [see Simon; "Devoir"]). Yet contrast is not enough.

The ethical ironist unmasks himself in the coda. The gently ironic "beau plaisant" becomes a caustic "magnifique imbécile" as the narrator explodes into righteous outrage that stretches to infinity: "Pour moi, je fus pris subitement d'une incommensurable rage contre ce magnifique imbécile, qui me parut concentrer en lui tout l'esprit de la France" 'As for me, suddenly I was seized with an incommensurable rage against that magnificent imbecile, who for me concentrated in himself the very essence of France's wit' (279; 5).

And indeed, the foundational target of Baudelaire's ethical irony is precisely *l'esprit de la France*, so difficult to translate (the French mentality, or French wit, intelligence, or humor). Without directly expressing respect for ordinary citizens, the enraged narrator proclaims his solidarity with oppressed beasts of burden, steadfast workers, while repudiating the cruelty of the self-centered artist.

Will Baudelaire resolve the opposition of the pleasure principle versus the reality principle? The next fable, "La Chambre double" ("The Double Room") reinforces a similar ethical lesson without giving vent to a democratic ideology. This is one of Baudelaire's best-known parables of the writer's irreducible duality, free imagination versus social, even professional, responsibility.

The ending of "La Chambre double" confronts that basic human contradiction. After evoking a seductive "rêverie" 'dream of paradise,' the "Spectre" 'Specter' of the urban writer's obligations destroys his freedom (281; 7), suggesting that "paradis artificiels" 'artificial paradises' (the vial of laudanum, opium dreams) mark his inescapable condition (377; my trans.). Students can debate whether that aesthetic conclusion is final.

Yet again, the fable's poetic closure reintroduces a relentless reality principle. Three parallel exclamations, each of which (after the initial "Et") contains four pronounced syllables: "Oui! le Temps règne; il a repris sa brutale dictature. Et il me pousse, comme si j'étais un bœuf, avec son double aiguillon.—'Et hue donc! bourrique! Sue donc, esclave! Vis donc, damné!'" 'Yes! Time reigns; it has recaptured its brutal dictatorship. And it drives me, as if I were an ox, with its double goad.—"So gee'up! Donkey! So sweat, slave! So live, damned one!"' (*Spleen* [Pichois] 282; *Parisian Prowler* 8). Such is Baudelaire's allegory of the human condition, tragically split by the duality of mind versus matter, but affirming life and labor. Is the ending relatively positive? At the very least, "La Chambre double" completes the ethical affirmation of "Un Plaisant" and the warning against excessive aestheticism of "Le *Confiteor* de l'artiste." But do students possess adequate life experience to appreciate this grim, heroic story of human fallibility?

The class has thus confirmed irony as an ethical affirmation. Such compassionate realism would seem to place Baudelaire in the same ideological camp as Houssaye, or even Pierre Dupont, the worker-poet whom Baudelaire sincerely admired.[4] Baudelaire's irony, however, subtly or brutally subverts reductive readings. Ethical irony repudiates sentimentality and wishful thinking by forcing us to decide for ourselves.

Sadist or Ethical Ironist?

The class is now prepared to confront examples of radical undecidability, immoral fables that nonetheless maintain an implicit ethical challenge. Students should be excited to root out the complex ironies of "Le Mauvais Vitrier" ("The

Bad Glazier"). Because of its autobiographical resonances, this tale is in large part responsible for Baudelaire's scandalous reputation.

The narrative entices readers with several markers of irony. After introducing the story with observations on "moralistes" 'moral philosophers,' the Parisian writer places himself at center stage. The entire plot flows from his initial state of discontent: "Un matin je m'étais levé maussade, triste, fatigué d'oisiveté, et poussé, me semblait-il, à faire quelque chose de grand, *une action d'éclat*" 'One morning I had awakened sullen, sad, and worn out with idleness, and I felt impelled to do something great, *a brilliant action*' (*Spleen* [Pichois] 286; *Parisian Prowler* 14; my emphasis).

A major indication of irony is the paragraph composed of a long, pedantic, and unwieldy sentence (in parentheses) that boils down to this: "l'esprit de mystification . . . participe beaucoup de cette humeur . . . qui nous pousse sans résistance vers une foule d'actions dangereuses ou inconvenantes" 'the spirit of mystification . . . has much in common with that humor . . . which drives us irresistibly toward a multitude of dangerous or improper actions' (286; 14).

Then begins the outrageous aesthetic experiment. A depressed artist hears "le cri perçant, discordant" 'the piercing, discordant cry' of a pitiable glazier. Assailed by the unmusical sounds, the artist shouts the peddler up to his garret and angrily reproaches him for not selling "des vitres magiques" 'magic panes of glass': "vous osez vous promener dans des quartiers pauvres, et vous n'avez pas même de vitres qui fassent voir la vie en beau!" 'You dare walk through poor neighborhoods, and you don't even have panes which make life beautiful!' As the glazier leaves the building below, the demented artist, "ivre de [sa] folie" 'drunk with [his] madness,' drops a pot of flowers—"perpendiculairement" 'perpendicularly' (a humorously long adverb)—onto the glazier's backpack while screaming the refrain, "La vie en beau! La vie en beau!" 'Make life beautiful!' (287; 15). The sadistic narrator is acting out, literalizing a cliché, as if in a charade: "voir la vie en rose" 'to see the world through rose-colored glasses.'

The narrative then confirms the fable's ethical irony as it repeats a keyword: "et il [the glazier] acheva de briser sous son dos toute sa pauvre fortune ambulatoire qui rendit le *bruit éclatant* d'un palais de cristal crevé par la foudre" 'and he ended by breaking his entire poor itinerant fortune under his back, which produced the *brilliant sound* of a crystal palace smashed by lightning' (287; 15; my emphasis). The depressed narrator has completed the "action d'éclat" to which he aspired upon awakening. A pun on the repeated word *éclatant* (brilliant, shiny, smashed) is the structural element that unifies the fable as the narrator claims (or pretends) to rationalize his own vicious (and literally deconstructive) act.

Here class discussion becomes imperative. The story having concluded, an interpretive coda appears to generalize this amoral (or immoral) quest for pleasure or beauty, while recalling its possible pathological cause. More difficult ethical questions come forward. Was the glazier really *bad* for not veiling reality, as he walked through a "poor neighborhood"? Is the crazed artist responsible for his act? He concedes, "Ces plaisanteries nerveuses ne sont pas sans péril, et on peut souvent les payer cher. Mais qu'importe l'éternité de la damnation à qui a trouvé dans une seconde l'infini de la jouissance?" 'Such neurotic pranks are not without peril, and one can often pay dearly for them. But what does an eternity of damnation matter to someone who has experienced for one second the infinity of delight?' (287; 15). The anxious, impecunious poet-narrator (who lives on the top floor) admits that his adventure is "a neurotic prank," but the final sentence appears to assert the towering priority of aesthetic pleasure over simple human decency. The gnomic formula highlights the ethical or even theological dilemma. Can we convincingly answer this rhetorical question? Does the narrator assert, without irony, that damnation is, literally, worth the pleasure of momentary ecstasy—the harmonic music produced by smashing glass crystal?

Students will passionately debate these oppositions, guided by the fable's title that condenses all ironies: from an ethical perspective the narrator is bad. The glazier is guilty only for an aesthetic misdeed, not selling colored panes of glass that symbolically deny reality.[5] Common sense tells us that this neurotic prank is not worth a damn (my pun is intentional). The narrator's act is not gratuitous, for it expresses "une espèce d'énergie qui jaillit de l'ennui et de la rêverie" 'a type of energy that springs from ennui and daydreaming'—a sort of depression the narrator implicitly condemns. Does the fact that both the glazier and the narrator are poor justify this relentless quest for aesthetic pleasure? We are forced, Socratically, to make a momentous moral and even religious decision, to approach a question that only each individual can answer. The fable is indeed a mystification whose ending serves not to enlighten but to perplex readers, to bewilder us—or to inspire us. The question now becomes, Is this aporia sufficient? Interpretation is both compulsory and unsatisfying.

The Italics of Irony

Several fables signal their ethical irony by italicizing a keyword. Two examples must suffice. The famous "Le Gâteau" ("The Cake") repeats its title at crucial moments of the narrative. A dreamy traveler encounters two destitute urchins who fight, viciously, for a meager piece of bread they call "gâteau" 'cake,' since their starving eyes transform the narrator's ordinary bread into an upper-class delight. At the end, the narrator, moved by the boys' suffering, claims to regret his loss of imaginative freedom:

> Ce spectacle m'avait embrumé le paysage, et la joie calme où s'ébaudissait mon âme avant d'avoir vu ces petits hommes avait totalement disparu; j'en restai triste assez longtemps, me répétant sans cesse: "Il y a donc un pays superbe où le pain s'appelle du *gâteau*, une friandise si rare qu'elle suffit pour engendrer une guerre parfaitement fratricide!"   (299)

> That performance obscured the landscape for me, and the calm joy glad-
> dening my soul before I saw those little men had completely disappeared.
> I remained saddened for quite a while, and I incessantly repeated to
> myself: "So there exists a magnificent land where bread is called *cake*, a
> delicacy so rare that it suffices to beget a perfectly fratricidal war!"
>
> (32–33)

Which values are primary, the aesthetic or the ethical ones? Only on the level of
plot does the fable deny the efficacy of philanthropy. The reveries of the awakened dreamer (during which he almost believed that people were created good)
mature into what Paul Ricoeur calls "the sadness of finitude," the recognition
of mortality and our fallible nature (123–24; see also Kaplan, "Baudelaire"). At
the same time, the repetition of the italicized *cake* ironically suggests that he
despairs of resolving the battle between his solipsistic dreamed freedom and
physical hunger, the universal frailty of life. The fable leaves us with a vigorous
skepticism and mistrust of all ideologies while deploring the "fratricidal" violence provoked by poverty.

"Le Joujou du pauvre" ('The Pauper's Toy'), another parable of fallacious perception, depicts a similar dead-end as the narrator appears to repudiate literature's ethical function. The irony here resides in the apparent reconciliation of
the poor and the wealthy as two boys share their "toy," a living rat. This might
become an edifying—albeit somewhat crude—egalitarian parable, were it not
for the typographically odd ending. As in previous pieces, this coda lifts its manifest democratic ideology to a theoretical level: "Et les deux enfants se riaient
l'un à l'autre fraternellement, avec des dents d'une *égale* blancheur" 'And the
two children laughed at each other fraternally, with teeth of *equal* whiteness'
(*Spleen* [Pichois] 305; *Parisian Prowler* 41). Implicitly, the narrator presupposes the sanctity of all people, but he refuses to assert that noble principle
directly. The italicized *equal*, echoing *cake* of the fable that heads the series, re-
affirms the objective limits of good will as well as the persistence of ethical ideals. The closure does not take sides in a class war. The grotesque irony of the rat
and the teeth undermines the edifying lesson. The moral of this fable is not facile. The boys' transient equality is a flimsy figment of desire, as is the beauty of
the rat entertaining them. Their tastes and their natural endowments (e.g., their
teeth) are the same—but not their true opportunities in the world.

Socratic Challenges to Ideology

The collection's penultimate fable, "Assommons les pauvres!" ("Let's Beat Up
the Poor!"), once again demystifies the dogma of social equality. The story is as
fierce and zany as a Monty Python sketch.

First, the narrator sarcastically denounces utopian schemes of 1848, "livres où il est traité de l'art de rendre les peuples heureux, sages et riches, en vingt-quatre heures" 'books dealing with the art of making nations happy, wise, and rich, in twenty-four hours' (357; 121). Then he goes out for a drink. As he encounters a pitiful beggar, he unveils the Socratic function of all his immoral tales: "Puisque Socrate avait son bon Démon, pourquoi n'aurais-je pas mon bon Ange?" 'Since Socrates had his good Demon, why shouldn't I have my good Angel?' (358; 122). Then, inspired by the inner voice of irony, he posits—or rather, acts out—his ethical solution to inequality: "Celui-là seul est l'égal d'un autre, qui le prouve, et celui-là seul est digne de la liberté, qui sait la conquérir" 'He alone is equal to another, if he proves it, and he alone is worthy of freedom, if he can conquer it.' So, instead of giving charity (pity or money) to the beggar, he beats the daylights out of the old man who then, symmetrically, beats up his "benefactor." Before continuing the text analysis, students can now discuss the stated affirmation of personal responsibility and self-help, still a widespread ideology in the United States.

But is the narrator serious? The mathematical description that follows reaches a higher theoretical level as it names theory as such:

> Tout à coup, —ô miracle! ô jouissance du philosophe qui vérifie l'excellence de sa théorie! —je vis cette antique carcasse se retourner, se redresser . . . et, avec un regard de haine qui me parut de *bon augure*, le malandrin décrépit se jeta sur moi, me pocha les deux yeux, me cassa quatre dents, et, avec la même branche d'arbre me battit dru comme plâtre. —Par mon énergique médication, je lui avais donc rendu l'orgueil et la vie.   (359)

> Suddenly, —Oh miracle! Oh delight of the philosopher who verifies the excellence of his theory! —I saw that ancient carcass turn over, straighten up with a force I would never have suspected in a machine so peculiarly unhinged. And with a look of hatred that seemed to me *a good omen*, the decrepit bandit flung himself on me, blackened both my eyes, broke four of my teeth, and, with the same tree branch beat me to a pulp. —By my forceful medication, I had thus restored his pride and his life.   (122)

The narrator has physically, literally applied an ethical principle just as he had applied an aesthetic one in "Le Mauvais Vitrier." Here, the Spartan therapy works, and yet we must question "la jouissance du philosophe qui vérifie l'excellence de sa théorie!" '[t]he delight of the philosopher who verifies the excellence of his theory!' Again we ask if the momentary *jouissance* is congruent with ethical truth. And for the first and only time in the collection, the narrator labels his strategy "Socratic," openly acknowledging that it forces readers to question political or ethical dogmas (Hadot). This method of enlightenment recalls Franz Kafka's parable, "In the Penal Colony," in which a machine surgically engraves an unjust judgment into the flesh of an innocent, though condemned, prisoner.

The coda, which italicizes a renewed cliché ("avoir le *plaisir* de faire ***" 'to have the *pleasure* of doing ***'), prevents us from taking Baudelaire's parable literally—as if we would:

> Et souvenez-vous, si vous êtes réellement philanthrope, qu'il faut appliquer à tous vos confrères, quand ils vous demanderont l'aumône, la théorie que j'ai eu la *douleur* d'essayer sur votre dos.
>   Il m'a bien juré qu'il avait compris ma théorie, et qu'il obéirait à mes conseils.   (*Spleen* [Pichois] 359)

> And remember, if you are a true philanthropist, you must apply to all your colleagues, when they seek alms, the theory I had the *pain* to test upon your back.
>   He indeed swore that he had understood my theory, and that he would comply with my advice.   (*Parisian Prowler* 123)

The repeated word *theory* is the ironic lesson conveyed to the "enlightened" beggar. The conclusion recalls the vicious solitary who bludgeons the "bad" glazier for not providing "des vitres de paradis . . . qui fassent voir la vie en beau" 'panes of paradise . . . that make life beautiful,' thus denying reality. It would be safe to assume that Baudelaire's other polemics against democracy contain appreciable irony (Godfrey, "Dandy") and that narrow-mindedness as such, *l'esprit de la France*, is his true target.

Students can appreciate these fables for their Socratic challenges to act humanely as well as their undecidability and skepticism. When understood as attacks against complacency—be it democratic or literary—we can respond with flexibility. When read in the light of their ethical dimension, their brutality constitutes a perilous polemic against moralistic literature—perilous, because readers can miss the irony and take their stated negativity in earnest.
   Baudelaire's preamble to *Exposition universelle* (1855) proposes such open-mindedness: "Un système est une espèce de damnation qui nous pousse à une abjuration perpétuelle. . . . Pour échapper à l'horreur de ces apostasies philosophiques, je me suis orgueilleusement résigné à la modestie: je me suis contenté de sentir; je suis revenu chercher un asile dans l'impeccable naïveté" 'A system is a type of damnation that urges us toward a perpetual recantation. . . . In order to escape the horror of those philosophical heresies, I have proudly resigned myself to modesty: I have been satisfied to feel; I have returned to seek asylum in impeccable *naïveté*' (577–78; my trans. and emphasis). Textual analyses should be "impeccable," philologically accurate, theoretically sophisticated, without losing sight of literature's "universal vitality," its down-to-earth ethical content. *Le Spleen de Paris* reminds us—postmodern, poststructuralist, postdeconstructionist interpreters—not to forget the passion for truth, and the compassion, behind the Parisian prowler's many masks.[6]

NOTES

[1] See Metzidakis, *Repetition*; Bernard. The present analysis is expanded in my book, *Baudelaire's Prose Poems*. For other studies of the unity of *Le Spleen de Paris*, see Lawler; Runyon.

[2] See also Hadot; Metzidakis, "Baudelaire"; Godfrey, "Dandy."

[3] See Kaplan, *Baudelaire's Prose Poems*, app. 2 (175–81).

[4] See Baudelaire, *Oeuvres complètes* [Pichois]: 26–36; 169–75.

[5] Must we embrace the position of Baudelaire's sonnet "La Beauté," which celebrates art's distorting glasses "qui font toutes choses plus belles" 'which makes all things more beautiful' (*Fleurs* [Pichois] 21; my trans.)?

[6] See Mauron for the first systematic treatment of the ethical dimension of Baudelaire's prose poems.

(Post-)Romantic Vision
in *Le Spleen de Paris*

Stamos Metzidakis

An important task for serious students of Baudelaire—from those in introductory and survey courses about poetry to those in graduate seminars—is to determine through a reading of his poetic works as well as of his art criticism and correspondence where he belongs within the general artistic milieu of his time. Doing so helps students better understand Baudelaire's aesthetics, his depictions of the world, and his place in it. At the same time, students must recognize the inherent slipperiness of such a determination, due to competing critical definitions of those aesthetic movements and trends that are deemed significant. Otherwise, they risk ignoring or underestimating various influences exerted on and by a given author—in this case, Baudelaire. Students must try to avoid this risk because while Romanticism and realism are the two major currents most often ascribed to Baudelaire's work, neither one captures fully the originality of his hybrid prose poetry.

The parenthetical prefix in my title thus aims to indicate two things about Baudelaire's prose poems. First, that they present narrative situations in which we see the world as Romantics often saw it: as mirrors onto which are projected their feelings, obsessions, and fears. In "La Soupe et les nuages" ("The Soup and the Clouds"), "Un Plaisant" ("A Joker"), "A Une heure du matin" ("At One O'Clock in the Morning"), "Le Mauvais Vitrier" ("The Bad Glazier"), "Déjà!" ("Already!"), and "La Chambre double" ("The Double Room"), for example, the poet projects personal emotions onto both narrators and characters. These sentiments extend from existential despair to marital frustration, from generalized loathing of bourgeois society to escapist enthusiasm and drug-induced ecstasy. In each of these "mirrors" the author idealistically lays bare his own complex subjectivity in hopes of finding some understanding and sympathy among his readers.

But my title also indicates that unlike many Romantic works, *Le Spleen de Paris* provides other windows through which the exterior world is explored, openings that sometimes reveal more problematic, less accessible meanings. Realist novels and paintings, too, use a myriad of details from the empirical world to produce their creative universes. Baudelaire's admiration for painters of modern life, like Constantin Guys, suggests that the author stayed largely faithful to this window-type, realist aesthetic as well. And many of his prose poems do depict real-life situations and beings, like the poor in "Le Joujou du pauvre" ("The Pauper's Toy"), "Les Yeux des pauvres" ("The Eyes of the Poor"), and "Assommons les pauvres!" ("Let's Beat Up the Poor") or racehorses and their handlers in "Un Cheval de race" ("A Thoroughbred") or gambling houses in "Le Joueur généreux" ("The Generous Gambler") or smoking rooms and prostitutes in "Portraits de maîtresses" ("Portraits of Mistresses").

Yet, beyond his clear affinities with both Romantics and realists, this essay shows that, thanks in large part to his prose poems, Baudelaire also invented a uniquely post-Romantic type of narrative window. So, rather than record only details observed through a window, he strove to suggest something else about his visions, something unfamiliar or often troubling, through biting sarcasm, black humor, irony, and paradox. In a deliberately visible manner my title thus underscores the fundamental ambivalence of the vision(s) in *Le Spleen de Paris*, the capacity of these prose poems to offer Romantic and post-Romantic perspectives on the world simultaneously. This ambivalence largely justifies here, too, a potentially useful metaphoric distinction sometimes made between mirrors and windows, which I borrow from a well-known 1978 photography exhibition. In that show works by Alfred Stieglitz and Eugène Atget were seen as instances of Romantic self-expression (mirror) and realist observation of the outside world (window), respectively.

Now, I hasten to add that neither the author of that exhibit's catalog, John Szarkowski, nor I wish to rely on this distinction to divide all modern photographs (or, in this case, Baudelaire's prose poems) into what he calls "discrete and unrelated bodies. On the contrary, the model suggested here is that of a continuous axis. . . . No photographer's work could embody with perfect purity either of the two divergent motives" (2). Yet, these metaphors do express very different photographic goals, which have interesting parallels with *Le Spleen de Paris*. If I use them here, therefore, it is because of the ever-growing importance of photographic, digital, and cinematographic imagery in contemporary academic discourse in general. In Susan Sontag's words:

> Insofar as photography does peel away the dry wrappers of habitual seeing, it creates another habit of seeing: both intense and cool, solicitous

and detached; charmed by the insignificant detail, addicted to incongruity. But photographic seeing has to be constantly renewed with new shocks, whether of subject matter or technique, so as to produce the impression of violating ordinary vision.   (97)

Baudelaire's prose poems appear to function alternatively, then, as mirror-like or window-like photographs because, while they often first conjure up conventional sights and ways of seeing, they often end by violating ordinary vision. Sontag writes:

> Photography, which has so many narcissistic uses, is also a powerful instrument for depersonalizing our relation to the worlds; and the two uses are complementary. Like a pair of binoculars with no right or wrong end, the camera makes exotic things near, intimate; and familiar things small, abstract, strange, much farther away. It offers, in one easy, habit-forming activity, both participation and alienation in our own lives and those of others—allowing us to participate, while confirming alienation.   (167)

In this way, scholars of Baudelaire as well as college-level students of French poetry (in translation or the target language) are invited to see the people and things described in them differently, to revisit many scenes portrayed in *Les Fleurs du Mal*, but with "beaucoup plus de liberté, et de détails, et de raillerie" 'much more freedom, detail and mockery,' as he put it in his 16 February 1866 letter to Jules Troubat (*Correspondance* [Pichois] 2: 615).[1] This is why we may assert that "Baudelaire shifted from a world dominated by art to one defined more blatantly by reality when he evolved from poetry to prose poetry; the eyes of *Les Fleurs du mal* deflect or recast the outside world, whereas the eyes of *Le Spleen de Paris* perceive and respond to it" (Mills 157).

Such an opinion about the quasi-photographic nature of this collection is further corroborated by the poet's description of it as a "volume romantique à images" 'a Romantic picture book' (qtd. in Blin, Introduction 32), even if, admittedly, Baudelaire was likely thinking more about drawings in Romantic illustrated books than about photographs or daguerreotypes per se. Romantic art aims nonetheless to distance people, places and things from normal representations of them, to place them at a remove from our usual perceptions. In the words of the German poet-theorist Novalis: "Everything at a distance turns into poetry: distant mountains, distant people, distant events: all become Romantic" (Eitner 286n16).

Yet, in passing from poetry to prose, Baudelaire suffered a type of symbolic fall reminiscent of that of both Icarus and Lucifer, images of whom occur at several points in Baudelaire's work. Our poet abandoned in the process a certain Romantic belief in some bright, immutable, and oftentimes joyous ideal. Whether artistic, sociopolitical, or religious, most previous humanistic ideals give way to far more depressing visions of modern life, which emphasize instead a darker *Spleen*-like side of human life. As "Le Mauvais Vitrier" demonstrates, this tone and style allow none of the characters in *Le Spleen de Paris* to "make life beautiful," to see "la vie en beau," without suffering dire, real-life consequences. Baudelaire thus transforms many of the late verse poems in *Les Fleurs du Mal*, specifically the aptly titled "Tableaux parisiens" ("Parisian Scenes"), into snippets that emphasize the less luminous side(s) of life. In J. A. Hiddleston's words, we move "from an attempt at synthesis to fragmentation, contradiction and uncertainty . . . what remains after our reading of the fifty pieces is an impression of perpetual clash and of sentimental and moral anarchy" (3).

Even so, students of Baudelaire should remember that in several important respects he remained a lifelong Romantic. Adhering to Victor Hugo's oft-repeated precept from the *Préface de Cromwell* (1827) to have "ni règles ni modèles" 'neither rules nor models,' except for "les lois générales de la nature" 'the general laws of nature' (Hugo 88), Baudelaire continued to insist, for example, that "[l]e romantisme n'est précisément ni dans le choix des sujets ni dans la vérité exacte, mais dans la manière de sentir" 'Romanticism lies precisely not in the choice of subject matter nor in exact truth, but in the manner of feeling' (*Œuvres complètes* 2: 420). In his letter to Arsène Houssaye, which serves as a mini-guide for most readers to *Le Spleen de Paris*, Baudelaire admits, however, that in his new work, he did imitate a model, one provided not by nature but by Aloysius Bertrand in *Gaspard de la Nuit*.

Yet Baudelaire clearly never completely abandoned Romantic aesthetics because in the same letter he admits that his final product remained "bien loin de mon mystérieux modèle" 'quite far from my mysterious model' (*Œuvres complètes* 1: 276). His prose poems thereby remain triply Romantic, as it were, since they deal with no privileged subject matter, per Hugo's precept; create new visions thanks to their distance ("bien loin de" 'quite far from') from earlier models; and, finally, never reveal the "exact truth" or nature of these new visions. In fact, Baudelaire wonders whether these new visions contain anything exact at all or can even be called something ("si cela peut s'appeler *quelque chose*" 'if that can even be called something' [*Œuvres complètes* 1: 276]), as if the entire project could be interpreted as some type of dream or even a joke.

At the same time, the new vision found in and produced by these "paradoxical fables" is, as this critic dubs them in the very same sentence, *"postromantic"* (Kaplan, *Parisian Prowler* vii). The narrator and protagonist who frequently appear in them, moreover, both act like *homo duplex*: a two-sided man torn between opposing aesthetic models or divergent tendencies. The poet himself wrote, "Il y a dans tout homme, à toute heure, deux postulations simultanées, l'une vers Dieu, l'autre vers Satan" 'There is in every man, at all times, two simultaneous tendencies, one toward God, one toward Satan' (*Œuvres complètes* 1: 682). The author of *Le Spleen de Paris* therefore depicts the world in continually ambivalent terms. His prose poems show us ever-shifting sides of an artist both blessed and cursed with what we might call with Françoise Meltzer "double vision." In her words, this vision turns out to be "less a matter of choice than it is the accurate rendition of his psychological as well as historical being-in-the-world" (249).

A perfect example of our three key points about these texts—the mirror-versus-window dichotomy they exemplify, the author's continuing Romantic streak, and his double vision—is "Les Fenêtres" ("Windows"). After his opening maxim, the narrator informs us that "[c]elui qui regarde du dehors à travers une fenêtre ouverte, ne voit jamais autant de choses que celui qui regarde une fenêtre fermée" '[h]e who looks from the outside through an open window never sees as much as he who looks through a closed window' (*Spleen* [Pichois] 339). What we can see in sunlight, he claims, is always "moins intéressant que ce qui se passe derrière une vitre" 'less interesting than what transpires behind a windowpane.' The maxim is then illustrated by the rest of the text, such as "Le *Confiteor* de l'artiste" ("The Artist's Confession"), "Enivrez-vous" ("Get Drunk"), "Les Foules" ("Crowds"), "L'Horloge" ("The Clock"), "Le Port" ("The Port"), and "N'importe où hors du monde" ("Anywhere out of the World"). While all these tales set out to illustrate various morals (as the fables of La Fontaine do), they never definitively prove them. That is, they never provide us with any "exact truth" because dream and reality overlap throughout the collection and prevent us from knowing for certain what is what or who is who. As Robert Kopp states:

> La réalité du rêve n'est guère distincte de la réalité de la veille[;] . . . si tous ces éléments sont présentés comme appartenant à une même réalité, les lois traditionnelles de la perception subissent une sorte de subversion. . . .
> (*Spleen* [Kopp] 93–94)

> The dream's reality is hardly distinct from the reality of the waking state[;] . . . if all these elements are presented as belonging to the same reality, traditional laws of perception undergo a sort of subversion. . . .

In any case, to explain his urban vision in "Les Fenêtres," the narrator then chooses a vocabulary that again, in several respects, recalls Romantic lyric, saying that "il n'est pas d'objet plus profond, plus mystérieux, plus fécond, plus ténébreux, plus éblouissant" (*Spleen* [Pichois] 339) 'there is no deeper, more mysterious, more fertile, more obscure, more dazzling object' than a closed window. From Alphonse de Lamartine to Hugo, adjectives like "mysterious" or "obscure" are frequently used to depict either the inner workings of the human heart or mind or the depth, vastness, and surface luminosity of an ocean teeming with unseen life forms. This is no doubt why metonymic traces of these same implied referents—their profundity, brilliance, and mysteriousness—immediately appear in the following sentences: "Dans ce trou noir ou lumineux vit la vie, rêve la vie, souffre la vie. Par delà des *vagues* de toits, j'aperçois une femme mûre . . ." (339) 'In that black or luminous hole life lives, life dreams, life suffers. Beyond the rooftop *waves*, I notice a mature woman. . . .' (my emphasis).[2] Thanks to the word "vagues" 'waves,' the words depicting the individual who lives, dreams, and suffers in this tiny dark or light hole thereby subtly evoke an object or place as rich, brilliant, mysterious, and deep as the ocean itself. The text unfolds as if the known and unknown, light and dark, big and small were merely different sides of the same existential coins.

In presenting this doubled vision of windows in "Les Fenêtres," the narrator simultaneously conjures up another related image, that of mirrors, by insisting, paradoxically, that the direct view of someone or something through a closed window is less interesting when seen through an open one, as if the windowpane itself made the person or thing inside the room more interesting. Yet what could that more interesting image be if not also the complete or at least partial mirror image of the observer? Everyone who gazes across a street from an apartment balcony or who window-shops (think here of the dazzling new department store windows in nineteenth-century Paris) knows that it is well-nigh impossible to look at a windowpane and not notice both oneself and what or who is illuminated behind the pane. Baudelaire's *I* in these texts thus often becomes *Thou*, and vice versa. And what could be more Romantic than that? Hugo memorably stated at the very start of *Les Contemplations*, "Ah! insensé, qui crois que je ne suis pas toi!" 'O insane reader who thinks I am not you!' (4).

Thus whereas Hugo idealistically invokes our common humanity and asks for empathy, in the post-Romantic universe of *Le Spleen de Paris*, Baudelaire points instead to two related problems: the way he sees himself as well as the way he views society at large. His subsequent double vision then affects almost every other text in *Le Spleen de Paris*, making its narrator act simultaneously as mirror and window. Consequently, what the realist or Romantic in Baudelaire sees through the window of "Les Fenêtres" does not complete his new vision. Beyond the old woman lurks some other presence: the poet himself. Instead of looking at the old woman as an autonomous being in the world, the narrator thus sees her as his own invention, an extension of himself, admitting, "j'ai refait l'histoire de cette femme, ou plutôt sa légende" 'I have refashioned that woman's history, or rather her legend' (*Spleen* [Pichois] 339). In the process, he suggests that whenever we moderns try to observe what is outside of us, an external reality, we ineluctably gaze into a sort of mirror in which we simply rediscover ourselves.

For these reasons, both realist dreams of attaining impersonal objectivity and Romantic dreams of exhibiting an authentic subjectivity are doomed in *Le Spleen de Paris*. The observing subject is continually conflated into the object of his gaze. Instead of worrying in "Les Fenêtres" about whether this other "legend" (etymologically, *legenda*, or "that which must be read") is real or not, Baudelaire thus asks, "Que m'importe ce que peut être la réalité placée hors de moi, si elle m'a aidé à vivre, à sentir que je suis et ce que je suis" 'Does it matter what the reality located outside of me might be, if it has helped me to live, to feel that I am and what I am?' In this decidedly post-Romantic manner, he demonstrates the impossibility of expressing his innermost self—à la Alfred de Musset—without, in the same instant, describing something or someone else.

A similar phenomenon is found in "Le Miroir" ("The Mirror"), one related to what Meltzer has dubbed "scopic syllepsis": "a process where the single notion of 'image' functions in two different, often incongruous contexts within the same glance" (97). After walking into a room, the so-called frightful man of that brief text glances into a mirror. He is then asked why he does this since he can see himself only with displeasure. Instead of a concrete answer, however, the narrator receives an inconclusive one, pointing out that, thanks to the immortal principles of 1889, he can gaze at himself all he wants, since "cela ne regarde que ma conscience" 'that only concerns my conscience' (*Spleen* [Pichois] 344). This prompts the narrator to admit: "Au nom du bon sens, j'avais sans doute raison; mais, au point de vue de la loi, il n'avait pas tort" 'According to common sense, I was probably right; but from the legal viewpoint, he was not wrong.'

A different example on this Baudelairean tendency to see two (often antithetical) things in place of one is found in "Les Bons Chiens" ("The Good Dogs"), the last piece in *Le Spleen de Paris*. There it is hard not to see the poet's attempt to reenvision a traditional ode as an anti-ode. Rather than sing praises of good dogs (i.e., elegant, refined dogs), Baudelaire rhapsodizes about "les pauvres chiens, les chiens crottés, ceux-là que chacun écarte" 'pitiful dogs, muddied dogs, those that everyone shuns' (360). This should not surprise advanced literature students since such a change in convention was already anticipated by Miguel de Cervantes, among others, in "The Dogs' Colloquy." The narrator even rejects the need for the ancient "[a]rrière la muse académique" 'academic muse' whom lyric poets typically invoke and prefers instead "la muse familière, la citadine, la vivante" 'the familiar one, the city muse, the lively muse (360). Even in the collection's first text, "L'Étranger" ("The Stranger"), readers are shown far less what a prose poem is rather than what it is not (cf. Murphy, *Logiques* 117). Thus it is possible to read that short text, too, as a false sonnet, since it only approximates the correct number of lines (fifteen instead of fourteen), the proper number of syllables in an alexandrine (counting the syllable in the word "dis" 'say'), and the usual give-and-take dialogue form between quatrains and tercets. What better way to present a strange new type of writing, a *foreigner* to literature, so to speak, than to subvert that quintessential poetic form?

The *homo duplex* in Baudelaire thereby once again reveals his double nature, one in which, as is so often the case in this *œuvre*, an individual's soul or presumed essence is masked, indeed imprisoned, within his body. Such is the case, too, in "Laquelle est la vraie?" ("Which One Is the True One?"), where a female midget suddenly appears out of nowhere and confuses the narrator, to the point where he does not know if she is the dead girl he just buried or a mere double, a kind of *Doppelgänger*, which students of nineteenth-century literature can find in many other works of the time. The narrator sees himself as attached "comme un loup pris au piège" 'like a wolf caught in a trap,' with one of his feet stuck in the "fosse de *l'idéal*" 'the pit of the *ideal*' (*Spleen* [Pichois] 342; my emphasis). Baudelaire's celebrated verse poem "L'Albatros" ends similarly, with an otherwise birdlike poet exiled on the ground, where his "ailes de géant l'empêchent de marcher" 'giant wings prevent him from walking' (*Fleurs* [Pichois] 10). Should we see him as a bird, in other words, which lyrically soars in the air, or merely as an impotent fake, whose human nature keeps him grounded, trapped by his own physicality?

Such double vision also appears in "La Fausse Monnaie" ("The False Coin"), in which readers are invited to consider whether one can ever really differentiate between the genuine article and a counterfeit. Likewise, in "La Chambre double," where what first appears as a pleasure dome fit for a Romantic poet like Samuel Coleridge is brutally transformed into something far different by the narrative's end. There the narrator suddenly finds himself again in a state of uninspired monotony reserved for everyday life, one characterized by "Le Temps règne," the return of time, which 'reigns supreme,' just as the narrator's idol did in the initial phase of this double room. What was first an ideal place thus turns back into his actual hovel, "ce séjour de l'éternel ennui" 'this abode of eternal ennui.' This all-too-familiar room is one in which he has to deal with the ultimate urban authority figure, the bailiff, "qui vient me torturer au nom de la loi" 'who had come to torture me in the name of the law' (*Spleen* [Pichois] 280).

When placing Baudelaire into the literary history of his century, attentive readers must therefore conclude that he was never only a Romantic. His "situation," as Paul Valéry called it, within the pantheon of French writers remains problematic, because Baudelaire never stopped looking backward as well as forward to contemporary poets and beyond. Nor did he stop moving downward and upward, giving voice to Satan and God, *spleen et idéal*, even though he visibly moved much closer to the "spleenetic" side of things as time went on. He also continually turned his gaze both inward and outward, so that like him his readers might one day be able to see themselves in others. As a result, in "Les Foules" he recommends that we take a "bain de multitude" 'bath among the crowds' with him:

> Il n'est pas donné à chacun de prendre un bain de multitude: jouir de la foule est un art. . . . Qui ne sait pas peupler sa solitude, ne sait pas non plus être seul dans une foule affairée. Le poète jouit de cet incomparable privilège, qu'il peut à sa guise être lui-même et autrui.   (291)

> Not everyone is capable of taking a bath among the crowds: enjoying crowds is an art. . . . He who does not know how to populate his solitude does not know either how to be alone in a busy crowd. The poet enjoys the incomparable privilege of being able, at will, to be both himself and another.

A final, essentially Romantic aspect of the prose poems to note is how the narrator of "Les Foules" assumes the role of a magus-like figure, in which he feels an almost sacred obligation to show a better path to us egotists, who incessantly gaze inward for all the wrong reasons:

Il est bon d'apprendre quelquefois aux heureux de ce monde, ne fût-ce que pour humilier un instant leur sot orgueil, qu'il est des bonheurs supérieurs au leur, plus vastes et plus raffinés. Les fondateurs de colonies, les pasteurs de peuples, les prêtres missionnaires exilés au bout du monde, connaissent sans doute quelque chose de ces mystérieuses ivresses. . . .

It is sometimes well to teach the world's fortunate ones, if only to humiliate their stupid pride for an instant, that there are forms of happiness superior to theirs, more vast and more refined. Founders of colonies, shepherds of peoples, missionary priests exiled to the ends of the earth probably know something of these mysterious intoxications. . . .

More than in *Les Fleurs du Mal*, then, the visions that ultimately emerge from the writing in *Le Spleen de Paris* have "to resist all resolution, and the contradictions [have] to be maintained; this aspect of double vision is willed in Baudelaire. But it is often unwilled—his writing can produce two images that do not communicate with each other, either in temporal or in conceptual ways" (Meltzer 6). The sometimes realist but far more often Romantic narrator in *Le Spleen de Paris*, who presents accurate windows into our world along with unflattering mirrors into his own, thereby continually metamorphoses into a post-Romantic insinuator, whose meanings are unstable and often uncertain.

NOTES

[1] Unless otherwise indicated, all translations from the French are mine.

[2] Murphy notes Kaplan's translation of the line in question—"Beyond the billowing rooftops"—but, curiously, does not comment on his figurative choice of "billowing rooftops" over the more literal "waves of roofs" or "rooftop waves," which I and every other translator cited by Murphy choose (*Logiques* 205).

The Poet's Lost Halo—Reading *Paris Spleen* with Walter Benjamin in Baudelaire-Ville

Beryl Schlossman

> Je suis assez content de mon *Spleen*. En somme, c'est encore *Les Fleurs du Mal*, mais avec beaucoup plus de liberté, et de détail, et de raillerie.
>
> I am fairly happy with my *Spleen*. In brief, it is more of *The Flowers of Evil*, but with much more freedom, and detail, and sarcasm.[1]
>
> —Baudelaire, letter to Jules Troubat, 19 February 1866 (*Correspondance* 2: 615)

Walter Benjamin's writing on Baudelaire is perhaps the most charismatic body of work in the history of Baudelaire criticism. It is also the most controversial work on the poet's achievement. It has been ignored, maligned, and misused before the widespread recognition of the power of Benjamin's thought allowed it, to some extent, to enter the canon of authoritative works of French studies, theory, and literary criticism (Miller, *Ethics*; Chambers, *Mélancolie*; de Man, *Rhetoric*). Contemporary theoretical and critical discourse around the themes on urban experience in the literature of modernity derives in large part from Benjamin. His innovations in literary theory, literary history, and cultural studies include explorations of the following topics: poetry and the impact of the city; the poet and the commodity; questions of exile, displacement, marginality, and the underground; the power of the image; the *flâneur*, the prostitute, and the crowd; history, memory, and the unconscious; tradition and innovation; and time, media, and technology (Weber, *Mass Mediauras* and *Benjamin's -abilities*; Miriam Hansen; Benjamin, *Baudelaire* [Agamben] 2013). All of these topics are relevant and indeed crucial to the study and to the teaching of *Paris Spleen* and other works (Schlossman, "Review Essay").

In the context of presenting Baudelaire texts to students, Benjamin's work is useful in the advanced undergraduate classroom and of particular importance for graduate students across disciplines. The trajectory of the poetry of modern experience extends from Baudelaire's verse poem "Au Lecteur" ("To the Reader"), the liminal poem that introduces *Les Fleurs du Mal* (*The Flowers of Evil*), to the two known versions of "Perte d'Auréole" ("Loss of Halo"), one of the last of Baudelaire's prose poems published in *Paris Spleen*. Here I focus on the interpretation of materials based on original texts in French and German, as well as on English translations of works by the poet and the critic. These works can be studied in undergraduate and graduate courses taught in French, English, or other languages. Benjamin's major essays on Baudelaire include *The Paris of the Second Empire in Baudelaire* (a completed section of *Charles Baudelaire: A Lyric Poet in the Age of High Capitalism*) and "On Some Motifs in Baudelaire." These major works were translated into English in the late 1960s and early 1970s. In addition to several other texts on Baudelaire and an essay by Michael W. Jennings, the general editor of the Harvard translation of Benjamin, the works are available in *The Writer of Modern Life*. Following a brief introduction of the challenges of Benjamin's presentation of the prose poetry in his unfinished work and the critic's general situation in the context of his magnum opus focused on Baudelaire, I will discuss Benjamin's observations on the principles of Baudelaire's city poetry and the critic's less obvious attention to the impact of *Paris Spleen*, illustrated by Benjamin's interpretation of "Loss of Halo."

In Benjamin's late essay "On Some Motifs in Baudelaire," "Loss of Halo" plays a key role in the critic's innovative exploration of the effects of modernity. Benjamin concludes the essay with a close reading of this prose poem in the context of his analysis of memory, tradition, and perception in the poet's writings. Often discussed but rarely contextualized in relation to the poet who inspired it, Benjamin's concept of the aura is one of the keys to understanding his writing on Baudelaire. The aura and its material evidence emerge from Benjamin's exploration of Baudelaire's poetic vision of the city (Weber, *Benjamin's -abilities*; Schlossman, "Images").

Theory and Poetry

On the terrain of literary theory and aesthetics as well as poetry, early reading of Baudelaire led Benjamin toward his own translations of some of Baudelaire's poems. This turn toward translation is an aspect of Benjamin's early work that has important consequences for his development as a literary critic, a theorist, and a memoirist. We can see the influence of his encounters with Baudelaire's writing in his approaches to modern French literature, translation theory and practice, the status and transformation of the image and the work of art, the impact of memory on modernity, and modern architecture and the urban culture of the arcades. The *Arcades Project* brings all these topics together in a bold new project, a book constructed like a city of citations: it is built of textual and theoretical passages that are arranged according to chapters (avenues) and intersections (cross-references).

Literary criticism is on firm ground when referring to Benjamin's exploration of verse, but Benjamin says relatively little about Baudelaire's prose poetry. On the one hand, he underscores the impact of Baudelaire's verse and maintains throughout his writings that Baudelaire's most powerful insights appear in his verse rather than in his essays and theoretical writings. On the other hand, Benjamin often refers to Baudelaire's verse and prose poems without emphasizing the formal distinction between the two. The result of this ambiguity is a generalized uncertainty about Benjamin's position in relation to *Paris Spleen*.

The role of *Paris Spleen* in Benjamin's work has received little critical attention, even though Benjamin explores the topics and themes that run throughout the work. There are several reasons for this general neglect, and foremost among them is the phenomenal role of *The Flowers of Evil* as the final work in a long poetic tradition and, simultaneously, the starting point in the poetics of modernity. In addition, Benjamin clearly defends Baudelaire against a set of accusations seeking to destroy his reputation as a poet. There is an oddly moving sense of déjà vu in Benjamin's defense of *The Flowers of Evil*, because it unconsciously recalls Baudelaire's impassioned and effective long-range rehabilitation of Edgar Allan Poe while it underscores the plight of the critic himself, whose bold work frightened even some of his friends and peers in the Frankfurt School and who consequently was abandoned by the few institutions and individuals who could have restored his livelihood and might have convinced him to leave Europe before it was too late.

A second important factor in Benjamin's strategy concerning the prose poetry is that Benjamin conceives of Baudelaire's reputation as the effect of a single book of verse published during the poet's lifetime. He takes a radical position: he sees Baudelaire's innovative thinking about modernity as it emerges from his poetry. Baudelaire's essays, translations, and works published in journals are of distinctly lesser importance in Benjamin's assessment of the poet's task, goals, and fame. Given the history of prose poetry in general, it is not surprising that its hybrid formal status seems to elude the distinction between Baudelaire's verse and prose that plays an important role in Benjamin's essays. But comments on "Loss of Halo" and other works give evidence of Benjamin's interpretive approach to *Paris Spleen* as poetry: his commentary places the work in the lineage of *The Flowers of Evil* and draws a clear trajectory from the verse to *Paris Spleen*.

Philosopher, memoirist, travel writer, and translator, Benjamin is above all an innovative critic and theorist of literature and culture. A large part of his work on modernity focuses on urban experience in the nineteenth century. A Berliner who adored his native city, Benjamin nevertheless chose Paris as the city most representative of modernity and consequently, in his theoretical exploration of modernity, as his capital of the nineteenth century. Benjamin's reading of Baudelaire converges with the theory of the modern city in his projected exploration of Paris. His work on and around Baudelaire's writing is perhaps the most remarkable critical work of nineteenth-century studies to emerge—perilously—from Western Europe in his own lifetime.

A brief biographical sketch contextualizes Benjamin's heroic work on modernity and his understanding of Baudelaire's contradictions. When Benjamin's Frankfurt School friends fled the Nazis, he hesitated to leave Europe. Under Nazi law, he could no longer earn a living from his writing in Germany. His financial situation and his health became increasingly precarious during several years leading up to his definitive departure from Berlin. In 1933 he went into exile, seeking shelter in several cities and islands before deciding to pursue his research on French culture in Paris, where he suffered many

hardships and deprivations among the émigrés, the Parisians who did not welcome them, and the Nazi invaders. Benjamin writes discretely about the political and personal horrors that engulf him, and he continues his work under
shattering circumstances.

With the notable exceptions of his early translations and his last completed
Baudelaire essay, "On Some Motifs in Baudelaire," published in the year of his
tragic death, most of Benjamin's works on Baudelaire were not published during his lifetime. In an early sketch of the major work that Benjamin called his
Arcades Project, the writer who represents and reproduces the modern city in
literature is Baudelaire. This is the premise of Benjamin's unfinished book on
Paris, "the capital of the nineteenth century." This astonishingly innovative work
includes a book-length essay on Baudelaire (intended as a trilogy with two other
projected sections that do not appear to have been written), several completed
essays, and a sprawling and complex book manuscript based on citation as a
critical principle. Benjamin's vast research project on Paris produced several
very different kinds of work, including essays that combine cultural, historical,
aesthetic, and materialist approaches to poetry and a predigital database of citations accompanied by commentary. Benjamin presents the work as a city built
of intersecting themes, texts, images, and disciplines. The themes appear to be
conceived like boulevards. The citations appear in a suggestive frame of display
and interpretation. It is impossible to fix the work's final form, but the unfinished manuscript appears to be a completely new kind of work that combines
two languages, many voices, and several types of writing, as Benjamin interprets
modernity through a range of texts, disciplines, and media.

This book has been published and translated, the work in progress suspended
in the form it had taken at the time of Benjamin's violent and tragic death.
Thanks to Georges Bataille and the Bibliothèque Nationale, the manuscript
was saved, but Benjamin, the author, was not saved—from poverty after the
Nazis cut off his livelihood in Germany, from more poverty and isolation in the
increasingly hostile environment of his dream city, and finally, after the terrify-
ing internment at Drancy, from a desperate attempt to escape the Gestapo that
ended in Benjamin's suicide. Given these extreme circumstances, the elaboration of the work on Baudelaire, the work itself, and the survival of the manuscript seem to take on the quality its author observed in some of Baudelaire's
best lines of poetry; they literally have emerged from an abyss.

"On Some Motifs in Baudelaire" begins with Baudelaire's understanding of
his reader, but it ends, dramatically, with a reading of "Loss of Halo" that reveals
the poet's insight into his contemporaries. Baudelaire writes them into his poems as the subjects of loss, invisibility, history, and exile. Baudelaire's reader is
self and other at the same time, a player in the poet's painting of modern life.

Benjamin's focus on the singular way that Baudelaire writes the modernity
of Paris into his poetry unlocks one of the fundamental mysteries, or difficulties, of reading Baudelaire: the contradictions in tone and mood in his works.
The abrupt and contradictory qualities that characterize Baudelaire's style recall

earlier literary periods and were not generally encountered among the works of the early-nineteenth-century writers before Baudelaire or those of his contemporaries. As an expert on the European baroque and an exceptional authority on some of the least approachable German baroque works, Benjamin appreciates Baudelaire's intense use of allegory and his affinity for Renaissance and baroque aesthetics. In addition to his in-depth exploration of the literary and historical contexts of Second Empire France and their impact on modernist innovations in the early twentieth century, Benjamin enters the frame of Baudelaire's thought and the poet's passion for images. This approach allows Benjamin to explore Baudelaire's perspective as it differs from most of the poet's contemporaries. Beginning with his literary and philosophical understanding of the baroque, Benjamin approaches his project of the literary construction of modernity. Baudelaire portrays major figures of modern life that Benjamin locates in the re-creation of the city. His study of Baudelaire's innovations in prose and especially verse shapes his new perspective on Paris as the most characteristically modern nineteenth-century city and Baudelaire as its essential and emblematic poet. Paris, the city of Benjamin's flight toward modern life, could be called Baudelaire-Ville.

In Baudelaire's poetry, the baroque, with its emphasis on Melancholia, brings modernity closer to antiquity. Baudelaire's poetry suggests that the two periods correspond with each other; Benjamin explores the connection between modern mass culture and the decaying city. Benjamin likes to use the term *verschränken* ("clasping"), his insightful translation of *correspondance* (Schlossman, *Orient* and "Benjamin's *Ueber Einege Motive*"). The emphasis on unexpected intersections or crossings undercuts the continuous flow of lyric poetry; the breaks in rhythm and the abrupt topical shifts from one sentence or paragraph to the next characterize Baudelaire's prose poetry. Even in contexts characterized by vigorous movement, something can happen to freeze the figures in their tracks. This also happens to the narrator or speaker of "À Une Passante" ("To a Woman Passing By"). He is in complicity with the narrators of many of the prose poems; his predicament, his reflections, his tenderness, and his bitterness make him their brother. The movements, undulations, and shocks that characterize the chance encounters of city life echo the "Tableaux Parisiens" ("Parisian Pictures") and underscore their status as counterparts of the prose poetry. From the complex lyric and tragic characters that inhabit them, Baudelaire extracts the more ordinary, quotidian, and prosaic figures of the Paris streets. The results are startling.

Benjamin observes the consequences of the link that Baudelaire forges between modern Paris and the enterprise of prose poetry. The defense of the new form that Baudelaire celebrates in the dedication of *Paris Spleen* shapes the aesthetic of modernity. This is especially interesting and convincing given the novelty of prose poetry and Benjamin's reservations about Baudelaire's prose in general. The dangerous freedom that Baudelaire attributes to the form influenced many writers in Benjamin's time and beyond it. His perspective is even

more striking because Benjamin was writing at a time when Baudelaire's reputation as a great modern poet was either affirmed or vigorously denied on the
sole evidence of *The Flowers of Evil*. The dossiers of the *Arcades Project* are
filled with critical evidence for or against the greatness of Baudelaire's poetry
identified with his verse. Serious interest in prose poetry as poetry and not as
short prose pieces does not seem to be on the critical horizon of either Benjamin or Erich Auerbach, the two theorists and critics of the period between
the wars who most clearly perceive the long-term impact of Baudelaire. It did
not escape their attention that Arthur Rimbaud, Stéphane Mallarmé, Maurice
Maeterlinck, Emile Verhaeren, and other writers in the avant-garde movements
of the late nineteenth and early twentieth centuries continued the explorations
that Baudelaire's *Paris Spleen* had taken to a level of literary accomplishment
that earlier French prose poetry could not have achieved.

In Baudelaire-Ville

Benjamin's observations of Baudelaire's trajectory lead the critic to the link
between prose poetry and the qualities of Paris as the ground of Baudelaire's
subjects and as a poetic object in its own right. One of Benjamin's first sources
of insight on Baudelaire's innovation in the writing of modern life is a passage
in the provocative dedication of *Paris Spleen* to Arsène Houssaye (*Œuvres
complètes* 1: 275–76). Originally intended to convince Houssaye to publish the
prose poems, Baudelaire's argument presents some of the criteria that have
transformed modern literature (Schlossman, *Orient*).

The dedication begins with an evocation of the individual prose poems as sections of a snake: in contrast to the claim that Baudelaire made for the narrative
order of *The Flowers of Evil*, the sections can be arranged in any order desired.
In a carefully worded meditation on literary style, Baudelaire presents his new
poetic enterprise following the publication of *The Flowers of Evil*: "Quel est
celui de nous qui n'a pas . . . rêvé le miracle d'une prose poétique, musicale
sans rythme et sans rime, assez souple et assez heurtée pour s'adapter aux mouvements lyriques de l'âme, aux ondulations de la rêverie, aux soubresauts de
la conscience?" 'Who among us has not . . . dreamed the miracle of a poetic
prose that would be musical without rhythm or rhyme, flexible enough and suf-
ficiently abrupt to adapt to the lyrical movements of the heart, the undulations
of daydreaming, the shocks of consciousness?'(*Œuvres complètes*: 275). *Paris
Spleen* is a product of the effects of a vast collective creature that is latent, almost
invisible, hidden among Baudelaire's fragments and poetic figures: the crowd. In
Benjamin's thought, the crowd appears as Baudelaire's central motif.

In the constellation of the poet's favorite rhetorical figures and visual images—words and things—many of them are related to the motif of the crowd.
Baudelaire's strategic meditation is unusually candid about the impact of the

city and its masses: "C'est surtout de la fréquentation des villes énormes, c'est du croisement de leurs innombrables rapports, que naît cet idéal obsédant" 'Above all, it is the experience of enormous cities, the intersecting of their innumerable connections, that gives birth to this obsessive ideal.' Loosely constructed, the book seeks "la description de la vie moderne, ou plutôt d'*une* vie moderne" 'to describe modern life, or rather *one* modern life.' That life is filled with melancholy and ennui, or spleen. Its depiction echoes the strategic opposition between spleen and ideal that is prominent in Baudelaire's verse.

The first incarnation of spleen that appears to the reader of *The Flowers of Evil* is personified as a monstrous creature smoking a water pipe at the end of "Au Lecteur" ("To the Reader")—"Hypocrite Lecteur! Mon semblable! Mon frère!" 'Hypocritical Reader! My semblance! My brother!' (17). The violent shock of this last line confronts the reader with the innovative qualities of Baudelaire's poetry. The shock at the end illustrates the poet's notion of the *poncif*— a somewhat enigmatic term, frequently translated as a stereotype or cliché, that resonates in Baudelaire's declared desire to compete with well-known French Romantic poets. Baudelaire's *poncif* is a mark, an icon, or a slogan that would establish the poet as creator of the brand-new. It might be a poetic equivalent of advertising (or branding). I would suggest that the *poncif* can be understood in connection with the visual insignia of the halo in "Loss of Halo," a prose poem that explicitly portrays the role of the poet in the city.

The image of the poet crowned with a strangely angelic halo communicates to readers the particular quality associated with the creation of poetry in the Second Empire. Benjamin explores the temporal and historical dimensions of Baudelaire's poetic fable as the moment of high capitalism when the act of poetic creation is marginalized. The halo is old, attached to the representation of tradition and the sacred; the mark or signature of the modern, on the other hand, is the latest thing. I would suggest that the *poncif* to which Baudelaire aspired forever replaces the poet's halo.

Benjamin quotes the passage from Baudelaire's dedication of *Paris Spleen* at the beginning of the third part of *The Paris of the Second Empire in Baudelaire*, titled "Modernity" (*Writer* 96–133). Benjamin is interested in exploring the connection between Baudelaire's writing of his city experience as a poet, in verse and in prose. The poet at work is engaged in minute invisible improvisations as he moves through the streets. Benjamin sees these improvisations in verbal construction as the gestures of a man fencing. The critic is intrigued by the notion of the writer at work in the street, unseen by his peers. It impresses him that the poet's friends never saw the evidence of his writing; desk, quill and ink, paper, dictionaries, and other implements of the writer's craft were not observed in Baudelaire's rooms. The lost halo is emblematic of the poet's hidden identity, his struggle with darkness and stormy weather, his elusive trajectory. Like the character in "Loss of Halo," the poet exposes himself to the world without the protection of his insignia; invisible, he blends into the jostling crowd. Unlike the poetic personae of Victor Hugo who see beneath the earth's surface with the bard's special vision, Baudelaire's fictional poet figures read themselves into the crowd, its fantasies, appetites, and pleasures.

The Poet's Halo and the Theory of Modernity

Baudelaire's poetic path leads from "Spleen and Ideal" to the stark cityscapes in verse and in prose poetry. One of the last cityscapes occurs in "Loss of Halo," near the end of *Paris Spleen*, published in 1869 (*Spleen* [Pichois] 352). This late prose poem, presumably written during Baudelaire's Belgian exile, was not published during the poet's lifetime, although Baudelaire had submitted it at least once to the *Revue nationale et étrangère*, which rejected the poem in 1865 (*Œuvres complètes* 1: 1347).

The striking contrast between the sketch and the prose poem provides a rare opportunity to observe Baudelaire's substantial revision of a major late text. Here is the early version that appears in *Fusées XI*, followed by my own translation:

> Comme je traversais le boulevard, et comme je mettais un peu de précipitation à éviter les voitures, mon auréole s'est détachée et est tombée dans la boue du macadam. J'eus heureusement le temps de la ramasser; mais cette idée malheureuse se glissa un instant après dans mon esprit, que c'était un mauvais présage; et dès lors l'idée n'a plus voulu me lâcher; elle ne m'a laissé aucun repos de toute la journée.
>
> (*Œuvres complètes* 1: 659)

> As I was crossing the boulevard, and as I tried to move faster to avoid the coaches, my halo got loose and fell into the mud of the asphalt. Fortunately, I had enough time to pick it up; but an instant later, an unfortunate idea slipped into my mind that it was a bad omen; and from that moment the idea would not let me go; and it gave me no rest throughout the whole day.

The short draft text differs substantially from the published version of the prose poem and may remind the reader of some of Baudelaire's borrowings and adaptations from Thomas De Quincey or Poe. Although several elements are discarded, the passage is clearly one of the sources for the prose poem in *Paris Spleen*. Baudelaire's published poem preserves the boulevard's atmosphere of danger and the subject's anxiety about losing his halo. The good fortune of saving the halo and the superstitious obsession with misfortune that follows the incident disappear completely in the published poem. The final text is completely transformed into a dialogue between two friends or acquaintances. The mishap of losing the halo, the miniature event that dramatizes the shock effects of city traffic, is offered as a kind of pretext that allows the poet to go underground. The interlocutor's response and the poet's emotions are portrayed with many exclamations of surprise, pleasure, and irony. The lively verbal exchange identifies the poem's two characters only as two men who know each other in a more dignified social context than the "mauvais lieu" 'bad place' where they unexpectedly meet. The clearest aspect of their identity is the vocation of the poet, who is expected to act according to higher standards than the ordinary man whose freedom he describes.

My translation of "Loss of Halo" is informed by several published translations but substantially differs from them in light of my discussion of the reading of modernity that Baudelaire continuously articulates in verse and in prose. The shifts in historical details add an additional challenge to the task of the translator of poems focused on the phenomena of modernity, since many of Baudelaire's starkly modern terms have a kind of archeological quaintness for readers in our time. My own translation seeks to emphasize the resonances of Baudelaire's vocabulary of modern life, the expressive intonations and ironic touches of the original, and the details that transform the first draft version into one of Baudelaire's most revealing and accomplished prose poems:

> Eh! quoi! vous ici, mon cher? Vous, dans un mauvais lieu! vous, le buveur de quintessences! vous, le mangeur d'ambroisie! En vérité, il y a là de quoi me surprendre.
>
> —Mon cher, vous connaissez ma terreur des chevaux et des voitures. Tout à l'heure, comme je traversais le boulevard, en grande hâte, et que je sautillais dans la boue, à travers ce chaos mouvant où la mort arrive au galop de tous les côtés à la fois, mon auréole, dans un mouvement brusque, a glissé de ma tête dans la fange du macadam. Je n'ai pas eu le courage de la ramasser. J'ai jugé moins désagréable de perdre mes insignes que de me faire rompre les os. Et puis, me suis-je dit, à quelque chose malheur est bon. Je puis maintenant me promener incognito, faire des actions basses, et me livrer à la crapule, comme les simples mortels. Et me voici, tout semblable à vous, comme vous voyez!
>
> —Vous devriez au moins faire afficher cette auréole, ou la faire réclamer par le commissaire.
>
> —Ma foi! non. Je me trouve bien ici. Vous seul, vous m'avez reconnu. D'ailleurs la dignité m'ennuie. Ensuite je pense avec joie que quelque mauvais poète la ramassera et s'en coiffera impudemment. Faire un heureux, quelle jouissance! et surtout un heureux qui me fera rire! Pensez à X, ou à Z! Hein! comme ce sera drôle!

"Oh! This is something! You here, my friend? You, in a backroom dive! You, the drinker of essences! You, the eater of ambrosia! This is truly a surprise."

"My friend, you know how terrified I am of horses and coaches. A little while ago, as I was crossing the boulevard in great haste and hopping in the mud through the moving chaos where death gallops in from all directions at once, at an abrupt movement, my halo slipped from my head to the filth of the asphalt. I didn't dare to pick it up. I decided it would be less unpleasant to lose my insignia than to have my bones broken. And then, I said to myself, even a misfortune has to be good for something. Now I can walk around incognito, act without conscience, indulge in vulgar behavior like an ordinary man. And here I am, as you see me—just like you!"

"You should at least put up a notice about your halo, or ask the police to find it."

"Good Lord! No. I'm fine here. You're the only one who recognized me. Besides, dignity bores me. And then it's a joy to think that some awful poet will pick it up and have the nerve to put it on. What bliss to make a man happy! And above all, the happy guy will make me laugh! Think of X, or Z! Hah! Won't that be amusing!"

A close reading of the prose poem and a comparison of the two versions of the poet's halo make it possible to see that "Loss of Halo" plays a major role in shaping Benjamin's theoretical approach to Baudelaire and his theory of modernity. Benjamin observes that earlier critics generally overlooked the poem. He compares it briefly with the untitled first draft version in Baudelaire's personal writings, in *Fusées*, and indicates the importance of the final version for an understanding of Baudelaire's single-minded pursuit of his poetic project, a portrait of modern life, even as the poet suffered its effects and consequences in his own experience. Anger and bitterness, betrayal, isolation, and exile are the aftereffects of the loss of auratic experience. Baudelaire's poetic shorthand for the predicament of modern life is the image of being jostled in the crowd. It is the essential experience of the modern city dweller, according to the poet.

In class, it is useful to point out that the first draft version explores the incident of a poet, speaking in the first-person singular, who loses his halo while crossing a busy street; the text uses a single narrative voice. The speaker picks up the fallen halo, but the draft concludes with the narrator brooding over the fateful significance of the incident. The draft ends with the suggestion that the momentary loss has become an idée fixe, an obsession that torments him.

In Baudelaire's rewritten version, "Loss of Halo" is expanded into an energetic dramatic dialogue with an ironic tone and a different ending. An atmosphere of sin and vice is introduced into the setting, where the interlocutor unexpectedly meets the poet. The acquaintance expresses exaggerated surprise at the poet's plunge from habitual refinement to the coarse pleasures offered within a vulgar setting. The poem uses the halo fallen to "the filth of the asphalt" as an image for an auratically powerful poetic identity that is suddenly subjected to the shattering forces of modernity. The omen disappears, replaced by the hyperbole of movement, chaos, and the baroque allegory of death on horseback. In another baroque touch, Baudelaire alludes to the proverbial gain from misfortune. This is not a moral imperative but rather its opposite: the freedom to act without conscience, in the anonymity created by city life. The poet's loss enters the realm of comedy or even farce, as the end of the poem fills with dark laughter and moral ambiguity, underscored in the poetics of modernity. The poem indicates that the halo is a mark of poetic identity, but the character of the poet forced to sacrifice it to modern life is nonetheless a true poet (unlike some of his acquaintances, who might fish it out of the mud). The poet who has lost his "insignia" proclaims his satisfaction now that the absence of the halo allows him to move through the city without being recognized. His acquaintance in the seedy place where they meet is surprised: now that his halo has disappeared, the poet does not feel impelled to behave more virtuously than other men. This extraordinary ending illustrates Baudelaire's power of sidestepping Romantic clichés and portraying the moral ambiguities of modern life (Culler, "Baude-laire and Poe" and "Baudelaire's Destruction").

This experience turns the figure of the poet into an unidentifiable man in an urban crowd. The poem is explicitly anchored within the larger framework of *Paris Spleen* in part through the offhand reference to the poet's ennui at play-ing the role of poet. He mocks the bad poet who might have found his halo in the muddy street and is now masquerading in it, presenting himself in the true poet's insignia. I would suggest that the capitalized title of Poet that appears in many of Baudelaire's verse and prose poems is comparable to the radiant power of the halo. Such instances are literary and visual examples of Baudelaire's prac-tice or use of allegory.

Dialectics of the Aura

The prose poem raises the question of the status of the halo (literally, an "au-réole"); Benjamin's comments implicitly raise the question of its connection to his theoretical concept of the aura. It is worth pointing out that Benjamin did not invent the word *aura* and that in French *aura* and *auréole* are related but distinct. Benjamin's original theoretical concept of the aura is based on several aspects of tradition and developed in the contexts of modernity. The theory appears in some of Benjamin's major texts written in 1929 and throughout the 1930s, including his work on Baudelaire, where it plays an important role. The discussion of the aura in "On Some Motifs in Baudelaire" is probably the last treatment of the topic in Benjamin's formal writing (*Writer* 170–210).

Benjamin, who considered his project on the nineteenth century as a kind of theater of dialectic, usually proposes the concept of the aura in a dialectical framework. In "On Some Motifs in Baudelaire," the extreme saturation of aura is evoked through "Correspondences," while the opposite position—the ruin or destruction of the aura—is explored through "Loss of Halo." Briefly, aura is associated with the plenitude of enduring experience, steeped in tradition, art, ritual, and nature, as well as the imagination and involuntary memory, whereas the ruin of the aura is associated with experience as mere data: the ruin of the aura takes place through commodification, shock effects, and technological advances (including the reproduction of the work of art) that shape the crises of modernity.

I would suggest that Benjamin's theory of the aura originates in part in his reading of Baudelaire; the poet's work shapes Benjamin's approach to modernity across the disciplines. His theory is grounded in questions of perception and art as well as history and technology. Benjamin proposes two notions of experience that shape the theory of the aura: *Erfahrung*, translated as "long experience," and *Erlebnis*, isolated or "immediate experience" (*Writer* 176–77). *Erfahrung* is experience as sensory plenitude, art, ritual, or the content of tradition, as illustrated in the concept of the aura. In contrast, *Erlebnis* is experience as mere data or the shocks that characterize the experience of the streets, the elbowing by the crowd. These encounters that Baudelaire portrays in the dedication to *Paris Spleen* are an indication of his innovation as a poet of modernity. Benjamin theorizes the experiences of the crowd that Baudelaire evokes as the "decay," "ruin," or "destruction of the aura" (205, 210). The richness of experience is at one end of the dialectical spectrum, its poverty at the other. Baudelaire is the poet of both forms of experience. Some of Baudelaire's most famous poems propose the Romantic transports of pleasure, intoxication, and involuntary memory, as well as the long experience that Benjamin proposes as prehistory. The ruin of the aura leaves traces that Benjamin associates with the clues uncovered in Poe's invented genre of detective stories. Poe's work was superbly translated by Baudelaire, who interpreted its urban contexts through his experience of Paris.

I would suggest that the concept of the aura is at the foundation of Benjamin's construct of Paris as Baudelaire-Ville. The figures of modernity, including the crowd, the masses, the figure of a woman passing by, and the artist as acrobat are hidden in Baudelaire's poems.[2] These figures emerge in Benjamin's interpretive sounding of Baudelaire's poems as traces of the lost realm of traditional, collective society and the plenitude of experience (Schlossman, "Images"). Benjamin explores the importance of "Loss of Halo" within the theoretical framework of Baudelaire's motifs as hidden figures. In the end, the poet describes himself most clearly as a man pushed around in the crowd. He surrenders his work to a future that he cannot imagine as other than a storm of modernity. The last words of "On Some Motifs in Baudelaire" indicate that this dissolving of the aura is the law of Baudelaire's poetry.

Baudelaire unobtrusively pairs the term *insignia* with the halo. There are several etymological echoes that reinforce the enigmatic prestige of the poet's emblem; the most obvious one is the presence of the sign in insignia. The French term, *insigne*, refers to a distinctive mark and takes on a surprising early-nineteenth-century variation in reference to the crowning of Napoléon. The term *insignia* is also related to the classical Latin origin of *enseigne*, which includes "decoration" among its meanings. Language, art, and a crown borrowed from the angels for a modern-day emperor unite in Baudelaire's staging of the halo.

Poetry leads Benjamin toward new and powerful concepts that continue to resonate in theoretical contexts. Baudelaire's late prose poem, which, according to Benjamin, nearly slipped away unnoticed after the poet's untimely death, is at the heart of the critic's thinking about modernity across the disciplines. In the original text of "On Some Motifs in Baudelaire," Benjamin translates "Loss of Halo" into German. It is the only prose poem quoted at length in his writings on Baudelaire. In Benjamin's essay, it is balanced by a limited number of verse excerpts and one complete poem, quoted in French. We may infer the importance of these texts for the author, constrained to limit his citations in this essay. Benjamin's translation and his commentary on "Loss of Halo" occupy the twelfth and final section of the essay. In the commentary, Benjamin emphasizes Baudelaire's reflections on the poet's situation in a prose poem that bears witness to the last years of the poet's life in exile.

According to Benjamin, Baudelaire arrives at the end of a poetic tradition that has its greatest impact in *The Flowers of Evil*. The major motifs of this work problematize the existence of lyric poetry itself. Baudelaire paid a very high price for his complicity with the destructive effects of the modern world. Benjamin names this particular form of destruction as the decay or the dissolution of the aura—a concept that he elaborates to explore the depth and duration of past experience. This form of experience is essentially collective, but it also occurs on the level of the individual, where it is anchored in the unconscious and lends its magic to our images of lost time. If it is the shock effects of modern life that destroy the plenitude of experience associated with the aura, then we can read "Loss of Halo" as the acceptance of modern life and the banishment of poets wearing halos into the realm of the old-fashioned. The world of fashion, novelties, and commodities furtively approaches the nouveau for which Baudelaire's narrators thirst.

"Loss of Halo" marks a decisive moment in Baudelaire reception; it confirms everything that Benjamin understands about Baudelaire in the poet's verse, the centerpiece of the critic's argument. It thus opens the path to the exploration of the poetic qualities of Baudelaire's prose poetry. Benjamin anchors these qualities in the perceptions of urban life that shape Baudelaire's images of experience.

The narrator of "Loss of Halo" has decided to go underground, into the crowd. He anticipates the anonymity of the blank-faced figures in paintings by artists like Kazimir Malevich, René Magritte, Marcel Duchamp, and Giorgio de Chirico or the infinite repetition of the crowd in avant-garde Soviet cinema. The prose poem demonstrates the power at work in Baudelaire's city poetry: it moves beyond the experience of poetry inherited from Romanticism and overtakes the life of the poet. In this sense, Baudelaire's aesthetic is "trans-romantic," and the loss of the halo signals the arrival of modernity under the suffocating skies of

Second Empire Paris. The impact of Benjamin's reading of the most enigmatic, influential, and magnetic nineteenth-century poet also lives on through its clear vision of Baudelaire's place in the modern world.

Shock, Spleen, and Modernity

Although prose poetry remains an elusive form, and arguments linger about the separation between *Flowers of Evil* and *Paris Spleen*, Baudelaire's prose poetry is firmly anchored in his verse masterpiece. *Paris Spleen* pursues the perspectives that can be observed in some of the most powerful poems of *The Flowers of Evil*, at the intersections of their urban context and the ideal of style. Among these perspectives are the poet's tasks, ideals, and roles and the difficulties faced by the artist in modern city life. Using poetic qualities of language that are outside the formal constraints of rhyme and meter, *Paris Spleen* continues to explore the questions raised in verse about the possibility of lyric poetry in urban modernity. Many of the difficulties that Baudelaire encountered in verse and in prose poetry derive from the unfamiliarity of his subjects, as perceived according to the strictly identified contexts of Romantic poetry. His famous and provocative remarks about the miracle of a poetic prose present *Paris Spleen* in a formulaic combination of the city, the work of art, and the perceptions of modern life. The perception of walking through the streets is characterized by the rhythms of movement and undulation, and the abrupt and shattering interruptions of thought and desire, as well as the shocks of exterior violence.

The emotional landscape is dominated by ennui (or spleen) and melancholy, the emotional and reflective responses to modernity that characterize Baudelaire's aesthetic. The city is the source of these related responses to modernity. The *flâneur*, for whom the city is a theater of entertainment and a welcome source of distraction, is a reassuring image of modernity that masks many other figures — heroes and heroines, in Baudelaire's terms of modern life — who are subjected to the relentless violence and shocks of life on the street, among the crowds. These figures include the lonely men and women in search of forms of consolation, love, or pleasure; the dandy eager to be seen; the criminal looking for prey; the hunted victim in flight from pursuers; and the poet-artist or prostitute seeking new opportunities and clients, new desires and pleasures, new consolations for melancholy ennui or spleen.

Borrowed from English, spleen mingles with the ideal as the modern intersects with the terms of classical antiquity: *Le Spleen de Paris* evokes the same combination of modernity and classical antiquity as the title of "Spleen et Idéal" ("Spleen and Ideal") in *The Flowers of Evil*. From Baudelaire's perspective, spleen represents the newest borrowed concept in French, the ideal, the oldest. Like "Parisian Pictures," the prose poem collection adds Paris to the abstract concept, as if the name of the city were itself the ultimate fusion of classical antiquity and the cutting edge of modern life. In this sense, we might think of the name of Paris as an example of Benjamin's dialectical image, combining the past and the future with the present, the now that flashes past us.

Benjamin's reading of modernity posits Baudelaire's poetry at its core and shapes its approach to perception and aesthetics in modernity through a theory of melancholy and allegory (de Man, *Rhetoric*; Starobinski; Chambers, *Mélan-colie*). In Baudelaire's theater of poetry and in Benjamin's critical responses to Baudelaire, the creation and destruction of illusion unfold in time and space. "Loss of Halo" allows for a compelling approach to these perspectives across the breadth of *Paris Spleen* and across the depth and range of its styles. The poem leads Benjamin toward the theory of modernity. Shock is the symptom, and aura is its antidote, according to a dialectical relation captured in the poetry of violence, solitude, and tenderness. It is played out repeatedly in Baudelaire-Ville, in the same streets where Benjamin walked the path of exile and exploration seventy years after the poet. Benjamin evokes Baudelaire moving at a rapid pace along the street and crossing the dangerous mud-filled boulevards. Benjamin's reading traces the path of a writer following his objects of desire, getting lost in a labyrinth, observing unknown women in public gardens, and listening to the music of momentary happiness.[3]

NOTES

The author gratefully acknowledges research support from the University of California, Irvine.

[1] Unless otherwise indicated, all translations from the French are mine.

[2] See Schlossman, "'Le Cygne'—Paris Downstream," "Baudelaire l'extravagant," and "Métamorphoses."

[3] See Schlossman, "Baudelaire l'extravagant" and "Métamorphoses."

Baudelaire Modern and Antimodern: *Le Spleen de Paris* in an Interdisciplinary Course on Modernity

Joseph Acquisto

For many, Baudelaire is a key figure in the inauguration of literary modernism, and the formal experimentation and innovative thematic material of the prose poems lends much credence to that view. When the aesthetic category of modernism is extended to the more broadly cultural category of modernity, the poet still has a crucial role to play alongside philosophers and other theorists of the modern, not least on account of his famous theorization of the modern artist as having the potential to "tirer l'éternel du transitoire" 'draw out the eternal from the transitory' ("Le Peintre de la vie moderne" [*Œuvres complètes* 2: 694]; my trans.). In this essay, I explore the way Baudelaire's prose poems can be used in an interdisciplinary course on European modernity. In such a course, Baudelaire is a crucial figure because he serves as a particularly marked example of a key paradox of those thinkers and writers most strongly identified with the modern—namely, that they were often highly skeptical about and critical of the modern world. The prose poems reveal a simultaneously modern and antimodern Baudelaire; they can serve as a disconcerting but accessible introduction to the paradox of giving voice to the modern in a way that expresses deep, and even reactionary, reservations about it.

The course I describe here is entitled Reading Modernity. It always carries an interdisciplinary course number; I have given versions of it, in English, as a sophomore honors seminar, an undergraduate lecture course, and a graduate seminar for master's students. (I focus in this essay on the undergraduate version.) There are no prerequisites for the course, which I describe as focusing on European modernity through broad readings in literature, philosophy, political science, sociology, and critical theory, along with some attention to painting and music. Our starting point is the paradox that most writers and thinkers centrally linked to the idea of modernity were in fact highly skeptical about and critical of the modern world. After a first day's lecture that explores various eras often considered the ones that gave birth to the modern, the course focuses on three periods: the Enlightenment (with readings from Kant, Voltaire, and Diderot), the high modern period of the late nineteenth and early twentieth centuries (Marx, Nietzsche, Freud, Weber, Mann), and what might be called the postmodern period (Jameson, Lyotard, Hutcheon, Bauman, Beckett, Hrabal).

The course explores a variety of characterizations of what the category modern might designate, acknowledging that there is no scholarly consensus about this question, either within or between disciplines. Students at the start of the course typically identify it with contemporary and often mention particular technological developments as characteristic of what the modern is, whereas some might successfully identify the intellectual or ideological roots of modernity in the Protestant Reformation or the dual revolution or perhaps identify progress as a key concept. Instead of adopting one particular theoretical lens through which to define the modern, the course attempts to put famous representatives of modernity in dialogue with each other and to see what emerges from the intersection of these texts from different countries, time periods, and genres.

While any contemporary theorist of the modern necessarily provides only a partial and limited view of a vast topic, good starting points for an undergraduate course such as this one include Matei Calinescu's *Five Faces of Modernity* and Antoine Compagnon's *Five Paradoxes of Modernity*. The latter gives attention to modernity as both a cultural and aesthetic category, a distinction some authors uphold by reference to modernity as opposed to modernism. The model that Compagnon identifies as German (*Five Paradoxes* x) is more familiar to American students; it is the one that emphasizes Enlightenment-style reason and is at the root of Americans' identification of modernity with progress. As students see in the course, there is ample evidence of this view in eighteenth-century France as well, but for the most part, exemplary moderns are, as Compagnon points out, figures such as Nietzsche and Baudelaire who are suspicious of the notion of progress and teleological visions of history.

It is at this point that the role of literature in shaping the modern begins to come more clearly into view. The literary works we read in the first part of the course, including stories by Voltaire and the dialogue *Rameau's Nephew* by Denis Diderot, serve as a kind of laboratory for testing the Enlightenment model of progress, their characters challenging the credibility of that model through philosophical objections and the portrayal of lived experiences at odds with the fundamentals of what the students later learn to call the Enlightenment's grand narrative. The micronarratives of fiction, featuring individual characters embedded in particular situations, work out the highly critical approach to modernity that will see its full theoretical flowering in thinkers such as Weber and Freud. Here Baudelaire comes into play, since, while he is often taken as a key inaugurator of the modern, in some ways he also fits in the category of antimodern as characterized by Compagnon, whose characteristics include anitrevolutionary politics, an anti-Enlightenment stance, and an emphasis on original sin and the sublime (*Antimodernes* 18).[1] This paradoxical stance is of course completely appropriate to Baudelaire, who famously claimed that we are double in nature ("Qui parmi nous n'est pas un *homo duplex*?" 'Who among us is not a *homo duplex*?' ["La Double vie par Charles Asselineau" [*Œuvres complètes* 1: 87]; my trans.]) and that we are under the constraining effect of a double postulation, one toward God and the other toward Satan.[2]

As Fredric Jameson has argued in an essay on Baudelaire as modernist and postmodernist, "there are . . . many Baudelaires" (223); for Jameson these Baudelaires are "of most unequal value indeed." He dismisses the "second-rate post-Romantic Baudelaire, the Baudelaire of diabolism and of cheap *frisson*, . . . of a creaking and musty religious machinery which was no more interesting in the mid-nineteenth century than it is today." I would argue that, while there are indeed many Baudelaires, it may not be as easy as Jameson suggests to dismiss the diabolism and "religious machinery" at work throughout both the verse and prose poems. Although space does not allow me to develop this argument here, Baudelaire's religious vision is a Christianity without salvation—that is, a Christianity deprived of its basic core belief.[3] In fact, it is this radical revision, or reappropriation, of a religious vision that is a major contributor to Baudelaire's particular modern antimodernism. His recourse to a religious vocabulary—one that is much more than a metaphor but something quite different from anything we would typically label belief—allows him to give voice to a particularly trenchant critique of modernity in the prose poems.

A reinterpretation of Christian vocabulary with an intensified focus on original sin and removal of salvation is only one aspect of Baudelaire's antimodernity, but it is one of the most complex and, in the context of the course I have been describing, highly present in students' minds given the moment at which we read the prose poems in the course. Students have already encountered Voltaire's and Diderot's dismissal and mockery of organized religion and have come to associate that attitude with the Enlightenment spirit. In excerpts from Karl Marx's "Economic and Philosophic Manuscripts of 1844," too, students will have seen a critique of religion as superstition and mystification, a major obstacle to seeing and knowing the world as it is (Marx and Engels 70–91). All the more surprising, then, to see that Baudelaire provides a rather different take on what it means to see things as they are and that his modernity is in some ways very much at odds with the otherwise coherent picture that had been emerging thus far in the course. While plenty of the prose poems invite dialogue with Marx's notion of urban alienation and the critique of commodity culture,[4] others complicate the picture and resist students' efforts to see Baudelaire simply as a kind of illustration of the worldview theorized by Marx. The prose poems complicate simple dichotomies and, in this way, force students to confront the complexity inherent in the very concept of the modern. From among the multitude of categories with which the prose poems engage, all of which are fruitful paths for class discussion, I focus first on the notion of self, which, perhaps surprisingly, leads back to a consideration of religion. In both cases, Baudelaire's modernity is inextricably linked with his antimodernity and is thus yet another instance of his troubling the very categories by which we would like to be able to evaluate his place in literary and cultural history.

In his autobiographical fragments *Mon Cœur mis à nu* (*My Heart Laid Bare*), Baudelaire writes: "De la vaporisation et de la centralisation du *Moi*. Tout est là" 'Of the vaporization and the centralization of *the self*. All is there' (*Œuvres complètes* 1: 677; my trans.). The centralization of self is a hallmark of the modern since René Descartes's positing of the *cogito*; any course on modernity would explore the ways in which the modern democratic state endows the individual political subject with individual rights at the same time that an individualist mentality emerges that would come to be associated with liberal capitalism and opposed to collective resistance to it. What is particular about Baudelaire's portrayal of selfhood is that it is a question not of alternating between presence and absence of self but of experiencing both *simultaneously*. As Leo Bersani has indicated, in Baudelaire, "the artist's, the lover's, and God's unconditional availability to otherness, their sacrificial prostitution of the self, is an openness to a *non-moi* that they already possess" (74). The prostitution of the self is explored both in *Mon Cœur mis à nu* and in the prose poems—most especially "Les Foules" ("Crowds"), where Baudelaire affirms that "le poète jouit de cet incomparable privilège, qu'il peut à sa guise être lui-même et autrui" 'the poet enjoys the incomparable privilege of being able, at will, to be himself and an other' (*Spleen* [Pichois] 291; *The Parisian Prowler* [Kaplan] 21). This capacity produces a "singulière ivresse" 'unique intoxication' drawn from what the poet calls "cette universelle communion" 'this universal communion.' The blending of religious and sexual registers escalates as the poem continues, culminating in an unfavorable comparison of what is typically labeled love to "cette ineffable orgie, . . . cette sainte prostitution de l'âme qui se donne tout entière . . . à l'inconnu qui passe" 'that ineffable orgy, that holy prostitution of the soul which gives itself totally . . . to the unknown which passes by.' The experience the poet describes here is distinct from the notion of vaporization and centralization of the self in that the poet enters, body and soul, into another, not so much creating a new composite subject as experiencing himself as both self and other simultaneously. This elaboration allows us to go back and reread this earlier assertion in the poem: "Multitude, solitude: termes égaux et convertibles pour le poète actif et fécond" 'Multitude, solitude: equal and interchangeable terms for the active and fertile poet.' It is not that the poet prefers one term to the other but rather that one experiences both at the same time and in terms of the other, so that the difference between the two is both canceled and operative. The fact that the poet can experience himself as same and other simultaneously also cancels, or at least calls into question, the notion of linear time, which is also flattened along with the self/other distinction. And here we have another crucial aspect of Baudelaire's antimodernity, a strong and consistent resistance to advancement in linear time and its concomitant notion of progress.[5]

To indicate whether this is a modern view is no simple matter. To the extent that it radically calls into question the notion of autonomous selfhood, it subverts existing categories and challenges the reader to become like the poet by seeing commonplace reality through a different lens and imagining how one might perceive the everyday world differently. This move is in keeping with the modern spirit of critique that students have already traced through the eighteenth-century authors they have read in the course. But at the same time, Baudelaire offers a critique of the complacency of the modern world in its standard, bourgeois manifestation (the appeal to what people call love), and to announce the critique he returns to Christian vocabulary, precisely the source of superstition and ignorance according to many of those same eighteenth-century *philosophes*. What is taking shape here, then, is a distinctive antimodernism that is not merely a reactionary attempt to return to prerevolutionary culture and politics, a tendency visible in thinkers such as Joseph de Maistre, whom Baudelaire admired but with whom he ultimately has little in common, perhaps especially on account of de Maistre's Catholic notion of a sacrificial victim, a view for which Baudelaire's unredemptive religious view has no room. And so with this return with a difference of a highly idiosyncratic para-Christianity, Baudelaire enacts yet another kind of simultaneity, the dismissal and advancement of the modern project. As students will come to realize, often an antimodern stance is necessary to articulate the modern, and not by simple opposition. Rather, the modern contains and depends on the antimodern, which emerges in Baudelaire (and others) as a fertile and creative, not merely reactionary, stance. This, one of the fundamental premises of the course, gets both its most complex and most accessible exposition in the situated experiences portrayed in Baudelaire's prose poems.

One of the most idiosyncratic of these experiences is the one related in "Le Mauvais Vitrier" ("The Bad Glazier"), which memorably concludes with the poet chasing a glazier out of his apartment because the former had dared peddle in a poor neighborhood without offering any colored panes of glass so that the residents might see something that renders life beautiful — "la vie en beau" (287). The poet then drops a flower pot on the glazier, causing him to fall and break the wares he was carrying, before concluding with the following rhetorical question: "Mais qu'importe l'éternité de la damnation à qui a trouvé dans une seconde l'infini de la jouissance?" 'But what does an eternity of damnation matter to someone who has experienced for one second the infinity of delight?' (287; 15). This is one of Baudelaire's richest prose poems, providing fertile ground for analysis of violence, irony, ethics, representations of social class, and more.[6] In our present context, an important feature of this conclusion is the way it unites, as "Les Foules" also does, religious and sexual vocabulary, the word "jouissance" suggesting not only delight but sexual climax. Linear time also seems vanquished in the single second of pleasure, which is then exchanged for an eternity that also cancels earthly time. Once again, Baudelaire appropriates Christian discourse in an unusual context, but to appreciate the full resonance of that appropriation we need to return to the perhaps less immediately memorable but crucially important first half of the poem, in which he ponders why otherwise passive people sometimes act "avec une rapidité dont elles se seraient crues elles-mêmes incapables" 'with a speed of which they would have not believed themselves capable' (283; 13)]. He admits that "le moraliste et le médecin" 'the moralist and the physician' would be powerless to explain the "force irrésistible" 'irresistible force' that acts on such people (285; 13), and in a parenthetical paragraph that serves as transition between this first section and the first-person anecdote about the glazier, he characterizes that force as "hystérique selon les médecins, satanique selon ceux qui pensent un peu mieux que les médecins" 'hysterical according to physicians, satanic according to those who think a little more lucidly than physicians' (286; 14).

Here we have a thoroughly antimodern Baudelaire who perhaps seeks to reclaim traditional religious notions of diabolical possession as an effective counterpoint to modern scientific explanations—but again, things are not as simple as they appear. Even putting aside the question of whether the speaker in the poem actually represents Baudelaire, there is more at stake, since the implied critique of science suggests the sort of nondogmatic skepticism that science adopts in its experimental attempts to establish causal relation. After all, a major test for the validity of a scientific theory, as played out dramatically in the debates around Darwin at the time when Baudelaire was writing, is the comprehensiveness of its explanatory value as opposed to what counterevidence it leaves unexplained or what phenomena it fails to account for. In the absence of further elaboration of why we should prefer the satanic explanation, we would not be wrong to presume that the scientific world of physical and material determinism is not simply unsatisfying but also inadequate. Once again, Baudelaire is not, like less remarkable antimoderns, suggesting we avoid science and return to a premodern Catholic worldview. His desire for satisfying and complete explanation suggests the limits of science and provides a warning about a misplaced faith in its methods and conclusions, which is not to be supplanted by a simple traditional Catholicism. In fact, in 1861, one year before "Le Mauvais Vitrier" first appeared, Baudelaire wrote in a letter to his mother: "Je désire de tout mon cœur (avec quelle sincérité, personne ne peut le savoir que moi!) croire qu'un être extérieur et invisible s'intéresse à ma destinée; mais comment faire pour le croire?" 'I desire with all my heart (with what sincerity, no one can know except me!) to believe that an exterior and invisible being is interested in my destiny; but what can I do in order to believe it?' (*Correspondance* 2: 151; my trans.).

So what can we make of this atypical antimodernity, a call for a return to the register of religious faith without actual belief or practice to sustain it? Herein lies a key feature that distinguishes Baudelaire from other more typically reactionary antimoderns and that impels us to reconsider Jameson's description of the "second-rate post-Romantic Baudelaire, the Baudelaire of diabolism." Baudelaire's diabolism in "Le Mauvais Vitrier" serves as a critique of the epistemological soundness of medical theory and thus arrives, through its very antimodernity, at a trenchantly modern skeptical view of the contemporary world worthy of a Marx, Freud, or Weber. Instead of reading the verse and prose poems that evoke or even glorify Satan as a puerile rebellion against God and the good, I follow Benjamin Fondane, poet and literary critic who wrote his book-length study of Baudelaire just before being deported to Drancy and then murdered at Auschwitz. The context in which he writes these words gives them an urgent, if not explicit, political charge:

> C'est sur un vaste canevas d'ennui que l'on brodera les cruautés, les crucifixions, que l'on terrassera l'ennemi, le diable, le néant, et quand la torture elle-même deviendra impuissante, . . . le tissu primitif reparaîtra à la

> surface et ce sera . . . *l'acedia*. "Absence de Dieu" . . . ; sans doute ! mais absence du diable également.   (Fondane 332)

> On a vast canvas of ennui one will embroider cruelties and crucifixions and knock down the enemy, the devil, nothingness, and when torture it-self becomes impotent, . . . the primitive fabric will reappear at the sur-face and it will be . . . *acedia*. "Absence of God" . . . without a doubt, but absence of the devil too.   (my trans.)

For Fondane, Baudelaire's diabolism is a refusal not of God but of nothing-ness, given that the poet eliminates salvation or paradise as a potential form of resistance to the void. Baudelaire's rebellion is "plus dangereux, plus noble que l'obéissance, et en regard de ce que le damné accepte de perdre (vertu, paix, con-naissance), Baudelaire refuse d'y voir un lâche consentement à ses plaisirs. . . . *Il sait*, lui, qu'il ne s'agit pas du consentement à un univers de joie, mais à un univers d'horreur" 'more dangerous, more noble than obedience, and in regard to what the damned person accepts to lose (virtue, peace, knowledge), Baude-laire refuses to see a cowardly assent to his pleasures. . . . *He knows* that it is not an assent to a universe of joys but of horrors' (243; my trans.).

Considered this way, Baudelaire's appeal to premodern religious discourse becomes the source of an antimodern stance that, by its idiosyncratic transfor-mation of tradition, is markedly modern in the patterns of thought it inspires. In the context of a course on modernity, students are better prepared, after struggling with these questions in the embedded form of represented lived ex-perience that the prose poems present, to grapple with more abstract complex formulations of antimodern modernity. In Nietzsche, for instance, students will recognize the reappropriation of Christian discourse for very different ends (what does it mean, for instance, that Nietzsche suggests that *we* have killed God and thus bear responsibility?); in Freud, a deep-seated cultural pessimism that, while adamantly dismissing traditional religious discourse, refuses to sub-stitute a concept of progress in the wake of the overcoming of superstition. The stakes of these debates, as students come to see in my modernity course and several others, are nowhere more intriguingly staged than in Baudelaire.

NOTES

[1] As Compagnon notes, underscoring the paradox I have identified about modernity as constituted by a critique of the modern, "The antimoderns are not just any adversaries of the modern, but rather the thinkers and theoreticians of the modern" (*Antimodernes* 24; my trans.).

[2] See Meltzer's study of Baudelaire's "double vision": "He saw two times, or things, at once—as though his eyes, used as they were to seeing one world, could not yet assimi-late, even as they focused on, a new one. He sees, in other words, both worlds simulta-neously—the Paris before Haussmann, and the Paris during and after its redevelopment;

France before the revolution of 1848, and France in the increasingly triumphant capital-ist culture that followed; the death throes of the *ancien régime* with its unraveling social fabric, and the preening bourgeoisie with its nouveau riche self-satisfaction that touted social utilitarianism and "good works" to repress political guilt and crass mercantilism. Baudelaire's aesthetic strabismus is born of an inability to integrate the dying world and the burgeoning one" (1).

[3] For a fuller argument, see Acquisto, *The Fall out of Redemption* 19–56.

[4] Poems that lend themselves to this line of interpretation include "À Une heure du matin" ("At One O'Clock in the Morning"), "Les Veuves" ("Widows"), "Les Yeux des pauvres" ("The Eyes of the Poor"), and "Perte d'auréole" ("Loss of Halo"), among many others.

[5] On modern pessimism and its critique of linear time, see Dienstag.

[6] For a list of some important readings of the poem in both English and French, see Murphy, *Logiques* 327n1.

How to Read (Women) in Baudelaire's Prose Poems

Maria Scott

Baudelaire's prose poems present particular challenges to their female readers. Where women are not associated in *Le Spleen de Paris* with inaccessible ideals, they tend to be presented as disappointing travesties of that ideal. In the eyes of the unreliable authorial spokesperson, women often reveal themselves as grotesque in their selfishness, narcissism, and vulgarity. I outline here an approach to teaching the prose poems that complicates their overt meaning and, specifically, their apparent misogyny.

Reading Baudelaire's Prose Poems

For some years I taught a final-year undergraduate course, Reading Baudelaire's Prose Poems, that tackled the question of how to read these multilayered texts. The course stressed that even the most easily accessible forms of poetry demand a different kind of reading from that required by other types of writing. The course was aimed at students of French language and culture and, despite its English-language title, was conducted in French. Classes looked at how the meaning of a given prose poem can seem very straightforward—even offensively direct—upon first reading but can become richer and more complex upon closer examination or when read alongside other texts. On the one hand, the module emphasized the importance of close critical analysis, or the advantages of slow over hasty reading. On the other hand, it challenged the traditional notion that literary texts are self-contained units by reading the prose poems within a larger context (textual and, to a lesser extent, historical). Assessment was designed to reward students who engaged in the close reading of individual texts as well as those who had read and reflected on a wide range of Baudelaire's prose poems from the perspective of the themes and techniques discussed in class. The classes incorporated as much group discussion as could be managed, to emphasize the plurality of ways in which Baudelaire's prose poems can be consumed.

As I have argued in *Baudelaire's* Le Spleen de Paris: *Shifting Perspectives* and in a number of articles ("Intertextes"; *"La Belle Dorothée"*), the prose poems systematically offer themselves to be read from incompatible viewpoints. This argument encourages discussion in class, and it also has the advantage of fostering a watchful or slow approach to even the most apparently unpoetic forms of poetry. I encourage students to consider each prose poem from a number of different angles, notably by reflecting on its overt message, its structural development, its poetic elements (such as phonetic and verbal repetitions, rhythmic effects, images), any resistance it poses to the reader's acceptance, and its intratextual dimension. The course uses some of the tools of traditional critical analysis but also disturbs the supposition of unity that underpins conventional analysis by emphasizing the importance of reading the prose poems alongside one another and alongside other texts. Small-group teaching for this course focuses on the close reading of individual texts, while lectures place their focus on historical, cultural, and textual contexts.

Baudelaire's prose poems often operate to seduce the reader into acquiescence. An approach to these texts that emphasizes context has the particular advantage of offering a means for the reader to take a critical distance from individual prose poems. This approach also encourages students to read the entire collection of prose poems and introduces students to Baudelaire's larger body of work as well as to the wider historical, cultural, and intellectual contexts of his time. Grouping the prose poems around selected themes makes it feasible to study them in dialogue with one another, with other texts in verse and prose where Baudelaire handles similar themes, and with a selection of pertinent works by other authors or artists. While such an approach inevitably produces oriented readings of the prose poems, it also has the merit of at least suggesting the possibility of multiple orientations.

Reading Women in Baudelaire's Prose Poems

The problem of how to read Baudelaire's prose poems is approached, in my course, through a few recurrent themes that repeatedly emerge from the pages of *Le Spleen de Paris*. One of these is the disappointing female love object. Women are frequently represented in the prose poems as unworthy mates who fall short of male expectations in some crucial way. In "Les Yeux des pauvres" ("The Eyes of the Poor"), for example, while drinking outside a sparkling new

Haussmann-era café, the narrator's female companion inspires his hatred by failing to mirror his own response to the poverty-stricken family who stands beside them, gazing at the riches on display within. The excessively demanding mistress of "La Femme sauvage et la petite maîtresse" ("The Wild Woman and the Affected Coquette") is virtually identified by the narrator with a caged, brutalized, savage woman and threatened with defenestration. The four men of "Portraits de maîtresses" ("Portraits of Mistresses") complain alternately about the excessive appetites—whether carnal or intellectual—or the oppressive desirelessness of their chosen partners; the fourth man all but admits to having murdered his too perfectly acquiescent mistress, while his interlocutors are represented as tacitly sympathetic. It is probably impossible, as educated citizens of the new millennium, not to be repelled by the blatant misogyny of some of the prose poems. If students are going to be persuaded that these texts are worth reading, then they may need to be convinced that there is more to the overtly woman-hating prose poems than meets the eye. There are several ways of suggesting this.

Intratextual Reading

A straightforwardly misogynistic reading of individual prose poems is complicated by the fact that, in a number of texts from *Le Spleen de Paris*, women are treated with something approaching sympathy and even worshipful respect. Frequently, women who are broken in some way—the enigmatic central figure of "Mademoiselle Bistouri" ("Miss Scalpel"); the poor, housebound woman of "Les Fenêtres" ("Windows"); the old lady of "Le Désespoir de la vieille" ("The Old Woman's Despair"); the servile woman described in "Un cheval de race" ("A Thoroughbred"); the solitary women of "Les Veuves" ("Widows"); or the prostitute figure of "La Belle Dorothée" ("Beautiful Dorothy")—are written about with something resembling compassion. Similarly, inaccessible female figures, such as the lunatic mistress-muse of "Les Bienfaits de la lune" ("The Moon's Benefits") or the statue of "Le Fou et la Vénus" ("The Fool and the Venus"), do not come under explicit attack in the prose poems. Yet even in these more apparently respectful representations of women there is an implied violence and will to domination: the interrogation of Mademoiselle Bistouri, the approving representation of a mature woman as an utterly spent and docile racehorse, the interest in solitary women, and the idealization of the female are never as innocuous as they might initially seem.

Close Reading

Another way of problematizing the explicit messages of the woman-hating texts is by examining their internal logic. As twenty-first-century readers of the prose poems, we are much more likely than our predecessors to be suspicious of their overt messages; thanks to feminist literary criticism and deconstruction, not only are we better trained to recognize and contest the misogyny of the male speaker(s), we are also better equipped to read texts against their grain. As it turns out, the texts themselves frequently undermine the legitimacy of the position adopted by the central male figures, whether the latter take the form of third-person characters, first-person narrators, or characters whose speech is reported in the first person.

The narrator of "Les Yeux des pauvres" thinks himself an expert reader of the eyes of others, but his initial misreading of his mistress's eyes casts doubt not only on his bizarrely aestheticized reading of the eyes of the poor family but also on the final judgment he passes on his female companion. The narrator's sketch of a beautiful African woman's vanity and vacuity in "La Belle Dorothée" is problematized by the final revelation that the woman is using her charms to try to buy her sister out of slavery. The male speaker of "La Femme sauvage" implicitly identifies with a savage, highly aggressive male, while the casual misogyny of "Portraits de maîtresses" reveals an act of murder that would be legally indefensible even in a jurisdiction that was notoriously sympathetic to homicidal husbands.

The narrator of "L'Horloge" ("The Clock") gives a lyrical description of his lover's eyes, which he invests with immortal, eternal qualities, that is deflated by his conclusion, which retrospectively debases the spiritual to the level of the *spirituel* ("witty"): "N'est-ce pas, madame, que voici un madrigal vraiment méritoire, et aussi emphatique que vous-même? En vérité, j'ai eu tant de plaisir à broder cette prétentieuse galanterie, que je ne vous demanderai rien en échange" 'Now is this not, Madam, a truly praiseworthy madrigal, and as exaggerated as yourself? I took such delight in elaborating this pretentious romance, that I will ask nothing of you in exchange' (*Spleen* [Pichois] 300; *Parisian Prowler* 34). By concluding the text with the word "échange" ("exchange"), Baudelaire underscores the self-centered nature of the narrator's lyrical gambit: his flattery demands a reward, whether it takes the form of the lady's favors or, as here, the pleasure of invention and self-admiration.

The disingenuousness of the central male figure is also a feature of "Le Galant Tireur" ("The Gallant Marksman"). The first paragraph introduces the "mystérieuse femme" 'mysterious woman' to whom the marksman owes "tant de plaisirs, tant de douleurs, et peut-être aussi une grande partie de son génie" 'so many pleasures, so many woes, and perhaps also a large part of his genius' (349; 109). The marksman-poet fails at his art until, spurred on by his companion's mockery, he takes aim at a doll that he designates as her simulacrum: "*je me figure que c'est vous*" '*[I] imagine that it is you*' (350; 109). The marksman promptly decapitates the simulacrum and then turns back to his companion:

> Alors s'inclinant vers sa chère, sa délicieuse, son exécrable femme, son inévitable et impitoyable Muse, et lui baisant respectueusement la main, il ajouta: "Ah! mon cher ange, combien je vous remercie de mon adresse!"

> Then bowing to his dear, his delectable, his execrable wife, his inescapable and ruthless Muse, and respectfully kissing her hand, he added, "Ah my dear angel! How I thank you for my aim!"

Although the marksman acknowledges that he owes the mastery of his art to his female companion, it is apparent that she was no help to him until he put in place a false image of her. And just as the abstracted replica is made to stand in for the mocking woman, the latter, instead of her abstraction, is thanked for being the marksman's ideal or muse. The supposedly "inévitable" 'inevitable,' unavoidable muse has been brought to life only thanks to a clever sidestepping or avoidance of the woman's reality. The poet-marksman thus perfects his art by subjecting the woman to a metaphorical transformation, effectively splitting her into two interchangeable parts, one worthy of adoration, the other of assassination. The repeated description of the woman as both "délicieuse" 'delectable' and "exécrable" 'execrable' also suggests this doubling. This antithesis would seem to capture Baudelaire's own ambivalence toward women and arguably his society's contradictory attitude toward half its members.

The very consistency with which the texts reveal the untrustworthiness of their male interlocutors serves, however, as a warning that we must not confuse their voices with that of Baudelaire, even and perhaps especially where the identification seems most obvious. Baudelaire's prose poems can, then, be read as explicitly misogynistic, but they can also be interpreted as implicitly (though not necessarily self-consciously) critical of woman-hating men.

Intertextual or Contextual Reading

A third way of suggesting that the misogyny of *Le Spleen de Paris* is more complex than it first appears is by surveying some broadly contemporaneous academic or *art pompier* images of woman as goddess. In my lectures I use the birth of Venus paintings by Alexandre Cabanel (1863) and William Bouguereau (1879). I also show students some very different images of women, dating from around the same time: Édouard Manet's *Olympia* (1863), Gustave Courbet's *L'Origine du monde* (1866; "The Origin of the World"), and Paul Cézanne's *L'Éternel Féminin* (1875–77; "The Eternal Feminine"). Similarly divergent verbal contexts could be offered, alternatively or in addition, in the form of selected passages from Jules Michelet's apparently idealizing *La Femme* (1860; "Woman") or Pierre-Joseph Proudhon's overtly misogynistic *La Pornocratie* (posthumously published 1875; "Pornocracy"). I ask students to reflect on the differences between idealized and anti-idealizing representations of women and to try to situate Baudelaire's presentation of women in the prose poems in relation to these other representations.

I go on to show how the poet's larger body of writing both idealizes women and deflates such idealizations, often as a function of the chosen mode of discourse: his intentionally artless autobiographical writing can present women as little more than beasts, while his love poems and letters can be reverential in the extreme. In fact, some of his texts simultaneously exalt and disparage women. In "Le Peintre de la vie moderne" ("The Painter of Modern Life"), for example, Baudelaire notes that, for artists, woman is "une espèce d'idole, stupide peut-être, mais éblouissante" 'a kind of idol, stupid maybe, but dazzling' (*Œuvres complètes* 2: 713).

The complicated relationship in Baudelaire's work between the divinization of the female and her debasement can be illustrated by reference to *Les Fleurs du Mal*. In a number of the verse poems, the lyric subject presents himself as singing the praises of a desired female, in the tradition of courtly or troubadour poetry, which began in southern France in the late eleventh century and which was developed and transformed by Petrarch in the fourteenth century. Petrarchist motifs, such as the attribution of divine or angelic qualities to the woman's person or gaze, are recurrent in Baudelaire's love poems, where the gaze of the woman is often represented as illuminating or reviving the lyric subject and ultimately as offering him spiritual salvation. Even in poems such as "À une Madone" ("To a Madonna") and "Une charogne" ("A Carcass"), where courtly and Petrarchist tropes are cruelly subverted, the female continues to be idealized, however sadistically she is nailed to her pedestal and however grotesquely she is made to perch there.

The reason for Baudelaire's preservation of the figure of the idealized female in his lyric poetry is often suggested within the verse itself, but it is perhaps most explicitly stated in the poet's letter of 8 May 1854 to Apollonie Sabatier, the courtesan who inspired his most reverential love poems. He tells her that his anonymous adoration of her enables him to exploit the artistic boons of unfulfilled desire: "De cette rêverie excitante et purifiante naît généralement un accident heureux" 'From this exciting and purifying daydream a happy accident is generally born' (*Correspondance* 1: 276). The frankness of Baudelaire's acknowledgment that his admiration is artistically rather than sexually interested is startling: "Je suis un égoïste, je me sers de vous" 'I am a selfish man, I make use of you.' Madame Sabatier, as it happened, refused to play the poet's game; it is clear from a letter sent some time later that their relationship had recently ceased to be platonic, a fact that occasioned both a change of register and a rejection on Baudelaire's part: "il y a quelques jours, tu étais une divinité, ce qui est si commode, ce qui est si beau, si inviolable. Te voilà femme maintenant" 'a few days ago you were a divinity, which is so convenient, so beautiful, so inviolable. Now you are a woman' (1: 425; 31 Aug. 1857).

Students are encouraged to reflect on the self-servingly deluded and ultimately bogus nature of idealization in Baudelaire's prose poems and on the strange compatibility between the idealization and denigration of women in the texts.

The following prose poems lend themselves particularly well to an exploration of the ironic treatment of the dynamics of idealization in Baudelaire's prose poems.

"*Le Fou et la Vénus*"

In *Le Spleen de Paris*, the most obvious figure of the woman as a divinity is the statue evoked in "Le Fou et la Vénus." A clown-lover sits in adoration, in the middle of a huge park, at the feet of his idol. The terms used to depict the scene are overtly sexual: "Le vaste parc se pâme sous l'oeil brûlant du soleil" 'The vast park swoons under the sun's blazing eye'; "L'extase universelle des choses" 'The universal ecstasy of things'; "c'est ici une orgie silencieuse" 'here is a silent orgy'; "les fleurs excitées brûlent [de] désir" 'Aroused flowers burn with . . . desire'; "cette jouissance universelle" 'this universal rapture' (*Spleen* [Pichois] 283; *Parisian Prowler* 11). The repeated evocations of expansive energy in the third paragraph, along with the vigorous, anaphoric rhythm of the French text, create an impression of sexual ardor and potency:

> On dirait qu'une lumière toujours croissante fait de plus en plus étinceler les objets; que les fleurs excitées brûlent du désir de rivaliser avec l'azur du ciel par l'énergie de leurs couleurs, et que la chaleur, rendant visibles les parfums, les fait monter vers l'astre comme des fumées.

> An ever-increasing light seems to make objects increasingly sparkle. Aroused flowers burn with the desire to outdo the sky's azure by the energy of their colors, and the heat, turning scents visible, seems to make them rise to the stars like smoke.

By contrast with the active verbs in the above sentence, the repeated adjectival use of the passive verbal form in the portrait of the clown indicates that he is acted upon rather than acting:

> Cependant, dans cette jouissance universelle, j'ai aperçu un être *affligé*.
>   Aux pieds d'une colossale Vénus, un de ces fous artificiels, un de ces bouffons volontaires *chargés* de faire rire les rois quand le Remords ou l'Ennui les obsède, *affublé* d'un costume éclatant et ridicule, *coiffé* de cornes et de sonnettes, tout *ramassé* contre le piédestal, lève des yeux pleins de larmes vers l'immortelle Déesse.   (283–84; my emphasis)

> However, amidst this universal rapture, I noticed an *afflicted* creature.
>   At the feet of a colossal Venus, one of those artificial fools, one of those voluntary buffoons *assigned* to make kings laugh when pursued by Remorse or Ennui, *rigged out* in a flashy and ridiculous costume, *capped* in horns and bells, all *heaped* against the pedestal, raises his tear-filled eyes toward the immortal Goddess.   (11; my emphasis)

In the courtly tradition, the passivity of the lover is actually a triumph over his desire, as his very inaction means that he can maintain his desire for the love object instead of risking its loss upon satisfaction. Through inaction, the idealistic lover could avoid the problem of Baudelairean ennui, described by Suzanne Guerlac as "a listless disinterest, an absence of desire" (96). From this perspective, the apparent hopelessness of the court(ly) jester of "Le Fou et la Vénus" converts into a form of superiority; the kings mentioned in the text, whose desires are rarely frustrated, pay clowns to relieve them of their ennui, but the clown depicted here is master of his own desire. As immutable as the stone of the statue at whose foot he worships, his passion recalls the love of poets as described in the verse poem "La Beauté" ("Beauty"): "Éternel et muet ainsi que la matière" 'Eternal, and silent as matter is timeless' (*Fleurs* [Pichois] 1: 21; *Flowers* [McGowan] 39).

Indeed, the buffoon's attachment to the object is a source of pride for him:

> Et ses yeux disent: "Je suis le dernier et le plus solitaire des humains, privé d'amour et d'amitié, et bien inférieur en cela au plus imparfait des animaux. Cependant je suis fait, moi aussi, pour comprendre et sentir l'immortelle Beauté! Ah! Déesse! ayez pitié de ma tristesse et de mon délire!" (*Spleen* [Pichois] 284)

> And his eyes say, "I am the lowest and the most lonely of humans, deprived of love and of friendship, and for that reason quite inferior to the most incomplete animals. However I am made, I as well, to understand and to feel immortal Beauty! Oh Goddess! take pity on my sorrow and my madness!" (*Parisian Prowler* 11)

Despite the reference to the clown's sorrow, the "cependant" 'however' in the above passage echoes, and implicitly overturns, the "cependant" that earlier introduced him as "un être affligé" 'an afflicted creature.' The apparent inferiority of the clown is called into question by his appreciation of beauty. His choice of an ostensibly inappropriate object of love may not be as asinine, therefore, as it first seems. Like the swan of Baudelaire's "Le Cygne" ("The Swan"), the buffoon is presented as "ridicule et sublime, / Et rongé d'un désir sans trêve!" 'both ridiculous and sublime, / Gnawed by his endless longing!' (*Fleurs* [Pichois] 86; *Flowers* [McGowan] 177). The unresponsive female love object is necessary to the sustenance of the clown-artist's passion.

"Le Désir de peindre"

The prose poem "Le Désir de peindre" ("The Desire to Paint") further testifies to the role of unfulfilled desire in Baudelaire's poetics. As in the verse poem "Je t'adore à l'égal de la voûte nocturne . . ." ("I love you as I love . . ."), the poet-persona's passion seems to be intensified by the woman's elusiveness. The text presents a description of a female figure who has appeared to the speaker only rarely and fleetingly and whom he aches to paint. That the narrator's nonpossession of the woman is voluntary is suggested by the opening two sentences of the text:

> Malheureux peut-être l'homme, mais heureux l'artiste que le désir déchire!

Je brûle de peindre celle qui m'est apparue si rarement et qui a fui si
vite, comme une belle chose regrettable derrière le voyageur emporté
dans la nuit.   (*Spleen* [Pichois] 340)

Unhappy perhaps the man, but happy the artist shattered by desire!
I burn to paint her who appeared to me so rarely and who fled so
quickly, like a beautiful lamented thing left by the traveler swept into the
night.   (*Parisian Prowler* 94)

The female figure has, apparently, fled, but she is also represented as having
been left behind by the narrator-traveler. The latter's unhappiness is therefore
at least partly self-inflicted. The first sentence of the text makes it very clear
that what interests the narrator is the artistic recompense offered by unfulfilled
desire and therefore by the conversion of the real, physical, sexual woman into
a fantasized woman.

"Laquelle est la vraie?"

The self-interestedness of idealization is a central theme of "Laquelle est la
vraie?" ("Which Is the True One?"), a version of which was posthumously published under the title "L'Idéal et le réel" ("The Ideal and the Real"). The first-
person narrator of this text eulogizes "une certaine Bénédicta, qui remplissait
l'atmosphère d'idéal, et dont les yeux répandaient le désir de la grandeur, de
la beauté, de la gloire et de tout ce qui fait croire à l'immortalité" 'a certain
Bénédicta, who filled the atmosphere with the ideal, and whose eyes spread
the desire for grandeur, beauty, fame, and everything which makes us believe
in immortality' (342; 98). A few days after the narrator meets her, the "fille mi-
raculeuse" 'miraculous girl' dies, a detail that he somewhat flippantly attributes
to her being "trop belle pour vivre longtemps" 'too beautiful to live a long time.'
It is telling that the narrator compares Bénédicta's coffin to a well-sealed Indian
chest and describes her grave as the site of his buried treasure; and it is equally
revealing that his eyes are described as "fichés" 'fastened' to the burial site, as if
they were nailing the woman into her grave. The woman's death, it is implied,
has been to the narrator's advantage. His repetition of the fact that it was he
who buried Bénédicta suggests that he may even have been instrumental in
her death: "C'est moi-même qui l'ai enterrée," "C'est moi qui l'ai enterrée" 'It
is I myself who buried her,' 'It is I who buried her.' The implication that it is
the narrator's idealization of the woman that has killed her recalls the symbolic
murder evoked in the verse poem "À une Madone."

If the soul of the dead Laura had a tendency to visit Petrarch in dreams, in
"Laquelle est la vraie?" the poet receives a visitation from a somewhat earthier
incarnation of the divinized love object: "une petite personne" 'a little person'
appears who, stamping and laughing on the grave, declares herself to be "la
vraie Bénédicta" 'the true Bénédicta.' The apparition accuses the narrator of

self-delusion ("ta folie" 'your madness,' "ton aveuglement" 'your blindness'), a charge corroborated by the concluding image of his self-entrapment in "la fosse de l'idéal" 'the grave of the ideal.' This final image, by associating the narrator's ideals with a grave, may highlight the dubiousness of his idealizations of Bénédicta. It may also, or alternatively, express the plight of the idealistic poet as evoked in the verse poem "L'Albatros" ("The Albatross"): the king of the aerial world is enslaved and grotesque at ground level. "Laquelle est la vraie?" can thus be interpreted as a mockery of the narrator's bogus art or as a celebration of the artist's ability to preserve his ideals despite the destructive forces that threaten to undermine them. In support of the latter reading, the poet claims, in the draft epilogue to *Les Fleurs du Mal*, the ability to extract "l'or" 'gold' from "[l]a boue" 'mud' ([Pichois] 1: 192; my trans.). Whether the idealization of the female in "Laquelle est la vraie?" is interpreted by the reader as phony or heroic, it is presented here — as in "Le Fou et la Vénus," "Le Désir de peindre," "Le Galant Tireur," and "L'Horloge" — as the product of willful self-delusion.

In "Laquelle est la vraie?," the idealized woman is in danger of being replaced by the real woman. The pressure of the real is evoked even more directly in the novella *La Fanfarlo* (*The Fanfarlo*), wherein Samuel Cramer expounds as follows on the fragility of idealistic love:

> "Ce qu'il y a de plus désolant," dit-il, "c'est que tout amour fait toujours une mauvaise fin, d'autant plus mauvaise qu'il était plus divin, plus ailé à son commencement. Il n'est pas de rêve, quelque idéal qu'il soit, qu'on ne retrouve avec un poupard glouton suspendu au sein. . . ."
>
> (*Œuvres complètes* 1: 561)

> "What is most grievous," he said, "is that all loves always end up badly, so much the worse if more divine and more winged at their beginning. There is no dream, whatever its ideal, that we recover without a gluttonous plump baby hanging from her breast."   (*Fanfarlo* [Kaplan] 19–20)

Baudelaire's prose poems highlight the tensions but also the continuities between two versions of femininity that were current in his day: the idealized, deified woman, on the one hand, and the excessively physical, sexual woman, on the other. The conjunction of apparently opposed attitudes toward women in the prose poems may be interpreted in a variety of ways — as illustrative of the dissonance and hybridity characteristic of prose poetry, as symptomatic of the poet's cynicism, as indicative of the extent to which Baudelaire typified his age, as suggestive of his ironic awareness of his own contradictions or those of his age. In class, I try to avoid privileging any one interpretation of the textual facts and generally encourage students to approach the prose poems with suspicion and, importantly, with the sense that everything has yet to be said about these texts.

What seems undeniable, however, is that the texts of *Le Spleen de Paris* repeatedly stage a willful misreading of the female love object, a forceful suppression—or sudden emergence—of her apparently unpalatable reality. By dramatizing acts of misreading other people, including women, the prose poems place the problem of reading at their center. An approach to teaching *Le Spleen de Paris* that gives central importance to the question of how to read has the merit of recognizing, if not actually avoiding, the danger of producing dubious interpretations of the kind that the texts both invite and stage. By tackling the prose poems as both self-contained units and interlinked products of a particular cultural context, idealizing and banalizing impulses can operate to keep each other in check, much as *Le Spleen de Paris* itself repeatedly confronts these impulses, not least in its representation of the female love object.

Pedagogies of Violence: A Tour through Baudelaire's Fight Clubs

Debarati Sanyal

Today's American undergraduate is bound to be shocked and intrigued by the politically incorrect violence of *Le Spleen de Paris* (*Paris Spleen*). A catalog of physical blows alone conveys the still timely provocation of these scenes of poetic abuse: the *coups de bâton*, or blows, that a fairground barker administers to his lawful wife (dressed as a beast and locked in a cage); the *coup de poing*, or punch, that instigates the exchange of blows between an intellectual and a decrepit old beggar; the *coup de tête dans l'estomac*, or head butt, with which a street urchin attempts to steal a piece of bread from a starving ragamuffin; the *coup terrible, lourd*, or the terrible, heavy blow of the external world, in the form of an infamous, whining concubine, experienced as *coup de pioche dans l'estomac*, or a pickax to the stomach. Walter Benjamin's portrait of the poet as a conspirator, secret agent, even terrorist captures the unpredictable energy of these poetic provocations. How does one reconstruct the aesthetic, historical, and ideological contexts for these literary blows while reanimating their subversive force within our contemporary cultural horizon?

This oscillation between past and present, between the reconstruction of a cultural formation and the reanimation of an artwork's critical force, is crucial to ensure that students do not view their objects of study as ossified museum exhibits. My aim in nineteenth-century French courses featuring Baudelaire's poetry is to make students familiar with the cultural production and lived experience of a remote past (temporal, linguistic, cultural) while provoking a sense of unfamiliarity in the world they inhabit. Sometimes this means making the past more present. From Baudelaire's Paris to today's New York or Mumbai, there are any number of paradigmatic ways in which each metropolis embodies modern life at different points in history. Current popular entertainment in the form of films, cartoons, and television shows can provide powerful, if ephemeral, points of entry into the particular conditions of Baudelairean urban modernity, opening up unexpected lines of inquiry while activating materials that at first seem distant.[1] To recognize the past in the present not only underscores the similarities between two times and sites but highlights what is distinctive about nineteenth-century urban life and its fabric of structural, symbolic, and material violence. Just as important, this recognition can defamiliarize apparently natural patterns of thought, desire, and consumption today. The challenge is to activate cultural artifacts without conflating the present and the past, so that different historical moments and cultural sites can be approached side by side, in relations of reciprocity and mutual illumination.

To this end, I propose here an itinerary through *Paris Spleen* that draws out the pedagogical function of Baudelairean textual violence, as a critical engagement with the Second Empire, its commodity culture, and its repression of the revolution's legacy. Textual stops include the preface dedicated to Arsène Hous-saye, "Perte d'auréole" ("Loss of Halo"), "Le Mauvais Vitrier" ("The Bad Gla-zier"), "Le Gâteau" ("The Cake"), and "Assommons les pauvres!" ("Let's Beat Up the Poor!"), which we read alongside clips from David Fincher's cult classic film *Fight Club*.[2] My aim is not to provide readings of these well-plumbed prose po-ems so much as to open up zones of resonance between their world and ours with the help of visual media from the nineteenth century and contemporary times. Whereas caricatures by J. J. Grandville enable a concise discussion of nineteenth-century commodity culture, reading "Let's Beat Up the Poor!" in tandem with *Fight Club* helps us grasp the ongoing relevance of Baudelaire's violence in its attempt to recover forms of historical agency and to reopen horizons for social change.[3]

A glance at the initial titles for *Paris Spleen—Poèmes Nocturnes* ("Noctur-nal Poems") or *La Lueur et la fumée* ("The Glow and the Smoke"), *Le Rôdeur parisien* ("The Parisian Prowler"), *Rêvasseries en prose* ("Musings in Prose"), or *Petits poëmes lycanthropiques* ("Little Lycanthropic Poems")—introduces stu-dents to the collection's eerie, crepuscular setting along with its distortion of the Romantic poetic subject. The *rêveries*, or lyrical contemplations, of Rousseau's solitary walker morph into *rêvasseries*, inchoate musings, of a vagrant prowler or werewolf. Clichés of the pastoral poet whose spirits quicken with a "correspon-dent breeze" (Wordsworth, *Prelude*, bk. 1) in Baudelaire cede to abject, impotent artist figures who haunt the city's seedy nocturnal labyrinth, or "les plis sinueux des vieilles capitales" 'the sinuous folds of old capitals' (*Spleen* [Pichois] 89; my trans.). Baudelaire's avatars of the poet as conspirator, ragpicker, or wolfman in-troduce students to the clandestine, nervous energy of his irony and its sabotage of a sovereign autonomous subject. Violence inhabits the very heart of the poetic self; "la vorace ironie" 'voracious irony' splits the "I" into self and other, into victim and executioner: "Je suis la plaie et le couteau! . . . / Et la victime, et le bourreau!" 'I am the wound and the knife! . . . / The victim and the executioner!' (79; my trans.).

In *Paris Spleen*, the poet's ironic doubling into subject and object of violence unfolds in the sensorium of capitalist urban modernity and against the back-drop of the Second Empire's politics of pacification and amnesia. Baudelaire's declaration toward the end of his life that "[n]on seulement, je serais heureux d'être victime, mais je ne haïrais pas d'être bourreau—pour sentir la Révolution de deux manières!" '[n]ot only would I be happy to be victim, but I would not hate being executioner—to experience the Revolution in two ways' maps irony's ontological doubleness onto social processes to unmask their underlying vio-lence (*Œuvres complètes* 2: 961; my trans.). By rendering historical experience from the stance of victim and executioner, as agent and recipient of its violence, Baudelaire resuscitates the covert relations of force that structure the Second Empire. Irony is a form of counterviolence that targets the Second Empire's repressive material and symbolic order. In its Sartrean sense, counterviolence des-ignates violence directed against institutionalized, structural oppression; its deployment is frequently (dis)qualified as illegitimate, insurgent, and terroristic (an apt characterization of Baudelaire's poetic practice, which Benjamin likened to a terroristic delirium). In the realm of representations, poetic counterviolence may be defined as a "symbolic, figurative, discursive force, wielded as a counterprinciple" with the aim to "undo metaphysical, institutional sedimentations of force, especially the violence exercised by instrumental reason with its logic and practices of exclusion" (Hanssen 9; see also Terdiman).

Baudelaire's preface to Arsène Houssaye gives an evocative image of reason's decapitation: *Paris Spleen* is envisioned as a serpent with "ni queue ni tête, puisque tout, au contraire, y est à la fois tête et queue, alternativement et réciproquement" 'neither head nor tail, since, on the contrary, everything in it is both head and tail, alternatively and reciprocally' (*Spleen* [Pichois] 276; *Parisian Prowler* 129). In this *mise en abyme* of reading protocols, we are warned that we may not be able to make head or tail of the volume. The crisis of signification harbored in these textual fragments, or *tronçons*, reflects the shock of modern cities and responds to the "croisements de leurs innombrables rapports" 'intersection of their countless relationships' (277; 129). Yet the hermeneutic violence done to the reader is also Baudelaire's concerted response to the structural domination of the marketplace. Indeed, literature's commodification in the age of cheap print reproduction has put the poet in the unenviable position of selling bite-sized textual pieces to be consumed on the go. Grandville's caricature of literature, reeled off like sheets of pastry and sold in chunks, conveys this commodification with forceful precision (fig. 1).

It reminds us that Baudelaire's prose poems were sold by the line and published in newspapers alongside *faits divers* ("news in brief") and advertisements. If Baudelaire accommodates these new conditions by producing a text that can be chopped into bits for the urban reader's convenience, we are nevertheless warned that these ironic morsels will not make for easy digestion.

Following Baudelaire's invitation to "cut wherever we want," we turn to four prose poems that illuminate facets of postrevolutionary, urban modernity and display a range of tactical counterviolences to the revolution's dominant values. Each of these poems dramatizes a fall into an aesthetic, economic, and social reality whose elliptical diagnosis foments various forms of conspiratorial or terroristic rebellion. Baudelaire's portrait of the poet as a prowler or werewolf and his definition of prose poetry in terms of urban, capitalist modernity prepare students to read "Loss of Halo." The poem stages the angelic Romantic poet's fall into the violence of modern life, his auratic halo literalized as a detachable accessory knocked off (like a top hat) by speeding carriages on a busy boulevard. The poet's descent into the refuge of a tawdry place, or *mauvais lieu*, reflects the halo's fall into the mire of the macadam. Just as the halo will presumably be picked up by a passerby and will circulate from one head to another, the "buveur de quintessences" 'drinker of quintessences' now mingles interchangeably with beer-swilling commoners (352; 113). The lyric poet falls from the heights of his ivory tower into the prose of the marketplace, the *mauvais lieu* of the

Fig. 1. Grandville, *La Littérature macaronique*. Lithograph illustration in *Un Autre Monde* (Paris: Fournier, 1843). Harry Ransom Center, University of Texas, Austin

lieu commun, understood as a promiscuous site of convergence and commonality but also a site of commonplace discourses: "Et me voici, tout semblable à vous" 'So here I am, just like you, as you can see!' From within this common crucible of language and experience, the prose poet fashions his tactics of counterviolence.

A brief reading of "The Bad Glazier" and its explosive end helps us imagine what this aesthetic counterviolence might look like as it emerges from and destroys cultural frames of representation. Like "Loss of Halo," 'the poem can be read as an allegory of art's fall into the degradation of urban modernity, the "lourde et sale atmosphère parisienne" 'heavy and dirty Parisian atmosphere' (286; 14). In a typical Baudelairean doubling of victim into perpetrator, the grumpy, impoverished hysteric who hails the glazier with a "Hey! Hey!" is mirrored by the docile, grunting peddler, himself an avatar of the poet who stumbles to the marketplace with his life-altering frames. The flowerpot grabbed from the windowsill and dropped on the glazier's wares is an ironic reminder of the rhetorical blossoms that were the flowers of evil. If poetry is banalized into potted prose as it falls into the *mauvais lieu* of the *lieu commun*, it nevertheless wields a destructive potency: the benign flowerpot mutates into an "engin de guerre" 'engine of war' that shatters the glazier's fragile wares (287; 15). The shattering of transparent panes—a stock figure for realist prose—signals the shattering of utilitarian representation and its illusion of transparency, ushering in a different aesthetic regime. The acoustic crash is a species of performance art that makes "le bruit éclatant d'un palais de cristal crevé par la foudre" 'the brilliant sound of a crystal palace smashed by lightning' (287; 15). We might recall that the iron and glass Crystal Palace was built for London's Great Exhibition in 1851 as a symbol of modernity and progress, a myth replicated in Napoléon III's world fairs yet belied by the narrator's derelict neighborhood, the polluted Parisian atmosphere, and the abjection of poets and glaziers alike. The violent *jouissance* of "The Bad Glazier" flouts the bourgeois myth of modernity as progress but also the certainties of utilitarian thought and instrumental reason. Yet that this destructive force is directed at an innocent victim also confronts us with difficult ethical questions on the relation of art and violence. Baudelaire's fantasy of art as creative destruction is an aestheticization of violence whose legacy can be discussed in the light of André Breton's declaration that "the simplest Surrealist act consists of dashing down the street, pistol in hand, and firing blindly, as fast as you can pull the trigger, into the crowd" (125). If there is adequate preparation for a further discussion of this aestheticization, we might also discuss "The Bad Glazier" and its explosive end in the light of the composer Karlheinz Stockhausen's shocking characterization of the Twin Towers' destruction on 9/11 as "the greatest work of art ever" (qtd. in "Attacks").[4] These excursions open up a meditation on the ambiguity of counterviolence as a contestation that, in its celebration of destruction's productivity, verges on nihilistic complicity with the violence it purports to contest.

These moments of complicity are the hallmark of Baudelaire's irony; they are the consequence of the poet's commitment to a critique from within the commonplaces of cultural discourses, by means of conspiratorial and terroristic tactics. It is from inside the dominant order that the poet seeks to disrupt both the comforts of bourgeois readerly digestion and the Second Empire's authoritarian repression and manipulation of historical memory. As many critics have noted, Baudelaire's prose poems are forms of memorializing that reanimate shards of the republican legacy in an attempt to shatter the empire's pacified facades. This resuscitation of revolutionary possibility from the stance of victim and perpetrator is staged in "The Cake," which opens with the poet-traveler soaring on the wings of *l'universelle analogie*, or universal analogy, to such heights that Rousseauesque clichés of man's essential goodness no longer seem absurd.

Yet hunger, or "la matière incurable renouvelant ses exigences" 'incorrigible matter renewing its demands' (*Spleen* [Pichois] 298; *Parisian Prowler* 31), interrupts this spiritual ascent, and the traveler pulls out a loaf of bread. His meal is interrupted by a starving little urchin, to whom the traveler offers a slice, when another ragamuffin, "son frère jumeau" 'his twin brother' (298; 32), wrestles the first one to the ground in a grab for the booty. The ritual of breaking bread mutates from an act with biblical, communal connotations into a Darwinian struggle in which the disputed property crumbles to nothing. Fraternity, figured in contemporary republican iconography as two cherubs locked in an embrace, mutates into fratricide. "Il y a donc un pays superbe où le pain s'appelle du *gâteau*, friandise si rare qu'elle suffit pour engendrer une guerre parfaitement fratricide!" 'So there exists a magnificent land where bread is called *cake*, a delicacy so rare that it suffices to beget a perfectly fratricidal war!' the poem concludes (298; 33), in an allusion to the proverbial "Let them eat cake" commonly misattributed to Marie-Antoinette in the face of the peasants' hunger.[5] "The Cake" is an ironic recollection of the revolution's inheritance that distorts the republican motto of freedom, equality, and fraternity into hunger, inequity, and fratricide. The children's portrayal as savages (executioner), reduced to bestial violence by hunger (victim), reminds readers of the body's incurable exigencies and of ongoing class inequity under the Second Empire. In a characteristic Baudelairean fall, the traveling philosopher plunges from the heights of idealism to embodied reality, from the promises of revolution to the reality of its imperial aftermath.

These readings of Baudelairean counterviolence as so many falls into urban, postrevolutionary modernity prepare students to embark on an analysis of "Let's Beat Up the Poor!" in the light of class struggle and the Second Empire's repression of its evidence. This central prose poem stages the post-1848 generation's disillusionment with revolutionary politics and the dream of equality, figured as the crushing irrelevance of past idealism. In Marx's words, "the tradition of all dead generations weighs like a nightmare on the brain of the living." In "Let's Beat Up the Poor!," the poet-intellectual is figuratively bludgeoned into a stupor by utopian theories of the 1840s, by "des livres où il est traîté de l'art de rendre les peuples heureux, sages et riches en vingt-quatre heures" 'books dealing with the art of making nations happy, wise, and rich, in twenty-four hours' (*Spleen* 357; *Parisian Prowler* 121). He tumbles out of his ivory tower in search of action and refreshments, again within the *mauvais lieux* of the *lieu commun*. Once on the streets, a beggar approaches him with "un de ces regards inoubliables qui culbuteraient les trônes, si l'esprit remuait la matière, et si l'oeil d'un magnétiseur faisait mûrir les raisins" 'one of those unforgettable looks that would topple thrones, if mind could move matter, and if a hypnotist's eyes could ripen grapes' (357; 121). Another double for the poetic subject, the beggar's gaze mirrors the aims of poetry and social thought alike: it would make thrones tumble if only spirit moved matter, if only theory unlocked praxis, if only poetry were a performative utterance that materialized dreams. The impotence of theory (or the socialist literature of 1848) is likened to the beggar's pleading gaze (or the glazier's inability to fulfill the request, "La vie en beau!" 'Make life beautiful!' [287; 15]), itself a mirror for poetry's inability to *remuer la matière*, to move matter, shift bodies, and produce social change.

The poem returns to the body, or, as "The Cake" describes it, to "incorrigible matter," as the primary site of social transformation, proposing clandestine physical violence as revolutionary praxis. The scrawny intellectual reacts to the beggar's plea by checking to make sure there are no police in sight before leaping on the old man and beating him up "avec l'énergie obstinée des cuisiniers qui veulent attendrir un beefteack" 'with the obstinate energy of cooks trying to tenderize a beefsteak,' until the "antique carcasse" 'antique carcass' finally rises up and retaliates in kind (359; 122). The mathematical precision of the beggar's retaliation in this cartoonish infliction of blows, which yields exactly twice as many counterblows, once again underscores the productivity of violence in Baudelaire's symbolic economy. Further, as in "The Cake," physical violence actualizes the relations of force masked by the theoretical rhetoric of equality. The hierarchies of the postrevolutionary social sphere are materialized as a collision between two bodies on the street. This physical encounter resuscitates forms of agency from within a regime that sought to suppress visible signs of social disparity and the revolution's legacy through Haussmannization, deportation, and censorship. The poet's terroristic tactics jolts the beggar out of his passivity and into an active conquest of his rights in an unjust world. Similarly, students might consider how reading becomes an exercise in agency rather than submission to textual authority.

An excursion into Fincher's film *Fight Club* illuminates the ongoing relevance of Baudelaire's counterviolence for historical junctures in which the energies of resistance seem co-opted or foreclosed. Based on a novel by Chuck Palahniuk, this dark satire of postmodern American consumerism narrates the encounter between an insomniac insurance claims adjustor and a renegade soap manufacturer. The two characters form a secret society in which men fight each other and recover their masculinity from the anesthetized conditions of corporate America. The Fight Club morphs into Project Mayhem, an anarchist paramilitary group that commits anticapitalist vandalism in the city. The film concludes with the discovery that the two characters are in fact one and the same. The schizophrenic narrator's alter ego has fomented a plot to blow up the city's financial headquarters in order to reset the national debt. The final images are of buildings exploding like dazzling fireworks against a night sky.

Fight Club's reflection on the sterility of contemporary consumerism allows us to revisit Baudelaire's critique of commodity culture in order to explore its contemporary resonances. In a central scene, as Fincher's protagonist-narrator orders furniture on the phone, his condo room takes the shape of a virtual three-dimensional Ikea catalog with product descriptions overlaid on the screen (fig. 2).

Fig. 2. Scene from *Fight Club*, dir. David Fincher. "Ikea boy"

"Like so many others I had become a slave to the Ikea nesting instinct . . . I'd flip through catalogs and wonder, 'What kind of dining set defines me as a person?'" ("Fight Club Ikea Catalogue Scene"). This reflection on brand identity and lifestyle marketing is pursued in Baudelairean fashion throughout a self-reflexive, ironic commentary on the film's own status as a commodity (witness the soap embossed with a Fight Club logo on all the publicity for *Fight Club*). We put the fantasy of an Ikea world in dialogue with nineteenth-century bourgeois *fantasmagorias* by turning once again to Grandville's images. *Les Poissons d'avril*, for instance, shows fish fishing for consumers by dangling watches, bottles, and other trinkets as bait (fig. 3).

An ironic portrait of nature's revenge on the consumer's instrumental rationality, it suggests man's impotent dehumanization under commodity capitalism. This image illuminates other poems by Baudelaire that depict the bourgeois subject's psychic colonization by commodity culture, such as the prose poem "L'Invitation au voyage" ("Invitation to the Voyage"), which stages a lavish, kitschy apartment from which all traces of a human subjectivity are banished. Of course, even as we note convergences in these collective fantasies of reification, we also recall the differences between the forms of subjectivity produced under high capitalism and those under late-capitalist postmodernity. If, as Benjamin suggested, the nineteenth-century interior's distinctiveness compensated for a subjectivity threatened by anonymous urban masses, *Fight Club*'s condo and its Ikea furnishings spell the demise of such individualization, pointing instead to the mass production of identity and desire under global capitalism. As the narrator's demonic other, Tyler Durden, declares, contemporary subjects are mere "by-products of a lifestyle obsession."

Despite these differences, however, from their respective historical junctures, Baudelaire and Fincher present us with a crepuscular, alienated lifeworld that must be blown up for the new to emerge. The abject Baudelairean figures encountered in our itinerary can be seen as analogous to the contemporary white-collar corporate wage slave in their shared oppression by a system that forecloses all forms of social agency but also in their sense of a missed encounter with history. In *Paris Spleen*, this missed encounter is, among other things, 1848 and its failure to usher in a world where theory and praxis may unite, where action may be the sister of dream ("Certes, je sortirai, quant à moi, satisfait / D'un monde où l'action n'est pas la soeur du rêve" 'For my part, I shall gladly leave / A world where action is not the sister of dreams' [Baudelaire, "Le Reniement de Saint-Pierre," 'The Denial of Saint Peter' *Fleurs* (Pichois) 122; my trans.]). Instead, revolution has spawned the benign authoritarianism of Napoléon III and the colonization of social and psychic space by commerce. *Fight Club*'s deadening corporate environment realizes Baudelaire's darkest vision of France's future: an authoritarian plutocracy, Americanized by technology, atrophied by the cult of materialism, and drained of all its vital energy: "La mécanique nous aura tellement américanisés, le progrès aura si bien atrophié en nous toute la partie spirituelle, que rien parmi les rêveries sanguinaires, sacrilèges, ou anti-naturelles des

Fig. 3. Grandville, *Les Poissons d'avril*. Lithograph illustration in *Un Autre Monde* (Paris: Fournier, 1843). Harry Ransom Center, University of Texas, Austin

utopistes ne pourra être comparé à ses résultats positifs" 'So far will machinery have Americanized us, so far will Progress have atrophied in us all that is spiritual, that no dream of the Utopians, however bloody, sacrilegious or unnatural, will be comparable to the result' (*Œuvres Complètes* 1: 665; *Intimate Journals* 58).[6]

In what serves as Fight Club's manifesto, the leader Tyler Durden declares:

> I see in Fight Club the strongest and smartest men who've ever lived. I see all this potential, and I see it squandered. God damn it, an entire generation pumping gas, waiting tables—slaves with white collars. Advertising has us chasing cars and clothes, working jobs we hate so we can buy shit we don't need. We are the middle children of history, man, with no purpose or place; we have no great war, no great depression; our great war is a spiritual war, our great depression is our lives.
>
> ("Fight Club Ikea Catalogue Scene")

The squalor of the urban underground in *Fight Club* provides the antidote to a tetanized lifestyle shackled by consumption. White-collar workers no longer spend evenings at home polishing their Scandinavian furniture set, but instead beat each other to a bloody pulp in the basement of a bar. "You aren't alive anywhere like you're alive in Fight Club," claims Durden, just as Baudelaire's Nietzschean philosopher claims, "Par mon énergique médication, je lui avais donc rendu l'orgueil et la vie" 'By my forceful medication, I had thus restored his pride and his life' (*Spleen* [Pichois] 359; *Parisian Prowler* 122). The "énergique médication" by which the Fight Club will restore "l'orgueil et la vie" to their petrified social space is similar to Baudelaire's prescription for the beggar: beat up random strangers on the street until they fight back. The fighters' first foray into broad daylight takes the form of a homework assignment in which each member picks a fight and loses to a random passerby.[7] What follows is a very funny sequence in which peaceable citizens in urban spaces are provoked, despite their obvious reluctance, into fighting back: a carwash man hoses down a priest who voices his indignation only to be sprayed again (fig. 4).

A scramble for the hose ensues, the incensed priest finally lunges forward in an awkward punch to his assailant, even if he then backs away in apologetic terror. Spliced into this sequence are two other scenes of strangers harrassed in public places until they cannot help retaliating. These confrontations intend to spur a docile citizenry into recognizing their physical force and social agency. As in Baudelaire's "Let's Beat Up the Poor!," revolutionary praxis is likened to a kind of anarchistic mimetic contamination. The Fight Club seeks to infect corporate America with lawless energy, just as Baudelaire's poet-narrators seek to reanimate the occulted savagery of the empire, thereby translating the structural violence of law and principles into embodied counterviolence.

The juxtaposition of these two historical moments opens up fascinating lines of inquiry into the politics of their representation, including the status of collective dreaming then and now. If Baudelaire's textual terrorism responds in part

Fig. 4. Scene from *Fight Club*, dir. David Fincher. "Homework Scene"

to the dashed hopes of revolutionary transformation, the anarchistic activities of Fight Club and Project Mayhem reveal a far less exalted source of disillusionment: the broken promises of neoliberal individualism and the crisis of masculinity in corporate, consumerist America. We might also note that both Baudelaire's poem and Fincher's film have provoked intense disagreement as to the politics of their (counter)violence. If, for some, their provocations are revolutionary in spirit, for others, their perspective is nihilistic and ultimately conservative. In their critical reception, both works have been linked to various forms of authoritarianism, whether as a prefiguration or a recollection of fascism. For Richard Burton, Baudelaire's encounter between the philosopher-poet and beggar anticipates a totalitarian hierarchy of power in which physical brutality transmits ideology: "Beyond 'Assommons les pauvres' duo of *bourreau* and *victime*, demagogue and lumpenproletariat, a still more fateful sado-masochistic pairing—Führer and Volk—comes dimly into view" (*Baudelaire and the Second Empire* 363). As for *Fight Club*, its protagonist has been compared with a "holdover of early-twentieth-century fascism" and its overall politics dismissed as dangerous, regressive, and profoundly misogynistic (Giroux and Szeman 97). In both cases, the works' ironic texture has polarized their audiences, an indication of counterviolence's slipperiness and potential mutation into the violence it contests. Yet this texture is precisely what enables a multiplicity of readings to emerge and to shuttle between past and present. In spring 2011, for example, one of my students likened the poet's doubling into victim and executioner to the Tunisian street vendor Mohamed Bouazizi and his self-immolation in response to persecution by the police, an act that catalyzed the Arab Spring. In her analysis of "Let's Beat Up the Poor!," the poem's call to conquer equality and restore pride captured the collective struggle for dignity and self-governance sweeping through the Middle East.

In the end, "Let's Beat Up the Poor!," like all of Baudelaire's textual fight clubs, resists the comforts of ideological closure. Its meditation on violence is a *mise en abyme* of the act of reading, materialized as an embodied confrontation between philosopher and beggar, text and reader, past and present. The translation of theory into practice is figured as the translation of reading into beating, into the application of violence and the incitement to counterviolence. It is an energetic transfer that actualizes the relations of force in a given historical moment, in what is also a paradoxal coercion of the reader into agency. Baudelaire's poem speaks to the endless reanimation of literature's force as it traverses readers and histories.

The objective of this itinerary through Baudelaire's fight clubs is to create the conditions for the possibility of what Benjamin described as a profane illumination, where fragments of a remote past are restored to their subversive vitality, and the present, no longer a petrified given, instead is layered with traces of an "it could be otherwise." We can work toward a modest version of this experience in the classroom setting, by foregrounding both the distinctiveness of Baudelaire's nineteenth century and a "synaptic" approach to its cultural material, one that sparks our students' imagination by highlighting circuits of exchange between the past and present (Belcher 182). The use of visual and cinematic imagery to shuttle between distinct historical moments and social formations helps convey the stakes of Baudelaire's pedagogy of violence in *Paris Spleen* and light up its relevance for contemporary cultural life.

NOTES

[1] I have relied on contemporary pop culture resources for courses such as *Sex and the City*: Passions and Fortunes in Nineteenth-Century Paris, where central episodes of the turn-of-the-millennium HBO series set in Manhattan were discussed in relation to forms of gender, ambition, and desire in Baudelaire, Balzac, or Manet.

[2] This selection is designed for undergraduate courses conducted in French, but I have also adapted it to courses in English.

[3] The use of caricature and cinema to unravel Baudelaire's scenarios of violence is a deliberate reminder that the prose poem as a genre harbors an uneasy kinship to the popular cultural forms such as the *feuilleton*, the *faits divers*, and the *roman policier*.

[4] The theme of art as productive destruction, and of counterviolence as oppositional complicity, returns in our discussion of *Fight Club*, which closes on the image of skyscrapers being blown up.

[5] According to Rousseau, the phrase was uttered by Louis XIV's first wife, Marie-Thérèse of Spain: "Enfin je me rappelai le pis-aller d'une grande princesse à qui l'on disait que les paysans n'avaient pas de pain, et qui répondit 'Qu'ils mangent de la brioche'" 'I remembered the comment by a great princess who was told that peasants had no bread and who replied, 'Let them eat brioche' (306; my trans.). The phrase was then misattributed to Marie-Antoinette during the French Revolution. For a reading of Baudelaire's "The Cake" in the light of the June Days, see Oehler.

[6] This fragment of Baudelaire's intimate journals continues thus: "Ai-je besoin de dire le peu qu'il restera de politique se débattra péniblement dans l'étreinte de l'animalité générale, et que les gouvernants seront forcés, pour se maintenir et pour créer un fantôme d'ordre, de recourir à des moyens qui feraient frissonner notre humanité actuelle, pourtant si endurcie ? . . . Quant à moi, qui sens quelquefois en moi le ridicule d'un prophète, je sais que je n'y trouverai jamais la charité d'un médecin. Perdu dans ce vilain monde,

coudoyé par les foules, je suis comme un homme lassé dont l'oeil ne voit en arrière, dans les années profondes, que désabusement et amertume, et devant lui qu'un orage où rien de neuf n'est contenu, ni enseignement, ni douleur" 'Need I describe how the last vestiges of statesmanship will struggle painfully in the clutches of universal bestiality, how the governors will be forced, in maintaining themselves and erecting a phantom of order, to resort to measures which would make our men of today shudder, hardened as they are? . . . For myself, who feel within me sometimes the absurdity of a prophet, I know that I shall never achieve the charity of a physician. Lost in this vile world, elbowed by the crowd, I am like a worn-out man, whose eyes see, in the depths of the years behind him, only disillusionment and bitterness, ahead only a tumult in which there is nothing new, whether of enlightenment or suffering' (*Œuvres complètes* 1: 666–67; *Intimate Journals* 58–59).

[7] Since most students have seen this cult film on DVD, I find that it is only necessary to show them the Ikea catalog sequence and the one that shifts from *Fight Club*'s manifesto to the provocation to fight on city streets. I usually fast-forward through the grisly fight sequence between those scenes, but occasionally I compare its hyperrealist representation of violence to the cartoonish unreality of Baudelaire's scenario.

The Glazier's Cry:
Dissonance in Baudelaire's Prose Poems

Aimée Boutin

There are many noisy street people in Baudelaire's prose poetry, not the least of whom is the glazier. In an upper-level French course focused on Baudelaire's verse and prose poetry, I dedicate considerable time to his evocations of encounters with lower-class workers and beggars on the noisy streets of Paris. While living in a big city today still entails unexpectedly meeting the poor and hearing the supplications and taunts of strangers, American students for the most part no longer have direct experience of the kind of street vendors that Baudelaire encountered daily. In fact, even seasoned city dwellers do not experience noise as one might have in the nineteenth century. The clamor of the city is a significant feature of the prose poems but not necessarily one that our students, habituated to urban noise, find audible or meaningful. (Students from immigrant families or who have traveled extensively could offer different points of view on this issue.) For this reason, Baudelaire's poetry can present a pedagogical challenge for those who have rarely heard the city, for those unaccustomed to listening to it, and for those who lack sociohistorical knowledge about pauperism and working conditions in nineteenth-century Paris. This essay helps teachers capitalize on students' unsettled reactions to "Le Mauvais Vitrier," which ranks among Baudelaire's most important and most jarring poems. Historical contextualization and comparison with Arsène Houssaye's contemporaneous prose poem are two strategies that aim to sensitize students to a range of ways of listening to the glazier's cry. "Hearing" the noise of Baudelaire's street poetry forces novice readers to confront issues central to both modern city life (urban encounters, social harmony, and violence) and modern art (shock, ambiguity, and dissonance).

The nineteenth-century city was a noisy place. Although we can no longer hear what Paris sounded like in the 1860s, we can sensitize our students to noise by asking them to tune their ears to their environments (indoor or outdoor, rural or urban), document what they hear, and organize their findings according to their affective responses (comforting, obnoxious, indifferent, variable). Such a prereading activity can help contextualize the ways Baudelaire's prose poetry repeatedly records the cacophony of urban sounds. Sounds are mostly disagreeable intrusions, especially when compared with the treatment of other sensations in the poems; tactile sensations are generally pleasing, whereas smells are either enjoyable scents or offensive stenches. The "aggressive onslaught on the ear of urban noise," argues Christopher Prendergast, "is a major consequence for his conception of what 'poetry' is and what it might be in the modern world" (127). In "Le Crépuscule du soir," for example, the din rising up to the narrator's balcony sounds like "une foule de cris discordants, que l'espace transforme en une lugubre harmonie" 'a multitude of discordant shouts, . . . transformed by the space into a dismal harmony' (*Spleen* [Pichois] 31; *Parisian Prowler* 50). In "Un Plaisant," the narrator identifies the big city as a delirium-inducing place made to "troubler le cerveau du solitaire le plus fort" 'disturb the brain of the most steadfast solitary' (279; 5). Accordingly, in "La Chambre double," noise threatens the speaker's reverie in the paradisiacal room, and in "Une Mort héroïque," a whistle interrupts the artist's enthralling performance. At other times, city noise is less a disruption than a consolation to the isolated city dweller: "Les Veuves" and "Le Vieux Saltimbanque" use street noise to heighten the protagonists' alienation. As Richard Burton summarizes in "Bonding and Breaking," citing "Le Tir et le cimetière": "It is difficult to imagine a better description of the *Petits poèmes en prose* themselves: a 'symphonie en sourdine' continually broken by explosive, disjunctive sounds, voices, and actions, a unique interweaving of the concordant and discordant, the lyric and the counter-lyric" (65).

Baudelaire referred to the formative role of urban noises in the genesis of his prose poetry in the dedicatory letter to Houssaye that served as preface to *Le Spleen de Paris.* In a statement that is not without irony, Baudelaire drew attention to the inspirational function of the strident cry of the *vitrier*, or glazier:

> Vous-même, mon cher ami, n'avez-vous pas tenté de traduire en une *chanson* le cri strident du *Vitrier*, et d'exprimer dans une prose lyrique toutes les désolantes suggestions que ce cri envoie jusqu'aux mansardes, à travers les plus hautes brumes de la rue?   (*Spleen* [Pichois] 276)

> You yourself, my dear friend, did you not try to translate the *Glazier's* strident cry into a *song,* and to express in lyrical prose all the woeful associations that cry sends all the way to attics, through the street's thickest fogs?
>   (*Parisian Prowler* 129–30)

Baudelaire discussed Houssaye's poem "La Chanson du vitrier" as an antecedent to his own work, but, as influential critics such as Ross Chambers ("Baudelaire's Dedicatory Practice"), Sonya Stephens (*Baudelaire's Prose Poems*), and Steve Murphy (*Logiques*) have explained, he did not respect Houssaye as an artist. Rather, he needed his support as a leading editor and critic; in fact, Houssaye edited the newspaper *La Presse* where "Le Mauvais Vitrier" appeared in 1862. Notwithstanding the double-edged flattery, the statement brings to the fore three points that invite further examination: first, Baudelaire evoked the glazier, a type known to his readers from literary guidebooks, if not from direct experience; second, he brought to mind the sense of desolation conveyed or aroused by the stridency of the cry while raising questions about the impact, if any, the cry had on the listener by describing *where* the cry is carried, not *who* hears it; third, the expression "traduire en une *chanson*" forces us to think about whether it is possible or warranted to harmonize this stridency into song or into lyrical prose. Although Baudelaire dismissed Houssaye's poem in the letter-preface, it is worth comparing "La Chanson du vitrier" and "Le Mauvais Vitrier" in class to give students a better sense of what Baudelaire was doing differently. Houssaye and Baudelaire diverged on how to translate the glazier's cry into poetry and how to orchestrate harmony ("song") and dissonance ("cry") in their poetics. Houssaye harmonized the glazier by sentimentalizing his song, thereby returning the poor to the social fraternity. In contrast, Baudelaire restored the primal sharpness to the cry, playing out its associations with unconscious desires, sensuality, hysteria, and even satanism.

What was the glazier's trade, and how did he practice it? What did his cry sound like? Answering these questions can help students become more sensitive to city sounds and their effects on listeners, as well as understand why writing poetry inspired by street noise is a thoroughly modern endeavor. An itinerant tradesman who sold panes of glass, the glazier wandered Parisian neighborhoods, carrying his "fragile marchandise" 'fragile merchandise' on his back (*Spleen* [Pichois] 286; *Parisian Prowler* 15), in a pack with hooks ("crochets" [287]), as described toward the end of "Le Mauvais Vitrier." The glazier called out his services to attract customers. Glaziers could be identified by their specific cry, always the same phrase sung on the same melody. Many believed the cries could faithfully be traced back to the Middle Ages (Boutin, *City* 35–60; see Fournel, *Les Cris de Paris*). High-pitched, the glazier's cry had to travel far and wide to reach the sixth-floor apartments and garrets where poorer occupants resided, such as those explicitly referenced in Baudelaire's poem. Glaziers, like other members of what Karl Marx referred to as the "lumpenproletariat" in chapter 5 of "The Eighteenth Brumaire of Louis Bonaparte" (149), were near-destitute themselves because itinerant trade, while never lucrative, could not compete with the development of the capitalist economy during the second half of the nineteenth century. Living on the fringe of society, these marginal workers gained a bad reputation as thieves and window breakers ("casseurs," or rioters), as Burton examines in "Destruction as Creation: 'Le Mauvais Vitrier' and the Poetics and Politics of Violence." Glaziers and other street types such as ragpickers, old-clothesmen, and flower vendors were frequently described and pictured in literary guidebooks, such as Léon Curmer's *Les Français peints par eux-mêmes*, whose images prove useful in class discussion of the type. Guidebooks such as these offered Parisian bourgeois readers opportunities to stroll the city streets as virtual *flâneurs*, or idlers. In this way, glaziers were idealized by readers who would never need their services but who valued their charm. In guidebooks, plays, and musical compositions, they became associated with the quaint and picturesque elements of Old Paris, the antithesis of Haussmann's sanitized city.

Houssaye's prose poem "La Chanson du vitrier" exemplified this kind of idealization of the glazier. The narrator strolls along rue du Bac in today's prestigious seventh quarter and hears the cry of the glazier. He stops to talk with him and invites him to have a drink in a bar. The poem's dramatic climax comes when the narrator fails to understand and act upon what the glazier tells him repeatedly—that he has not eaten and needs money to provide food for himself and his family. Although such moral detachment was fairly typical of *flâneur* literature, in which bourgeois idlers did not dwell on the socioeconomic significance of what they perceived, Houssaye muddied the waters by also evoking a sentimental discourse on pauperism (Murphy, *Logiques* 342). "La Chanson du vitrier" attempts unsuccessfully to reconcile detachment and empathy. The tensions in the text lead Murphy to claim rightly that Houssaye "n'a justement pas pu maîtriser les intentions directrices de son *propre* texte" 'was not able to control the implied meanings of his own writing' ("*Le Mauvais Vitrier*" 341; my trans.).

The lack of clear direction in the poem is related to the type of sound it transposes, since cries defy control and are subject to semantic drift (by its intensity the cry can mean distress as well as elation). Houssaye's poem dramatizes a peddler whose cry goes unanswered: although the cry in the poem is supposed to be an attention-getting and effective advertising tool, those in the marketplace ignore it. The narrator evokes the voices from the apartments above he would expect, in vain this time, to reply, but no one echoes the glazier's cry. Even the narrator fails to properly respond to the cry as an economic signal; instead of purchasing windowpanes, he breaks them. The cry has lost its efficacy as a sales strategy.

Although no characters respond to the glazier's cry, the poem repeats the cry as a refrain. This is important because the refrain converts distress into pathos. Although it is no longer functional, it is still beautiful and symbolic of the picturesque quality of Parisian streets. Throughout Houssaye's prose poem, different characters repeat "Oh! Vitrier!" so that the refrain works to ensure the circulation of melancholic feeling, ultimately covering over the socioeconomic causes of the desperation we hear; the pathos of the cry neutralizes its potential radicalism. Similar attempts at aestheticization were common in literary guidebooks and musical ethnographies. What did the glazier's cry sound like in these accounts? It is of course hard to determine today, especially when Houssaye could describe what he heard as a "chanson pleine de larmes" 'song full of tears' (*Œuvres poétiques* 287), whereas Baudelaire perceived the same cry as "perçant, discordant" 'piercing, discordant' (*Spleen* [Pichois] 286; *Parisian Prowler* 14). Students may gain a better understanding of the pitch of the glazier's cry by listening to an audio clip of Jean-Georges Kastner's symphony *Les Cris de Paris* (1857) from the CD compilation *L'Écrit du cri* by Ensemble Clément Janequin and noting the use of falsetto. Nineteenth-century musical ethnographers such as Joseph Mainzer spent considerable effort attempting to convey and transcribe the sound of the cry, as in this passage from *Les Français peints par eux-mêmes*:

> Il serait difficile d'indiquer par la notation en usage la mélodie *Au vitrier !* Ces deux mots subissent des variantes, et deviennent quelquefois incompréhensibles pour ceux qui ne font que les entendre sans voir les marchands, comme, par exemple, lorsqu'ils se transforment en ceux-ci : *Au i-tri-i !* Ils sont généralement moitié chantés, moitié parlés. La première syllabe *au* est chantée très haut et fortement criée, tandis que le mot *vitrier* est dit très bas, et se trouve presque couvert par le premier son.
>
> (Mainzer 913–14)

It would be difficult to indicate the melody of *Au vitrier!* with the notation style in use. These two words undergo variants, and sometimes become incomprehensible for whomever hears but does not see the vendors, as for example when the words are transformed into these: *Au i-tri-i!* They are also half-sung, half-spoken. The first syllable, *au*, is sung very high and cried out loudly, whereas the word *vitrier* is spoken softly and is almost muffled by the first sound.   (my trans.)

Whether the cry takes the form of the prepositional phrase "Au vitrier" that Mainzer identified or the more song-like apostrophe "Oh! Vitrier!" that Houssaye and others opted for, it seems clear that Houssaye was not aiming for sonic realism because he avoided the syncope that both Kastner and Mainzer emphasized. The contraction of "vitrier" reduces it to its most strident phoneme [i]. The fact that Houssaye avoided syncopation in his translation of the cry further shows his interest in harmonization.

In "Le Mauvais Vitrier," Baudelaire did not attempt to "translate" (the term he used in the dedicatory letter) the glazier's cry as Houssaye had. Indeed the poem does not cite the glazier's cry at all. Rather, the poem describes the perverse effect that hearing the piercing and discordant cry has on the poet-speaker, allegedly prompting him to drop a flowerpot on the glazier, shattering his panes of glass in an explosive noise. Houssaye went to some length to describe—even to elicit—the emotional impact that hearing the glazier's cry has on the narrator, and he detailed the dolorous music of the glazier's as well as the quality of other characters' voices. In contrast, Baudelaire's poem explored the sensation of sound as a mental construct and the behaviors sounds elicit. The sound the poet actually hears is less relevant than the effect the sound has on the listener. The first half of the poem sets the focus not on the material or substantive world but on the mysteries of the mind, the "impulsion mystérieuse et inconnue" 'mysterious and unknown impulse,' the "folle énergie" 'crazy energy,' the forces that motivate people to act (*Spleen* [Pichois] 285; *Parisian Prowler* 13). In fact, the dramatic entrance of the glazier is delayed by the litany of shocking anecdotes about incidents in which the narrator's friends committed absurd and dangerous actions. These sketches of impulsive behaviors contribute to the digressive structure of the narrative that, as Cheryl Krueger has shown ("Telling Stories"), can be interpreted as a means of frustrating hermeneutics. How the cry is interpreted is indeed at issue.

What effect does the glazier's cry have on the Baudelairean narrator? The answer appears in the interrelation of the first and second parts of the poem separated by the parenthetical statement. Indeed, in both parts, the narrator reflects on the inability to explain what motivates people to take action. Students can be asked to list all the references in the poem to the lack of rational motivation and the vagaries of chance occurrences and to consider the rich lexicon of causes listed, ranging from "impulsion mystérieuse" and "caprice" to idleness, fatigue, drunken madness, fury, and hysteria (*Spleen* [Pichois] 285; *Parisian Prowler* 13).

The narrator also ponders the abilities of moralists, physicians, and "ceux qui pensent un peu mieux que les médecins" 'those who think a little more lucidly than physicians' to accurately diagnose the internal or external source of motivation (286; 14).

One of the forces identified in the poem that leads the speaker to act is the influence of the devil. The implicit correspondences between the first and second parts of the poem suggest a clear analogy between the influences of the cry and of the "Démons malicieux [qui] se glissent en nous et nous font accomplir à notre insu, leurs plus absurdes volontés" 'malicious Demons [who] slip into us and, without us knowing it, make us carry out their most absurd wishes' (286; 14). Baudelaire's satanism surfaced in *Les Fleurs du Mal* (*The Flowers of Evil*); Jonathan Culler notes that in lyrical poems such as "Au Lecteur," the devil is the name given to the impersonal, external forces that control our will against our better judgment ("Teaching the Devil" 144). I often invite students to ponder how the devil figures into reflections on human agency in *Le Spleen de Paris* by pointing to links among "Le Mauvais Vitrier," "Les Tentations, ou Éros, Plutus et la gloire," "Le Joueur généreux," and "Assommons les pauvres!" or even Edgar Allan Poe's "The Imp of the Perverse."

We can also explain what motivates the speaker's actions and the role of the cry in eliciting impulsive behaviors by returning to the interrelation of "Le Mauvais Vitrier" and "La Chanson du vitrier." Baudelaire's poem responds to what we might call repressed content in Houssaye's text. If we read Houssaye against the grain, as Murphy does (*Logiques* 357), and view the apparent philanthropic and benevolent intentions of the author (to write a poem about Christian charity and fraternity) as their repressed opposite, the poem conveys an implicit violence and cruelty, even satanism, toward the working class. Like Mephistopheles, Houssaye's narrator befriends his victim (unwittingly) to secure his downfall. "Le Mauvais Vitrier" then explicates satanic violent impulses left unacknowledged in "La Chanson du vitrier." Moreover, both Baudelaire and Houssaye drew on commonplace allusions to the violent, fantastic, and sinister overtones of the cries in panoramic texts about the glazier and other street criers. Indeed, street cries surface in childhood memories, which can easily be infused with superstitions dating back to times immemorial or with the fantastic and the magical. These associations are all the more powerful because criers are often heard in the early morning hours while the listener is still half asleep, as is the case in Baudelaire's poem, where the narrator hears the glazier in the morning shortly after waking up in a bad mood.

Students undoubtedly will find Baudelaire's narrator's behavior toward the glazier unsettling because it is random and unprovoked. It is therefore helpful to interpret the actions narrated as an overt rebuttal of Houssaye's sentimentalism. In "Le Mauvais Vitrier," as in "Les Yeux des pauvres" and "La Fausse Monnaie," Baudelaire exposed the social hypocrisies that Houssaye remained blind to. Rather than risk not knowing what aggression he commits under the guise of a philanthropic and fraternal encounter, Baudelaire's narrator makes explicit his "hatred" for the "bad" glazier ("bad" because he bears bad-quality windowpanes, according to the narrator) and shouts loudly, if ironically, how delightful pranks feel even though he knows not why he does what he does. By encouraging students to keep "La Chanson du vitrier" in mind, I provide a strategy for them to disengage from their identification with the I-narrator. Indeed, it is worth reminding them, first, that we should be wary of confusing the first-person narrator-protagonist with the author (Stephens, *Baudelaire's Prose Poems* 61–65) and, second, that Baudelaire's prose poems "exploit our susceptibility as readers to be manipulated" (M. Scott 3). The poem's title, for example, in duplicitously identifying the "bad" window breaker, conveys the full complexity of the interaction (Stephens, *Baudelaire's Prose Poems* 68). The narrator's "guerre" 'war' on the glazier is calculated rather than accidental. The references to pink, red, blue panes of glass, to "vitres de paradis" 'panes of paradise,' to the expectation that people living in poorer neighborhoods want to "voir la vie en beau" 'make life beautiful' could refer (ironically) to the glazier's obliviousness to beauty and art, a wrong the speaker aims to right by shattering the glazier's merchandise in an "éclatant" 'brilliant' sound and light show (*Spleen* [Pichois] 287; *Parisian Prowler* 15). The poem ends with the speaker's crying "La vie en beau!," which inverts the vowel sounds [i] and [o] in the glazier's cry, "Au i-tri-i." The violence, however, turns on itself when the reader is forced to confront his or her own assumptions about art's ability to harmonize social consciousness with violence. The ear-piercing or heart-moving glazier's cry calls out to us: how would we respond?

Another interpretation of the narrator's actions limits our reach outside the text. In Baudelaire's poem, no other characters hear the cry, which becomes subsumed in the actions of the narrator ("Une action d'éclat" 'brilliant action' [286; 14]) and the glazier ("un bruit éclatant" 'brilliant sound' [287; 15]). A reading of "Le Mauvais Vitrier" as a self-contained narrative accounts well for the playful self-reflexivity of the poem. The actions of the speaker are determined by the words he uses to describe his motivation, even before the glazier arrives on the scene: an irresistible force pushes him to commit "une action d'éclat" 'a brilliant action.' The poem, as Culler comments in "Baudelaire and Poe," using an expression Baudelaire coined, is a "calembour," or pun in action (70–71). In a parodic gesture, Baudelaire substitutes Houssaye's "verre" with a "pot" ("prendre un pot," "prendre un verre" are informal expressions meaning "to have a drink"), which each poet uses quite differently, but both encounters end by aggravating the glazier's destitution. The flowerpot that the narrator throws down on the glazier also recalls Poe (the pun "pot"/"Poe") and Baudelaire's own "flowers of evil" (Culler, "Baudelaire and Poe"). Other puns, clichés, and references to stock phrases such as "la vie en rose" and "qui casse les verres les paie" 'if you break it you buy it' suggest the prose poem parodies bourgeois discourse (Stephens, *Baudelaire's Prose Poems* 68–69). I might add that the colloquialism "vitrier" 'glazier' in French and English refers to a person obstructing the view, inherently justifying the narrator's perception of him as a nuisance. Although "Le Mauvais Vitrier" does exhibit the self-reflexivity Culler and others ascribe to it while referring punningly to its literary intertexts (Poe, Houssaye), this interpretation seems to silence unduly the poem's coming to terms with the rich discourse on street cries as a collective memory and more broadly with the reality of urban noise, which breaks through throughout *Le Spleen de Paris* (as it already had in *Les Fleurs du Mal*) and resounds beyond it, in much of the poetry on the city that was inspired by Baudelaire.

The differences between Houssaye's euphonious glazier's song and Baudelaire's embrace of strident dissonance are evidence of the latter's modernist attention to noise. Rather than shut out noise and escape into a silent inner world of contemplation as the Romantics did or harmonize noise by translating it into "song" as Houssaye did, Baudelaire breaks the melodic line by forestalling idealization with strident interruptions. As a modernist, he "understood well the connection between the aesthetics of fragmentation and the effort to come to terms with the cacophony of the modern urban environment" (Cowan 134). Listening to the city is part of a new attention to the transitory as distinct from the eternal, the two components of "modernity" according to Baudelaire's definition of the term in *Le Peintre de la vie moderne* (695; *The Painter of Modern Life* 12). "Le Mauvais Vitrier" in fact ends with the tension between eternal and infinitesimal time and between the spontaneous fury of the speaker's cry and the appeal to an aesthetic ideal: "la vie en beau." A class discussion of "Le Mauvais Vitrier" can spur students to hear the city differently and reflect on the poem as a sound clip of modernity.

NOTE

This essay is adapted from chapter 4 in my *City of Noise.*

Worlding Baudelaire:
Geography, Genre, and Translation

Françoise Lionnet

In an age of globalization, increased interest in world literature, and widespread awareness of the composite nature of individual and collective identities, advanced undergraduate students at my large public university are easily impatient with narrow approaches to French literature. When the author is Baudelaire, whose early travels to the Mascarene Islands of the Indian Ocean marked his poetic sensibility and inspired his abiding yet ambiguous interest in distant places and racial difference, the challenge consists in presenting the poet as actively engaged with questions of culture and understanding that intersect with our contemporary pedagogical and interpretive issues. It is important to link the poetry to historic, geographic, and textual realities that make Baudelaire's travels both compelling for twenty-first-century readers and generative of critical perspectives that can broaden national(ist) paradigms of literary history. In a class that I have taught in either French or English, and in which I focus on the Indian Ocean, travel, genre, and translation, my goal is to contribute to a timely and judicious pedagogical movement—the one that aims to globalize French studies and to develop a "new approach to literary history" (McDonald and Suleiman) that stresses the "becoming-transnational" of the field (Lionnet, "Introduction" 784; Hargreaves, Forsdick, and Murphy 2).

French modernist aesthetic conventions have encouraged critical approaches that privilege the Parisian and European elements of Baudelaire's trajectory to the point of ignoring the basic biographical facts of his youth: his avid reading of travel narratives about Africa and the Indian Ocean and his nine months' journey to the islands of Mauritius (Isle de France) and Réunion (Bourbon) in 1841. Baudelaire was always vague about these travels, and, as his friend Ernest Prarond suggests, he "obligingly fed the public rumors of his long peregrinations in fabulous countries because it gave him the mysterious appearance of having returned from distant lands" (qtd. in Lionnet, "Reframing" 64). Having settled for the little-known islands of the Mascarenes instead of the great continent of Africa or India, Baudelaire actively maintained an aura of ambiguity about that phase of his life. Yet, to bring in these salient global elements of his life and work is to better focus the attention of students, even the ones who are initially recalcitrant to close readings of French poetry. It is to enable them to relate more concretely to a tradition of nineteenth-century literature they might otherwise find irrelevant, if not downright offensive, because of its problematic engagement with the rhetoric of exoticism and orientalism in the representation of embodied, concrete others (Ahearn). To bring in his history of global encounters is to prod the students into a real appreciation of the poet's idiosyncratic way of resorting to irony in his encounter with, and subtle denunciation of, the violence of colonization (Sanyal).

My pedagogical approach is part of an interpretive strategy that aims to "actualize" reading and update the interpretation and reception of old texts, to use Yves Citton's terminology (*Lire*). I find this to be a productive way to urge students, on the one hand, to look for omissions and lacunae in past critical practice and, on the other hand, to read confidently from the perspective of their concrete standpoints or contemporary epistemologies and sensibilities. My aim is not merely to provide a sociohistorical and biographical context that might seem antithetical to Baudelaire's ironic modernist stance, commitment to the autonomy of poetry, and fierce defense of the independence of the artist. Rather, I challenge students to think about what European modernism owes to the colonial realities and literary production of francophone places distant yet not entirely separate from nineteenth-century Paris. I suggest that the local and the global, text and context, biography and criticism are so completely intertwined in Baudelaire's writings that we need to begin by understanding that broader picture before we can do serious textual analyses.

Geographies of Modern French Poetry

Francophone sites across the globe continue to be connected to Paris's publishing and editorial scene, given the city's declining but still robust cultural capital. Paris wields a great deal of controversial influence over that wider world. I want students to note this problematic influence but only as one element within a network that is never unidirectional, never simply from a presumed center to a so-called periphery, as in most models of world literary history indebted to the dominant ideology of the West (Moretti; Lionnet, "Universalisms" and "Critical Conventions"). I argue that influence is generally a two-way process that becomes fully visible only if we take into account the cultural dynamics of colonial peripheries. Baudelaire's life and work give ample evidence to support that larger point. The methodological point I emphasize, however, is that to avoid oversimplistic biographical correlations we must anchor his poetry in a cultural and discursive field that takes into account other narratives about the region he visited. I want students to be aware that discourses connected to a particular geography inevitably form a network that can reveal a writer's physical experience of that geography as well as his intellectual interest in how it had previously been represented by other writers and storytellers.

The history of travel writing in the Indian Ocean as well as the elegies of early Creole poets form part of such a discursive web; both genres—travelogues and lyric poetry—provide a crucial context for understanding Baudelaire. Poems that are remembrances of his visit to the Mascarene Islands are known to specialists of the Indian Ocean as *poèmes mascarins* ("Mascarene poems"). To read these poems with that discursive context in mind is to have a clearer sense of what it means to teach the history of a national language literature in our age of translation and global circulation. From both a conceptual and a hermeneutic point of view, such historical and discursive contextualizations enable deeper understanding of earlier patterns of world-scale exchanges that can then put twenty-first-century globalization into perspective.

Travel memoirs and eighteenth-century Creole poetry (see Racault) have left many traces on Baudelaire's work. These "minor" genres have been instrumental to the development of a poet who was often thought to have inaugurated the form of the prose poem. Yet it is the Creole Évariste Parny (1753–1814) from Réunion who first made innovative use of the prose poem, incorporating elements of Malagasy orality into his poetry (Moore; Seth). Baudelaire's combined interest in the genre and the region can be traced directly to Parny: Baudelaire suggests as much in a letter to his sister-in-law in which he asserts that his grand ambition is to follow in the footsteps of "un Pétrarque ou un Parny" 'a Petrarch or a Parny' (*Correspondance* 1: 135).[1] In *Les mystères galants* ("Mysteries of Sexual Intrigue"), he casually mentions Parny (*Œuvres complètes* 2: 1001), whereas in the essay "De l'essence du rire" ("Of the Essence of Laughter"), he makes an indirect allusion to the latter's 1804 scabrous epic *Goddam!* to illustrate his point about caricature and the Isle de France's "virginale Virginie," the heroine of Jacques-Henri Bernardin de Saint-Pierre's *Paul et Virginie* (*Œuvres complètes* 2: 529). Immensely popular across Europe during his lifetime and admired by Aleksandr Pushkin, who loved his *Élégies*, Parny is hardly known today, but he remains nonetheless a crucial piece in the puzzle of sources that can shed light on Baudelaire's creativity as a traveler, a reader, and a poet. Praised by François-René de Chateaubriand, Alphonse de Lamartine, and Charles Augustin Sainte-Beuve, Parny is absent from most modern poetry anthologies, although he was elected to the Académie française in 1803, the first non-European francophone poet to be so honored (Lionnet, "'New World' Exiles").

It is by using Parny to teach Baudelaire that I can best outline for students the historical conditions of production of norms and canons (according to Pierre Bourdieu's social theories in *Les Règles de l'art*, for example) and the place of the francophone within them. I suggest that reading is a historically situated activity for writers as it is for critics: for Baudelaire, Parny belonged to a set of fashionable writers who inspired his youthful desire for distant lands, whereas for us, today, Parny can serve to reinforce twenty-first-century postcolonial perspectives as we recover the racialized elements of his poetry that had been summarily dismissed by generations of literary historians (Lionnet, "'New World' Exiles"). The intertextual echoes between Baudelaire and this minor predecessor thus become the precondition for more precise close readings of the prose poems, readings that can now take into account the archive of narrative and poetic forms developed by European travel writers but also by the oral cultures they encountered and by the Creole poets whose impact on modernity remains woefully underresearched.

Among the Mascarene poems, the prose pieces "Un Hémisphère dans une chevelure" ("A Hemisphere in Tresses"), "L'Invitation au voyage" ("Invitation to the Voyage"), "Les Projets" ("Plans"), "La Belle Dorothée" ("Beautiful Dorothy"), "Déjà!" ("Already!"), and "Le Désir de peindre" ("The Desire to Paint") have obvious references to the region and its female figures, habitat, and natural landscapes. But the full extent of Baudelaire's debt to that region and to those who represented it before him can only be made explicit when we add selections from these earlier works to the syllabus. Doing so presupposes that we are prepared to recognize Baudelaire's foreign debt not just to the well-known Edgar Allan Poe, whom Baudelaire translated, but also to those who wrote on themes related to the same tropical latitudes where he acquired firsthand knowledge of the ecological and human diversity that haunt his poetry. These writers include, in addition to Parny, the traveler Melchior-Honoré Yvan, author of the 1855 *De France en Chine* ("From France to China" [Lionnet, "'The Indies'" and *The Known* 162–217]). Selections from Parny and Yvan prepare students to approach the surface rhetoric of exotic and racialist discourse from a more complex perspective than they might otherwise adopt if they were to remain wedded either to a modernist aesthetic of mere distanciation or to a postcolonial critical and political approach that immediately renders suspect the European poet's engagement with race and the tropics.

Once this critical problem has been laid out, it becomes easier to discuss issues of poetic irony, authority, experience, and the violence of representation without stacking the deck for or against Baudelaire or relying only on biographical details to make my case. I want students to be able to appreciate the fact that no single theory can be adequate to a complete understanding of the work: neither aestheticism nor historicism, neither the ideology of art for art's sake nor the reductive Sartrean critique that assigns only bad faith, avoidance of ethical responsibility, and lack of *engagement* to the poet. I argue that poetic representation of tropical landscapes and colonial violence is itself a crucial form of *engagement* with the realities of colonialism, as is clear from the contemporary work of the Mauritian writer Ananda Devi, whose short stories I also assign because of their intertextual responses to Baudelaire (Lionnet, "Littérature-monde"). By pointing out that Baudelaire's text is a vehicle for geographic and cultural realities—and that his travels as well as his readings about the region fueled his creativity—I stress both the importance of his global vision or cosmopolitan reach and what each contributes to our present moment of *mondialisation*. I situate Baudelaire in a genealogy that includes Parny and Yvan and explain that his legacy survives in contemporary francophone literature, especially in the works of authors such as the Haitian Jacques Stephen Alexis, the Martinican Édouard Glissant, and Devi, whose ironic style amplifies and critiques Baudelaire's gendered colonial scenarios as well as the feelings of productive discomfort they continue to generate today.

Travel and Critique

I begin by assigning the last poem of the 1861 edition of *Les Fleurs du Mal*, "Le Voyage" ("The Voyage"), in the poet Keith Waldrop's translation of *The Flowers of Evil*, which recasts the alexandrines into versets. I pair the poem with Baudelaire's "Méthode de critique" ("Critical Method"), the first section of his essay "Exposition Universelle – 1855 – Beaux Arts" 'The Universal Exhibition of 1855,' available in the 1981 Cambridge edition *Selected Writings on Art and Artists*. Together, these serve as introductory evidence of the poet's self-reflexive appreciation of the cosmopolitan and the worldly. I read them as methodological statements meant to guide our close readings by revealing the poet's self-reflective strategies of representation. The last lines of "Le Voyage" 'The Voyage' encourage us to "plonger au fond du gouffre . . . / Au fond de l'Inconnu pour trouver du *nouveau*" (*Œuvres complètes* [Pichois] 1: 134) 'to plunge the depth of the abyss . . . to the heart of the Unknown to find the *new!*' (*Flowers* [Waldrop] 182). I ask students to keep an open mind as they journey into the writings and toward the new interpretive possibilities that Baudelaire's critical texts invite.

"Méthode de critique" 'Critical Method' theorizes what travel does to the intelligent "homme du monde" 'man of the world' who may either be graced with sophisticated worldliness or who will soon become so, having learned to appreciate difference and diversity thanks to his encounters:

> Si, au lieu d'un pédagogue, je prends un homme du monde, un intelligent, et si je le transporte dans une contrée lointaine, je suis sûr que, si les étonnements du débarquement sont grands, si l'accoutumance est plus ou moins longue, plus ou moins laborieuse, la sympathie sera tôt ou tard si vive, si pénétrante, qu'elle créera en lui un monde nouveau d'idées, monde qui fera partie intégrante de lui-même, et qui l'accompagnera, sous la forme des souvenirs, jusqu'à la mort.   (*Œuvres complètes* [Pichois] 2: 576)

> If instead of a pedagogue I were now to take a man of the world, an intelligent one, and were to transport him to a distant land, I feel sure that though his surprises on disembarking would be great, though his process of acclimatization might be more or less long, more or less difficult, his sympathy would sooner or later become so keen, so penetrating, that it would create in him a whole new world of ideas, a world that would become part and parcel of him and accompany him as memories till his death.
>
> (*Selected Writings* 116)

When read with an adequate understanding of the poet's travels, this essay gives ample clues about Baudelaire's projection of his experiences of distant lands and how they have become an integral part of his own self. He values firsthand knowledge and common sense over the bookish kind imparted in the classroom by "une espèce de tyran-mandarin" (2: 578) 'a species of tyrant-mandarin' (118), and he entices students to think for themselves, to question the received wisdom dispensed by the "*modernes professeurs-jurés*" (2: 577) '*modern self-appointed aesthetic pedants*' that he decries because their interpretive "system" is unable to "keep up with universal man" (117, 118).

Using Baudelaire's words to undermine the authority of experts, students can begin to identify with his creative project and develop greater awareness of his implicit and explicit poetic goals. I try to let them come to the conclusion that rather than apply theories of criticism or models of interpretation derived from extraneous systems of thought, we can use the evidence of this essay to understand the fundamental role of Baudelaire's travels even in a poem such as "Le Cygne" 'The Swan,' which showcases the kind of critical and classical "érudition" (2: 579) 'erudition' that the poet sets up against the "impeccable naïveté" (578) 'impeccable naïveté' and "*ignorance*" (579) '*ignorance*' (119) that, as he argues, can in contrast feed the reader's affectivity, pleasure, and sense of identification (118, 119).

The style of the essay is reminiscent of Jean-Jacques Ampère's 1834 inaugural lecture at the Collège de France when he was elected chair of the history of literature. Ampère was the first French historian of literature to adopt a "global" or comparative perspective (Lionnet, "Critical Conventions"). In the same vein, Baudelaire denounces parochial judgments and "utopie pédagogique" (*Œuvres complètes* [Pichois] 2: 576) 'pedagogic utopia' that mask "la complexe vérité" (576) "the complex truth" and prevent critics from appreciating art on its own cultural terms (*Selected Writings* 116). Baudelaire's attention to context motivates his insistence on the embeddedness of the foreign within frames of meaning that can transform the viewer's (or reader's) understanding of the various instances of universal beauty encountered in the world. If a foreign object or work of art is to be properly understood, Baudelaire insists, the prerequisite is simply that

> le critique, le spectateur opère en lui-même une transformation qui tient du mystère, et que, par un phénomène de la volonté agissant sur l'imagination, *il apprenne de lui-même à participer au milieu qui a donné naissance à cette floraison insolite*.   (2: 576; my emphasis)

> the critic, the viewer, must bring about within himself a transformation, which is something of a mystery, and, by a phenomenon of will-power acting on his imagination, *he must learn by his own effort to share in the life of the society that has given birth to this unexpected bloom*.
>   (116; my emphasis)

Baudelaire points to the "transformation" that needs to occur in the critic if he is to be receptive to diverse paradigms of beauty. He understands the importance of the ground from which any art springs and stresses that one must, through efforts of will and imagination, attempt to coincide with, or to participate in, that milieu rather than try to apply exogenous theories of interpretation—as do those he calls "*professeurs-jurés*" (2: 577) '*aesthetic pedants*' (117). His statements resonate across the centuries with those of postcolonial critics who today demand native theories for native texts. This 1855 essay on method can therefore allow me to justify a critical approach that is modeled on the poet's own. I argue that to do so is to legitimize a process of worlding that can keep our reading in line with Baudelaire's strategies of interpretation as an art critic eager to understand "une contrée lointaine" (576) 'distant land' (116) and its forms of cultural production.

Despite his stated appreciation of cosmopolitan ideals of difference and worldliness, Baudelaire rarely gave details of his 1841 voyages to the little-known multiracial islands of Mauritius and Réunion, the *vieilles colonies* ("*old colonies*") of ancien régime France. But we can see that both his critical and poetic sensibilities were indelibly marked by his encounter with the otherness of Creole cultures that became an integral part of his self. These gave him "un monde nouveau d'idées" (576) 'a whole new world of ideas' (116) that accompanied him "sous la forme de souvenirs, jusqu'à la mort" (576) 'as memories till his death' (116) and allowed him to develop an appreciation for beauty (116). As he also insists, beauty is always "*bizarre*" (578), strange: it produces distance, defamiliarizes the real world. It is by being open to such transformative experiences and reflecting on them that Baudelaire developed his context-specific critical stance. I can then suggest that our encounter with his poetry must similarly be unfettered by aesthetic biases and unmediated by rigid academic conventions of genre and period.

Genre and Translation

Some discussions of the prose poem assert that Baudelaire invented the form with *Le Spleen de Paris*, but recent scholarship demonstrates otherwise. According to Fabienne Moore, the genre originates with eighteenth-century nostalgia for forms of expression capable of translating authentic modes of feeling increasingly displaced by revolution, modernity, and emerging scientific knowledge grounded in reason and logic. For her, "prose poems are one of the least known 'inventions' of the French Enlightenment" (2). She traces a genealogy grounded in the century's ambiguous fascination for *métissage*, when "hybridity became the reality of modernity . . . in art as in life" (13), when generic and class instability created aesthetic and social tensions that needed to be translated into new poetic forms. These tensions were in no small measure triggered by colonial discoveries and the presence of new others in the cultural imaginary. The 1788 success of Bernardin de Saint-Pierre's *Paul et Virginie* introduced the Indian Ocean islands to a large public, but it is Parny's prose poem *Chansons madécasses* ("Songs of Madagascar"), published in 1787 after the success of his 1778 *Poésies érotiques*, that fueled a new desire for the primitive (Meitinger) and inaugurated the association of Creoleness with a seemingly natural talent for poetic languor and eroticism. Parny's evocation of sexualized black voices in the *Chansons* is as much a precursor of Baudelaire's "La Belle Dorothée" 'Beautiful Dorothy' as are the quasi-ethnographic travel narratives of Yvan. Set to music by Ravel, these *Chansons* are better known to musicologists than to literary critics, but they form part of a popular eighteenth-century genre of pseudotranslation that ventriloquizes native voices. In "La Belle Dorothée," Baudelaire's use of indirect discourse and Creole vocabulary—for example, the word "Cafrines" (*Œuvres complètes* [Pichois] 1: 317) 'Black Women' (Lionnet, "Reframing" and *The Known* 179–82)—is also an effort to ventriloquize or translate local terminology into French contexts.[2]

Parny's *Élégies* and *Chansons* reveal a modern sensibility that announces Baudelaire's. "J'aime et je maudis les voyages" 'I love travel and I curse it,' Parny confessed in a 1785 letter to his brother (Boucher 149), and his experiences in Rio de Janeiro, the Cape of Good Hope, and Pondicherry confirm his own worldliness and ironic use of (post)colonial paradigms (Lionnet, "'New World' Exiles"). But if his role in the evolution of the French Romantic tradition is generally acknowledged, it is seldom studied critically, and his influence on Baudelaire remains obscure. This lacuna provides me with an opportunity to encourage undergraduates to develop original research projects and to think about the role of literature as an important source of muted local knowledge.

Parny provides rare and ironic insights into colonial melancholia. To trace his legacy, I assign his short elegy "À la nuit" 'To the Night' along with Baudelaire's "Crépuscule du soir" (*Fleurs* [Pichois] 1: 311) 'Twilight' (*Parisian Prowler* 51). Parny's "Ô nuit, favorable aux chagrins!" (Boucher 60) 'O night that promotes sadness' announces the overall atmosphere of Baudelaire's "Recueillement" (*Fleurs* [Pichois] 1: 140–41), 'Meditation' (*Flowers* [McGowan] 346–47) as well as the verse "Ô soir, aimable soir" 'O evening, friendly evening' in the versed "Le Crépuscule du soir" (Pichois 94) 'Evening Twilight' (*Flowers* [Waldrop] 125) and his "Ô nuit, ô rafraîchissantes ténèbres" (Pichois 312) 'O night! O refreshing darkness!' (*Parisian Prowler* 51). Baudelaire's "Les Projets" ("Plans"), on the other hand, with its tropical imagery and search for a "seashore" where he might find "intimacy" and "dwell to cultivate the dream of [his] life" (55) evokes Parny's "Projet de solitude" ("Plan for Solitude") and his desire for "une île ignorée / Interdite aux vaisseaux, et d'écueils entourée" 'a neglected isle / whose surrounding reefs keep away all ships,' and where smells and sounds create the ideal but now lost conditions for love, happiness, and "paisibles journées" 'tranquil days' (Boucher 58).

We discuss the descriptive precision of Baudelaire's prose: "le chant plaintif des arbres à musique, des mélancoliques filaos" 'the doleful songs of musical trees, of melancholy filaos,' as Edward Kaplan translates it (*Spleen* [Pichois] 315; *Parisian Prowler* 56). I point out that the melancholy "filaos" also feature as the title of a twentieth-century novel *Les Arbres musiciens* ("Musician Trees"), by Alexis. It takes a great deal of familiarity with the francophone tropics (and their literatures) to know that "filaos" are referred to as "musician trees." This connection gives the class an opportunity to discuss problems of cultural as well as linguistic translation. I ask students to compare Kaplan's English translation with the *kreol morisien* ("Mauritian Creole") rendering of the prose poem by Emmanuel Richon and Vimala Rungasamy.

The French version of the poem, "Les Projets," reads as follows: "et la nuit, pour servir d'accompagnement à mes songes, le chant plaintif des arbres à musique, des mélancoliques filaos!" (*Spleen* [Pichois] 315). Kaplan's translation reads "[a]nd, at night, lending accompaniment to my dreams, the doleful song of musical trees, *of* melancholy filaos" (*Parisian Prowler* 56; my emphasis). His use of the second "of" creates disjuncture, whereas the use of the definite article "the" would have been more appropriate both grammatically and poetically. The Creole translation is "[a]swar, avek zot fason plenye la, bann filao pu santé et pu akonpany mwa dan mo ban rev!" (*Poèmes mascarins* 169), which can be rendered literally as "at night, true to their plaintive ways, the filaos would sing and keep me company in my dreams." The tone is more matter of fact than melancholic here, and this version highlights the variety of possible affective responses that an original can produce for differently situated readers and translators.

Richon and Rungasamy's translation provides a way to discuss the response of readers in the Mascarene Islands to Baudelaire's representations of their world. Though transformed into imaginary sites of modernity, the islands of Mauritius and Réunion have left concrete traces in the prose poems. Creole translations make these traces even more "real": like other unexpected ways of "conferring meaning on the original," this Creole version can serve as "a bold interpretive gesture that captures readers' attention and provokes a reaction," as Jonathan Culler has argued about translation in general ("Teaching Baudelaire" 97). The pedagogical challenge is that my students typically do not know Mauritian Creole, and I have to retranslate the *kreol* into French or English to emphasize the intentional slippages that occur in that vernacular, but this exercise is well worth the small effort.[3] The following culinary lines from "Beautiful Dorothy" give rise to a discussion of both Creole cooking and individual agency:

> Et que la marmite de fer, où cuit un ragoût de crabes au riz et au safran, lui envoie, du fond de la cour, ses parfums excitants?
>
> (*Œuvres complètes* [Pichois] 1: 317)

> and her iron pot, simmering a crab stew with rice and saffron, from the back courtyard, sends her its arousing aromas.   (*Parisian Prowler* 59)

> E li abitye kui dan so marmit enn buyon krab ki ena byin safran ek duri, e ziska lwin dan lakur laba u ti pu kapav gany sa bon loder la!
>
> (*Poèmes mascarins* 175)

In the French original as in the English translation, the food appears to be cooking itself ("lui envoie . . . ses parfums excitants" 'sends her its arousing aromas') while Dorothy preens in front of her mirror. In the *kreol* rendering, however ("e li abitye kui dan so marmit enn buyon krab" 'and she usually cooks crab soup in her pot'), it is Dorothy's activity of cooking that is foregrounded, along with its impact on the visitor's (and writer's) sense of smell ("u ti pu kapav gany sa bon loder la!" 'you would be able to smell . . . the wonderful aroma'). The addressee "u" 'you' thus becomes the actual beneficiary of the woman's labor. This translation reveals an interpretive leap that makes visible the active contribution of the woman as producer, not just of food but also of material suitable for poetic appropriation. Following these translators' lead, I argue that Baudelaire's travels and his encounter with the labor of others played a major role in the evolution of the genre of the prose poem. The students become better able to understand his debt to a Mascarene culture that, far from being imagined, is alive and well today.

I assign a short excerpt from Alexis's novel to give the class a sense of the Haitian writer's poetic prose: "Les filaos étaient là, hautes cascades de filaments vert bleuté sous la lumière du jour. Les arbres fredonnaient à chaque souffle de l'air leur complainte languide, mélodieuse, rêveuse et diaprée" 'The filaos were there, tall cascades of bluish green filaments in the daylight. With every breeze, the trees would hum their languid, melodious, dreamy, and iridescent lament' (336). This tree imagery is an occasion to discuss the *"beau . . . toujours bizarre"* or the seeming exoticism of Baudelaire's representational practice (*Œuvres complètes* 2: 578). Since "filaos" and palm trees belong to the realm of the exotic for the European reader of his time, I take this opportunity to talk about the fact that exoticism is in the eye of the beholder and that Baudelaire's description of the natural world he had encountered belongs instead in the category of magic realism. As a case in point, I use the first two pages of Glissant's *La Lézarde*. There, terms such as "rêves épars" 'scattered or sprawling dreams,' "boue" 'mud,' "azur" 'azure,' "dais" 'canopy,' and "pourpre du flamboyant" 'the crimson of the flame tree' easily evoke the "fantômes épars" 'sprawling phantom' of Baudelaire's "À une Malabaraise" ("To a Malabar Woman") or the "dais d'arbres tout empourprés" 'the canopy of crimson trees' of his "À une dame créole" ("To a Creole Lady") (*Fleurs* [Pichois] 173, 162).

A broader discussion of what European realism actually owes the representation of so-called exotic locales can be generated at this point, especially with advanced students who have good notions of literary periodization. They are eager to engage in a productive discussion about the aesthetics and the politics of descriptive categories, the literary movements to which these correspond and into which authors like Baudelaire are assigned.[4]

Baudelaire's life experiences and his discovery of the colonial regime of power and of the lush natural landscapes of the tropics provided a shock to his youthful sensibility. But the poem represented them in terms of both extant exoticist rhetoric and realistic descriptive details true to the landscapes that fascinated him, as they had Bernardin de Saint-Pierre and Parny before him. To bring in these environmental, cultural, and textual contexts is to give students a better appreciation of how Baudelaire's writings provide a way to engage with what we can now think of as a world or transnational literary history that puts French texts in close dialogue with francophone ones from different historical periods, from those by the Réunion poet Parny who inaugurated the genre in the Indian Ocean to those by the Mauritian Devi.

NOTES

[1] Translations are mine unless otherwise specified.

[2] For an important historical clarification about the identity of the real Dorothy, see Alexander Ockenden. His research in the *Archives départementales de la Réunion* demonstrate that Dorothée Dormeuil was a Creole slave who had been released from slavery in 1838 by her owner Auguste Lacaussade. I prefer not to translate "Cafrines" by "Kaffir women" as Kaplan does in *Parisian Prowler* (59), since the word is a local Creole term widely used, then as now, to refer to dark-skinned Creole women in Réunion. Derived etymologically from the Arabic كافر (*kāfir*; or "infidel"), Kaffir was used in English in Southern Africa to refer to Blacks. "Cafrine" is a Creole adaptation of that term, with none of the original Arabic meanings nor the derogatory connotations of the English.

[3] On the two occasions that I have had undergraduate Mauritian students in my classroom, I have invited them translate the *kreol* back into French or English for the class. Their role as native speakers and peer experts enriched the discussion on matters of context and interpretation.

[4] Students from Southern California immediately understand the positional nature of such -isms, since they are familiar with the reality of palm trees and tropical flowering trees, which do not qualify as exotic in this region.

"L'Invitation au voyage": A Multiliteracies Approach to Teaching Genre in an Advanced Writing Course

Heather Willis Allen and Kate Paesani

As has long been recognized, undergraduate students entering advanced-level foreign language courses in institutions of higher education in the United States do not always possess advanced-level language abilities. To overcome this problem, many scholars have underscored the importance of attending to linguistic development in conjunction with the teaching of literary-cultural content (Allen; Byrnes, Maxim, and Norris; Donato and Brooks; Ortega and Byrnes; Paesani; Polio and Zyzik). Yet integrating these foci is a complex undertaking: typically, the study of language forms is relegated to advanced courses focused on language (e.g., phonetics, composition, grammar) and the study of content to advanced courses focused on literature and culture. This language-content divide present in many collegiate language programs poses a number of pedagogical challenges (MLA Ad Hoc Committee). We address two here: understanding how we can encourage students to see connections between the study of language and literary-cultural content, and determining what texts and pedagogical approaches might facilitate these connections. We argue that the multiliteracies framework is an appropriate pedagogical approach and that Baudelaire's prose and verse poetry are appropriate texts to create connections between language and content while developing students' linguistic competencies in an advanced French writing course.

Writing Development in the Advanced Undergraduate Foreign Language Curriculum

A perusal of French course listings at universities in the United States reveals that advanced writing is often treated alongside other language-focused subjects such as grammar or conversation. Moreover, the tables of contents for textbooks typically used in such courses are focused more on the development of discrete-point knowledge of language than on connections between language and literary-cultural content or on students' interactions with foreign languages texts (e.g., Gerrard, Rusterholz, and Long; Loriot-Raymer, Vialet, and Muyskens). Yet as Elizabeth Bernhardt points out, a relatively small percentage of what learners need to understand foreign language texts is language oriented. Indeed, grammar and vocabulary make up only thirty percent of this knowledge; other sources are first-language literacy (twenty percent) and unexplained variance (fifty percent) such as background knowledge, motivation, or strategy use (140). When advanced writing textbooks do focus on connections between language and content through texts, literature plays little if any role (e.g., Oukada, Bertrand, and Solberg). One exception, *Tâches d'encre* (Siskin, Krueger, and Fauvel), presents literary texts in five of seven chapters as a basis for the study of language forms and stylistic devices that prepare students for writing in various genres.

Despite this exception, advanced French writing courses are typically not centered on literary texts and, moreover, do not always provide students the opportunity to engage in creative writing tasks. According to Richard Kern (referencing Linda Flower), this minimal focus on literature and creative writing means that

> American students are trained primarily to recall and reproduce factual content, leading to a brand of literacy that emphasizes the consumption of information . . . [they] perform most adequately at straightforward informative writing tasks (factual reports, descriptions) and least adequately at persuasive and imaginative writing tasks.   (*Literacy* 33)

As a result, the development of students' advanced foreign language competencies may be hindered because we do not expose them to a broad scope of writing tasks, nor do we make explicit that what they read may serve as a model for what they write. This dynamic makes it challenging for students in advanced-level courses to respond to the cultural and linguistic content of literature in a variety of ways (e.g., summarizing, analyzing, arguing) in the foreign language.

To address this problem, we describe here an advanced French writing course that has students create literature rather than write about it. Reading literature is therefore a gateway to authoring that allows students to develop advanced foreign language competencies (Kern, *Literacy*). In this course reading and writing are thus viewed as complementary rather than separate modalities, and students learn that "what you read and the ways you read it influence the ways you write and the resources you possess" (Allen 372). Baudelaire's poems offer fertile ground for developing students' ability to be readers and authors of literature. Furthermore, the multiliteracies approach provides a framework for designing instructional activities that develop these abilities and highlight connections between language and literary-cultural content. In the remainder of this essay, we outline the multiliteracies approach and then demonstrate it through a pedagogical sequence treating three versions of Baudelaire's "L'Invitation au voyage": the prose poem from *Le Spleen de Paris*, the verse poem from *Les Fleurs du Mal*, and the animated poem by David Gautier.

Teaching Genre Using a Multiliteracies Approach

Recent research has advocated situating texts as the focal point of instruction across the foreign language curriculum; in particular, the construct of literacy has been proposed as an organizing principle for this kind of curricular reform (e.g., Byrnes, Maxim, and Norris; Kern and Schultz; Swaffar and Arens) and the multiliteracies approach as a pedagogical framework for teaching texts in foreign language classrooms (e.g., Allen; Allen and Paesani; Kern, *Literacy*). Within this scholarship, literacy is conceived of more broadly than reading and writing, which are often considered separate skills to be mastered. Instead, literacy entails

> the use of socially-, historically-, and culturally-situated practices of creating and interpreting meaning through texts. It entails at least a tacit awareness of the relationships between textual conventions and their contexts of use, and ideally, the ability to reflect critically on these relationships. Because it is purpose-sensitive, literacy is dynamic—not static—and variable across and within discourse communities and cultures. It draws on a wide range of cognitive abilities, on knowledge of written and spoken language, on knowledge of genres, and on cultural knowledge.
>
> (Kern, *Literacy* 16)

In addition to its focus on texts, key to this definition are its sociocultural, linguistic, and cognitive dimensions. Instead of seeing meaning as fixed, it is dependent on sociocultural contexts relative to specific communities, beliefs, or practices. Moreover, because of its focus on the interrelation of words, phrases, discourse, and the world, language is conceived of broadly rather than simply as sets of vocabulary words and structures. Finally, literacy and related acts of textual interpretation (reading) and creation (writing) involve cognitive processes such as critical thinking and analysis. As such, in addition to using language to express personal experiences and opinions, learners make form-meaning connections to build personal readings and writings of texts (Kern, *Literacy*).

By positing literacy development as an overarching goal of foreign language curriculum and instruction, we open the door to a different view of genre that moves beyond traditional types of literary production (e.g., prose, poetry, drama) to include a range of oral and written discourse forms. Janet Swaffar and Katherine Arens define genre as "an oral or written rhetorical practice that structures culturally embedded communicative situations in a highly predictable pattern, thereby creating horizons of expectations for its community of users" (99). Indeed, although genres are socioculturally variable, they are nonetheless characterized by certain norms of language use, style, and conventions that allow readers to "make connections between particular instances of discourse and others we have experienced previously" (Kern, *Literacy* 87). As learners interpret foreign language texts, they analyze rhetorical moves of a genre and gradually become aware of the norms and conventions that characterize it. This writing apprenticeship in turn helps learners understand the essential features of a genre and apply them in creative writing activities (Allen; Kern, *Literacy*; Hall).

Also related is intertextuality, which, in "draw[ing] attention to the potentially complex ways in which meanings (such as linguistic meaning) are constituted through relationships to other texts (real or imaginary)" (New London Group 82), underscores the links between texts and how textual resources have been repurposed to fit a new sociocultural context (Barthes; Kristeva). This conception of intertextuality makes clear connections between foreign language reading and writing that can contribute to improved student writing. Moreover, these connections provide "[p]erhaps the most advantageous route for learners to position themselves in the complex literate world of the language they are engaged in learning: learning to speak, read, understand, and write it a high levels of ability in order to convey content and knowledge that is meaningful to themselves and to others" (Byrnes, Maxim, and Norris 40).

The concepts of literacy, genre, and intertextuality can be translated into classroom practice through the multiliteracies framework (Cope and Kalantzis; Kern, *Literacy*; New London Group), a pedagogy that facilitates students' critical engagement with the linguistic, literary, and cultural content of foreign language texts and encourages "a discovery approach to genres in which students first become aware of the importance of genres in communication, and then are taught how to identify the characteristic features of genres by themselves" (Kern, *Literacy* 199). An important aspect of teaching genre within this framework is exposing students to multiple texts and identifying similarities and differences across them. This intertextual approach gives learners a multifaceted view of genre and of how common themes and linguistic conventions are expressed.

Key to multiliteracies pedagogy is the act of meaning design, which involves creating form-meaning connections through the related acts of textual interpretation (reading) and transformation (writing). Engaging in meaning design entails attending to the various Available Designs of a text, which include linguistic (writing system, vocabulary, syntax, coherence, cohesion) and schematic (organizational patterns, genre, style, background knowledge) resources for meaning making (Kern, *Literacy* 67). Because the process of meaning design draws on knowledge about language, conventions, genre, and culture to interpret, analyze, and reflect on the content of texts, form and meaning are viewed no longer as separate from one another but as closely intertwined. Textual interpretation is the act of moving beyond comprehension of surface-level facts to synthesize, explain, or analyze messages in a text and to reveal cultural perspectives and points of view. Textual transformation involves shaping and reworking meaning gleaned through interpretive activities to establish new connections among existing Available Designs. According to Kern, "this means creating new texts on the basis of existing ones, or reshaping texts to make them appropriate for contexts of communication other than those for which they were originally intended" (133–34).

In the context of an advanced French writing course, certain Available Designs necessary for textual interpretation and transformation, particularly those related to recalling and reproducing factual information through description or narration, may be more obvious to students given that they have been interacting with these resources throughout their foreign language studies. Less transparent may be the Available Designs necessary for interpreting and creating literature. One strategy for making these more overt is to have students engage in creative writing activities. In addition to expanding their language competencies, this kind of writing makes "it possible to create imagined worlds of their own design. Symbolic play, and the recombining of elements in fresh, inventive ways can be highly motivating and can help to prepare language students to read poetry and other forms of literary expression with greater sensitivity" (172).

Four pedagogical acts, or learning activities, serve to organize multiliteracies-based instruction and facilitate engagement in textual interpretation and transformation. *Situated practice* activities such as previewing a text or writing summary sentences focus on the act of experiencing; they provide learners the opportunity to immerse themselves in spontaneous use of appropriate Available Designs without explicit reflection. Learners build on Available Designs in *overt instruction* activities such as identifying stylistic or linguistic features in a text. Overt instruction entails the act of conceptualizing and encourages learners to analyze form-meaning connections found in texts. The resources identified in overt instruction can then be used to interpret or transform meaning in subsequent activities. *Critical framing*, or analysis, directs learners' attention to the relation of language use and meaning in various sociocultural contexts. Examples include instructional conversations related to an author or genre comparisons. Finally, *transformed practice* activities such as creative writing focus on the act of applying; they engage learners in meaning design through creation of texts appropriate for different discourse contexts (Cope and Kalantzis; Kern, *Literacy*; New London Group).

Teaching "L'Invitation au voyage" in the Advanced French Writing Course

In keeping with the aims of the multiliteracies approach, the advanced French writing course described here was designed to emphasize the complementarity of reading and writing as acts of meaning design. The course's primary objectives include sensitizing students to the relation of form and content, or why and how certain linguistic devices are used in particular textual genres; providing students with experience in creative writing in French for communicative purposes; and furthering students' abilities to speak in French at advanced levels.

The course is organized into four modules, each focused on a different author and textual genre. These include descriptive tales from Philippe Delerm's *La Première Gorgée de bière et autres plaisirs minuscules*, ethnotexts from Annie Ernaux's *Journal du dehors*, prose and verse versions of Baudelaire's "L'Invitation au voyage," and short stories from Anna Gavalda's *Je voudrais que quelqu'un m'attende quelque part*.[1] A previous version of the course used several excerpts from Raymond Queneau's *Exercices de style* to frame the third module, but, because of students' stated interest in poetry, *Exercices de style* was replaced with the Baudelaire texts. By so doing, the course incorporates a more varied selection of textual genres including the prose poem, a genre that is most likely unfamiliar to students and that can facilitate new understandings of what defines both prose and poetry.

For each module, after reading, analyzing, and discussing the thematic and stylistic content of several texts, students use the linguistic and schematic Available Designs of those texts as the starting point for creating written work. Over a period of several class sessions, these texts are drafted, discussed in peer review and individual conferences with the instructor, and compiled in a digital portfolio. Thus, a familiar progression from reading-focused to writing-focused activities occurs in each module, whereas the textual genres increase in complexity during the semester. We detail next the course module for "L'Invitation au voyage"; all instructional activities are conducted in French.

Stage 1: Situating the Author and "L'Invitation au voyage"

The instructional sequence begins with critical framing to sensitize students to contextual information related to Baudelaire's *Le Spleen de Paris* and *Les Fleurs du Mal*. Students are divided into three groups. Each group reads about and presents one element of the context of the texts. These elements are represented in a cultural reading (focused on elements of mid-nineteenth-century French life that informed the central themes of the two collections), a historical reading (a summary of political upheavals at the time "L'Invitation au voyage" was written and their influence on Parisian life), and a biographical reading (a chronological snapshot of Baudelaire's life and literary production) of one to two pages each. As they read at home, students complete a text matrix to map the reading's main themes to specific phrases wherein each theme is reflected (Swaffar and Arens 87). The instructor provides some of these themes in the matrix (e.g., political upheaval, literary influences, family life, *la bourgeoisie*); yet, as students read, they may list additional themes and accompanying textual support found in their assigned text.

Next, students participate in a brief in-class oral comparison of the content of their matrix with that of other students who have read the same text. Whereas identification of appropriate citations related to themes provided by the instructor tends to be a simple matter, arriving at consensus on the textual themes students identified entails problem solving and collaboration. Each group of students, aided by their completed text matrix, then presents a summary of their reading to the other two groups, who write down major themes using a simplified version of the text matrix.

The final step in the activity involves a teacher-led instructional conversation, a technique aimed not only at conveying content but also at promoting students' communicative development through strategies such as questioning, modeling, feeding back, and explaining (Hall). The intent of this interactive discussion is to highlight connections among the cultural, historical, and biographical elements students presented and how those linkages relate specifically to the prose and verse versions of "L'Invitation au voyage."

Following this critical framing, the focus of the first class of the module shifts to situated practice and predicting the content of the first text students will read. This is accomplished by introducing a visual image, Henri Matisse's "Luxe, calme et volupté," inspired by a line from the verse version of "L'Invitation au voyage." Students are asked to silently reflect on the relation of what they see in the painting and its title, taking notes on their ideas before sharing them with peers and the instructor. Once students have shared their interpretations, they are asked to share their expectations of the content of the poem, given what they now know about the writer's biography, the historical and cultural context of his writing, and the images depicted in Matisse's painting.

The first class concludes by modeling a situated practice activity that students complete at home to prepare for discussing the thematic content of the prose version of "L'Invitation au voyage." Together, the instructor and students read and create a one-sentence summary of the text's first paragraph and then brainstorm useful expressions for beginning other summary phrases (e.g., "Dans ce paragraphe, il s'agit de . . . , Ensuite, on voit . . ." 'This paragraph is about . . . , Next, we see . . .'). As homework, students summarize each of the remaining eleven paragraphs of the text in one phrase and identify the "mots clés" 'keywords' for each to help them understand the main ideas and themes of the poem.

The critical framing and situated practice activities completed as part of the first class are designed to provide students with new schematic Available Designs (e.g., background knowledge) relevant to the poems they will be reading and with strategies for mapping their initial understandings of the prose text through a summarizing activity. Intertextuality plays a key role in these activities as students familiarize themselves with resources that may be meaningfully repurposed and thus connected to the poems they read. Furthermore, constant overlapping of reading or viewing texts, responding to texts through informal in-class writing, and sharing textual interpretations orally contribute to developing students' advanced language competencies.

Stage 2: Analyzing the Thematic Content of Two Versions of "L'Invitation au voyage"

The second class of the module begins with situated practice that builds on the reading summaries students completed at home. First, students work in pairs to further condense their summaries into five parts (paragraphs 1–2, 3–5, 6–7, 8–9, and 10–11) and identify key words in each; the instructor and students construct a summary sentence and select key words for the first part together, to model the activity. The purpose is to work from the poem's micropropositions to its macropropositions—that is, from its details to its main ideas (Swaffar and Arens 87). As follow-up, the teacher leads an instructional conversation to determine, in collaboration with students, the text's main themes and how those themes are developed from the text's start to its end.

After the thematic contours of the prose poem have been established, a second situated practice activity serves to preview the content of the verse version of "L'Invitation au voyage," which students will later read and compare with the prose version. Students examine an animated version of the verse poem (D. Gautier): a three-minute video in which the text is read aloud and accompanied by a series of color illustrations. As they first watch the video without sound, students predict the content of the verse poem and reflect on how this differs from the prose version. Once they have discussed their ideas with the instructor, they watch the video a second time with sound and share how their initial hypotheses regarding the text's content differed from the audio text. Finally, in preparation for comparing the two versions of "L'Invitation au voyage" during the next class, students are instructed to read the verse poem at home, write a one-phrase summary for each stanza of the text, and note key words in each, just as they had done for the prose poem.

The first half of the third class of the module focuses on similarities and differences between the content of the verse and prose versions of "L'Invitation au voyage." First, in a situated practice activity, students use their completed text summaries to facilitate a detailed comparison of primary themes of the prose poem, the verse poem, and themes shared by both texts using a Venn diagram. The instructor provides a possible starting point for students' reflections by suggesting a focus on the poet's aim in each text, the person who is being addressed, and in what terms. Reading, writing, and speaking overlap as students first work independently before sharing their interpretations with the class. The instructor then fills in a master Venn diagram with students' ideas. This situated practice activity moves students away from discussion of generalities related to the texts toward a more critical comparison of the two. This comparison is further developed in a follow-up critical framing activity in which students focus on the image of the woman and of the exotic country represented in both poems (Harrington 111) and made explicit in the lines "Au pays qui te ressemble" in the verse poem (*Fleurs* [Pichois] 53) and "Il est une contrée qui te ressemble" in the prose poem ("A land exists resembling you"; *Spleen* [Pichois] 302; *Parisian Prowler* 37]).

Students are thus led to consider final questions of interpretation such as which content in the two texts represents the place, the woman, or both and what is the relationship between the woman and the place in these texts.

Stage 3: Focusing on Form-Meaning Connections in "L'Invitation au voyage"

The transition from discussing thematic content in the verse and prose versions of "L'Invitation au voyage" to identifying key linguistic and schematic Available Designs and how they express meaning occurs during the second half of the third class period. The goal of the following overt instruction activities is for students to analyze how meaning is made within the texts under study and to become aware of new Available Designs for later use in creating their own prose poem.

To draw students' attention to certain Available Designs in the poems, the instructor gives a list of specific types of linguistic and stylistic features to focus on (e.g., pronoun choice, verb forms, repetition, metaphor, interrogative forms). Students are asked to find examples of each feature in both texts and relate them to themes of the place, the woman, or both. In addition, students must identify one other notable linguistic and stylistic feature in both texts and examples of each. After completing this activity alone, they compare their findings in small groups and then with the whole class to verify that all instances of targeted linguistic and stylistic devices have been found and understood. Once the list of textual features has been compiled, students consider the question of how specific linguistic or stylistic choices made by the poet affect meaning, particularly regarding how meaning shifts from one version of the poem to the other.

The second element of overt instruction turns attention to the preface of *Le Spleen de Paris*, in which Baudelaire wrote of aspiring to "une prose poétique, musicale sans rythme et sans rime, assez souple et assez heurtée pour s'adapter aux mouvements lyriques de l'âme, aux ondulations de la rêverie, aux soubresauts de la conscience" 'a poetic prose, musical without rhythm and without rhyme, supple enough and choppy enough to fit the soul's lyric movements, the undulations of reverie, the jolts of consciousness' (275–76; 129). Based on this description of the poet's aim, students find instances in the prose poem that correspond to being "musicale sans rythme et sans rime" 'musical without rhythm and without rhyme' and simultaneously "souple" 'supple' and "heurtée," 'choppy' first individually and then with the whole class. Students then use these examples to decide if they agree or disagree with the poet's claim of his failure to meet his aims ("je restais bien loin de mon mystérieux et brillant modèle" 'I remain quite far from my mysterious and brilliant model' [276; 130]), justifying their opinion with references to the text.

At the close of the third class, the instructor prepares students to complete an at-home critical framing activity. Students must compile a list of ten essentials for writing a Baudelairean prose poem based on their personal understandings of "L'Invitation au voyage." In so doing, students synthesize the meanings they have ascribed to the text and narrow down those linguistic and schematic Available Designs that they deem most consistent with the poem. To begin the fourth class period, the instructor synthesizes these ideas, particularly ones common across several students, as the final activity leading to writing their own prose poem. This cycle of textual analysis, interpretation, and collaborative discussion sensitizes students to how meaning emerges through key Available Designs in both genres. Furthermore, given that the prose poem is a genre whose conventions are typically unknown to undergraduate students in the United States, these activities seek to make its associated Available Designs as transparent as possible to provide a smooth transition from reading-focused to writing-focused activities.

Stage 4: Moving from Interpretation to Creating a New Text

As a first step in creating their own prose poem, students complete a situated practice activity during the fourth class to map initial ideas using a graphic organizer. The focus is on generating content-related ideas about their version of "L'Invitation au voyage": the narrator and his or her aims, the place to which one travels, the person invited to this place, and key descriptive words associated with each. Because this is a creative writing assignment, students may opt to narrate the poem from their own viewpoint or someone else's and, likewise, may employ a register of French different from that in Baudelaire's poem, so long as it is consistent with the narrator's identity. After they have completed initial written brainstorming independently, students collaborate with a partner, using the graphic organizer to explain the main ideas of their poem. In turn, their partner poses questions, asks for clarifications, and makes suggestions related to these ideas. After collaborating on the content of the poem, students then discuss its form—that is, how they plan to tell the story of their poem using Available Designs to shape the text's meaning. They are advised to refer to both their list of ten essentials for writing a Baudelairean prose poem and their completed text matrix as tools to help them plan their poem's content.

At the close of the fourth class, students are ready to engage in the transformed practice activity of writing their own version of "L'Invitation au voyage." The instructor provides them with detailed instructions for the assignment and criteria for assessment, and they are asked to prepare an initial draft of the text for the fifth class. The rest of the module entails participation in peer review and individual writing conferences with the instructor to facilitate editing and revision of their poem over several class sessions. A *table ronde* completes the module, wherein each student makes an informal presentation of his or her text by briefly summarizing its focus and reading it aloud. Class members are invited to ask questions and make comments on their peers' texts.

This final stage of the instructional sequence culminates in students' "creat[ing] imagined worlds of their own design" through writing prose poems (Kern, *Literacy* 172). Yet this creative venture is also constrained in the sense that students are required to respect the conventions of the textual genre, which they now better understand given the previous stage's attention to form-meaning connections in "L'Invitation au voyage." The connection between reading and writing is further reinforced as students become readers and interpreters of their peers' writing and collaborate in refining one another's texts.

The four-stage model we have elaborated for teaching the prose and verse versions of the poem "L'Invitation au voyage" takes students beyond writing about literature to creating literature, based in large part on the knowledge they glean from textual analysis and interpretation. Although the instructional sequence described herein pertains to specific literary content and instructional goals, the pedagogy within the sequence can be tailored to a wide variety of courses or aims, including cultural studies courses, advanced language courses, or literature courses with a primary focus other than creative writing. In all these contexts, the multiliteracies approach provides ample opportunity for exploring the linguistic, stylistic, and cultural content of literary texts and for developing students' advanced-level language competencies.

NOTE

[1] A detailed description of the course's fourth module (Gavalda's short stories) is provided in Allen.

The Rhetoric of Intermediality:
Teaching Baudelaire's "L'Invitation au voyage" in a Translation Class

Larson Powell

The challenges of teaching Baudelaire's prose poems in creative writing courses are often quite different from those encountered in literature courses focused on reading and interpretation without creative production. Few creative writing students have much exposure to foreign languages, and their most important goal is to be published in journals, meaning that their knowledge is focused on current North American taste. Even the history of English poetry is often not familiar to students whose judgment often remains intuitive and subjective rather than linked to any craft traditions. This unfamiliarity is especially marked in relation to forms (such as the sonnet) or metrical patterns. Many creative writing students now seem to think poetry consists only of metaphor and not of the shape of lines; few have ever tried to work with strict forms. Teaching them to listen to poetry, to pay attention to sound and rhythm, to the ear and not only the eye, is thus an important part of the course. Close reading of poetry in a foreign language may also alert students to the possibility of greater syntactic freedom than our current Anglo-American domination of colloquial naturalness tends to allow.

I recently team-taught Baudelaire as part of a new course titled The Practice of Translation, together with a poet from the English department; it was cross-listed with my home department of foreign languages and literatures. Many of our students were creative writing students, but some were foreign language and linguistics students; some were undergraduate and some graduate, including local high school teachers. Our mixed student body necessitated a flexible methodology. Most of our students had had no more than a year or two of a foreign language, meaning that few had ever read a poem in a language other than English. Approaches to texts began with a literal paraphrase that we then turned into a poem through assignments analyzed in workshop discussions. The practice of translating poetry was accompanied by readings on the theory of translation, the purpose of which was to encourage student reflection on the translator's practice, and especially to get them beyond the idea of language as merely a neutral medium. One of the most important but also most difficult texts on translation theory was Walter Benjamin's "The Task of the Translator," originally intended as a preface to Benjamin's own translations of Baudelaire. Having students first compare the relative merits of extant translations made the point that their work as a translator did not take place in a historical void but must define itself relative to previous efforts. This criticism of other translations also helped bring out working rules of practice and freed the students from merely private judgments ("I really liked this line") that might otherwise dominate discussion.

Baudelaire was a central figure in the course (others included Rainer Maria Rilke, Eugenio Montale, César Vallejo, and Zbigniew Herbert—the last two of whom also wrote prose poems). Typically we began discussion by introducing historical and contextual background for a poet, including specific aspects of the particular poetic and linguistic tradition (e.g., the alexandrine in French). We then moved on to close reading of the original—including reading it out loud—and comparative discussion of students' prepared translations. I have also argued for Baudelaire's centrality to the class through his prose and verse versions of poems.

The prose versions of verse poems present students with an additional problem: how do we understand a work whose independence seems diminished by its coexistence with a poetic model? What was Baudelaire's purpose in producing prose versions of his own poems? Was he proposing a possible model of their translation—into other languages or other media? Could adaptation theory help us here? The two versions of "L'Invitation au voyage" serve as a pedagogical test case for this problem.

Verse poetry is, for many of these students, less unfamiliar than prose poetry. I begin by asking them how we define the prose poem as a genre. Does it fit traditional generic definitions? Why or why not? How might prose poetry inherently open up poetry to other media? In a previous class, we have already discussed the verse poem "Correspondances," and I introduced the idea that Baudelaire's overall work, with its references to painting and music, is a development of the Romantic idea of a "progressive universal poetry" (Schlegel 182) that absorbs other arts within it. How does "L'Invitation au voyage" suggest effects from other arts and media? Is it harder for us now to visualize Baudelaire's poem in an age of film and TV (as Friedrich Kittler has argued)? One topics has been that "the route through translation" helps us "raise questions about the formal features of the poem" (Culler, "Teaching Baudelaire" 92). The prose "L'Invitation" further extends this opening up of form, since "the process of revision and transformation is constantly thematized" in it (Johnson, "Poetry" 54). Now, in another interpretative step, the class moves from translation between languages to that between different media, whether from poem to prose or from literature to the other arts. Another central aspect of Baudelaire's poetics now emerges: that one aspect of his bid for a modern autonomy of art—freed from morals or utility—was the linkage of the arts with one another. Intermedial borrowings have often been a paradoxical vehicle for heightening artistic autonomy, whether in late-nineteenth-century notions of music as "queen of the arts"[1] or modern painting's reference to ideas of écriture. Translation's connection to intermediality may also be seen as an aspect of world literature or comparative literature. Thus Erin Schlumpf has argued that "intermediality" should "apply to the translation and negotiation between works in different languages from and to different cultures" and asked if "comparative work" is "necessarily intermedial" (2).

Having opened up a number of large and ambitious questions about the text, we move to historical specification. Just as late-twentieth-century critics of Baudelaire corrected the old tendency to swallow up the doctrine of "Correspondances" into a broad Romantic genealogy, stressing instead its modernist discontinuities (de Man, *Rhetoric*), so we should now beware of swallowing up

Baudelaire's intermedial poetic into the soup of a premature Wagnerian *Gesamt-kunstwerk* aesthetic. I might point out to students that Baudelaire was also defining his poetic in rivalry with other media, such as photography and journalism, and not only through absorbing them. Intermediality can thus be an agonic and not only a harmonic relation, contrasting aspects that we may correlate to Baudelaire's combination of "surnaturalisme et ironie," or ideal and spleen (Broome 178). Here it is important to bring a historical dimension back into the theoretical context that has been set up. We could mention Baudelaire's art criticism and his interest in Wagner, on the one hand (as a way to contextualize the musical and visual aspects of his poetry), and note, on the other, that literature's emergence as an autonomous art since the eighteenth century took place in a context of competition with other media (Schmidt). Students will be familiar with this phenomenon from our current televisual and digital media environment, but it is worth pointing out to them that Baudelaire was one of the first poets to respond self-consciously to it.

So far, however, we have not yet defined what a medium is. The term is notoriously loose and hard to pin down, especially since it can be used either in a material or technical sense — as a channel of communication — or a semiotic one, through a code (Wolf). *Medium* can overlap with *genre* or can refer to different ways of organizing information (Nünning and Nünning 132–33). If we do not include the semiotic dimension of media, we risk a technological determinism that marginalizes the content of literature (as in the work of Kittler). For literature is itself also a medium (Jahraus) and can thus respond to or even anticipate the effects of other media, as so many theorists of modernity have argued.[2]

To see how Baudelaire engages with this question of media, we need now to get closer to the text of the two versions of "L'Invitation." Students notice both its painterly visuality, heightened by the demonstrative pronouns in the verse poem ("Vois sur ces canaux" 'See on these canals'; *Fleurs* [Pichois] 53; *Flowers* [Waldrop] 71) and the wealth of specific detail in the prose poem, and its proximity to music, especially in the verse (Fraser 112). I note that it has been argued that Baudelaire is referring to Dutch landscape painting in the verse poem (Beauverd; Cohn), but here, too, we need to be careful with our terms. What is *intermediality*? What is it that is brought over from one medium or art into another? Baudelaire is not simply pasting a reproduction of a Dutch painting into his poem, in the manner of a collage; as Cheryl Krueger has pointed out, "the prose poems contain no verbal representations of paintings" (*Art* 92). Werner Wolf has suggested how we might distinguish between more recent forms of intermediality (such as graphic poetry or digital literature) and that of the nineteenth century: "In contrast to plurimediality, intermedial reference does not give the impression of a medial hybridity of the signifiers, nor of a heterogeneity of the semiotic systems used; rather, intermedial references represent a medial and semiotic homogeneity and thus qualifies as "'covert' intracompositional intermediality" (5). Jens Schröter proposes a contrast between "synthetic intermediality" that fuses different media (as in Wagner) and "transformational intermediality: a model centered around the representation of one medium through another medium" (2). Baudelaire's practice here can be seen as an instance of the latter: the poet is both representing art and music through poetry and then transforming verse into prose. The translating work of the class thus receives a new dimension and depth for the students, since it has become an extension of Baudelaire's own self-consciously comparativist and transformational practice.

When we read the two versions of "L'Invitation au voyage," we are also acknowledging that Baudelaire's practice was intermedial and that intermediality is a form of his characteristic critical self-consciousness. As Sonya Stephens has put it, in the prose poems, "[t]he sense of questioning poetry is, of course, twofold: the creation of a new genre clearly questions the limits or limitations of poetry; and these are poems that question, not only through their formal experimentation, but in a very real sense of being interrogative" ("Prose Poems" 72). The prose poem transforms the imperative commands of the verse into rhetorical questions: "quel est celui qui composera l'*Invitation au voyage* . . . ?" "Ne serais-tu pas encadrée dans ton analogie . . . ?" "Vivrons-nous . . . ?" 'Who will compose the *Invitation to a Voyage* . . . ?' 'Would you not be framed in your analogy . . . ?' 'Will we ever live . . . ?' (*Spleen* [Pichois] 302–03; *Spleen* [Waldrop] 33–34). Barbara Johnson has argued that the prose "L'Invitation" exposes the codes of poetry on which the verse depended ("Poetry" 37). The rhetorical questions are a good instance of this reflexive aspect of the poem and also of how figures from one medium (verse) are transposed into another (prose). We could extend Johnson's argument to assert that the prose poem, perhaps ironically, exposes the medium of verse, if we conceive medium in the aforementioned semiotic sense. Code and medium are in fact inseparable aspects of literature's self-definition (Luhmann); I remind the class of the historical emergence of literature as autonomous and note that Baudelaire is polemically and reflexively pointing precisely to this autonomy. As many readers of Baudelaire have remarked (e.g., Johnson, "Poetry"; Benjamin, "Task"), the irony or paradox of Baudelaire's poetic, very much in evidence in "L'Invitation," is the simultaneity of poetry's autonomy with its reference to very specific contemporary social realities. Baudelaire's overall poetic project of *Les Fleurs du Mal* points to just this differentiation of literature's code from that of morality. But even the code of poetry, whether we see it as beautiful versus ugly or interesting versus dull, must (parasitically) draw on various other codes, whether culinary, financial, or touristic. The metaphors of the poem depend on metonymies (Johnson, "Poetry" 38–40), and its autonomous self-reference cannot be separated from its reference outside itself. That is, the form of the poem depends on its medium.

When we come to the actual practice of translation, we quickly run into the limits of English as a medium for translating French. In the verse "L'Invitation," it is very difficult to imitate the form in English, a language that lacks the shifting stress patterns of French. Rhyming translations tend to remind us of Edgar Allan Poe or of Lewis Carroll's Jabberwocky, which may be why Robert Lowell, justifying his use of freer verse to imitate Baudelaire, referred to them as "stuffed birds" (xi). Our ears no longer respond to the hypnotic, repetitive rhythms typical of Poe (although we may be familiar with them from popular music). This change in our relation to nineteenth-century poetics, which we feel so palpably in our relation to language, is an instance of the historicity of the medium of language, "a medium that itself is always in the process of changing" (Weber, *Benjamin's-abilities* 67) and thus also changes our relation to Baudelaire. When Wallace Fowlie translated the verse poem's "[d]es meubles luisants" as "[h]ighly polished furniture" (*Selected Poems* 57), is this not already as prosaic as the lists of luxury commodities in the prose "L'Invitation?" Richard Howard's "[f]urniture gleaming" preserves more of Baudelaire's meter while still having something of the concreteness of prose (*Fleurs* [Howard] 58). We end up with the paradox that some of the best student versions of the verse "L'Invitation" were those that allowed prosy moments to disturb regular metrical patterns and avoided the mechanical or sing-song feel of too-regular meter while not lapsing into complete anarchy. Free-verse translations allow for a "necessary freedom of expression and research" (Bonnefoy, qtd. in C. Scott 200)—necessary also in the context of a translation course that is concerned with exploring the boundaries of different linguistic media, as exemplified in a particularly striking student translation:

> We would see drowsy ships
>   in the canals
> and couldn't we say *To see them*
>   *back from every adventure is*
> *to satisfy all desire?*

Here, the student imitation has transposed Baudelaire's imperative—"Vois sur ces canaux" (*Fleurs* [Pichois] 53)—into a rhetorical question, just as the prose "L'Invitation" often does. The striking effect of the prose interpolation derives from its interruption of the rhythm, somewhat as Howard's version does:

> On these still canals
> the freighters doze
> fitfully: their mood is for roving   (*Fleurs* [Howard] 59)

The strength of the student's version is also that it manages, through a prosaic gesture, to capture the force of Baudelaire's assertion: "C'est pour assouvir / Ton moindre désir / Qu'ils viennent du bout du monde" (*Fleurs* [Pichois] 53). The force of the translation is one of surprise, which we can link back to Baudelaire's own poetics of gambling and shock. This element of surprise and novelty, of translational freedom, is a recurring theme of the course, one which we have explored with reference to Benjamin's "The Task of the Translator."

Thus already in working on translation of the verse "L'Invitation," the class has begun to approach the prose version. That approach begins through the question of transposition or translation from poetry to prose. What has Baudelaire brought from one to the other? Since, according to his famous letter to Arsène Houssaye, he wanted "une prose poétique, musicale sans rythme et sans rime" 'a poetic prose, musical without rhythm and without rhyme' (*Œuvres complètes* 1: 276; *Parisian Prowler* [Kaplan] 129), it is not the features specific to verse that could be transposed. Here, too, the paradoxical formulation—"musicale sans rythme et sans rime"—forces us to think in intermedial terms. The old Romantic paradigm of "verbal music" seems no longer adequate, for the same reason that a direct transposition of painting into literature is not either. What structures the prose version is in large measure rhetorical: not only the rhetorical questions but also the use of syntactical inversion, which is greater than in the verse (Fraser), along with the use of parallelism. Rhyme, in the verse, is replaced by anaphora in prose. Thus I suggest that it is the (rhetorical and poetic) figurality, as much as content or theme, that is intermedially transposable. Iris Llorca and Valérie Thévenon have described this transposed figurality as that of the arabesque, with reference to the famous poetological thyrsus from the prose poems, and it is helpful to quote a line or two of "Le Thyrse" ("The Thyrsus") to the class to give them an intuitive sense of how Baudelaire combines structure and freedom, repetition and variation: "Ligne droite et ligne arabesque, intention et expression, roideur de la volonté, sinuosité du verbe, unité du but, variété des moyens, amalgame tout-puissant et indivisible du génie, quel analyste aurait le détestable courage de vous diviser et vous séparer?" 'Straight line and arabesque line, intention and expression, tautness of the will, sinuosity of the word, unity of goal, variety of means, all-powerful and indivisible amalgam of genius, what analyst would have the hateful courage to divide and separate you?' (*Œuvres complètes* 1: 336; *Parisian Prowler* 87). I point out to the class that this prose poem was dedicated to Franz Liszt, hinting at another element of intermedial cross-fertilization. This example shows students that elements often thought of as merely ornamental can have a structuring role in writing.

The prose poems and verse poems offer different obstacles to comprehension. Where the verse "L'Invitation" created difficulties of finding equivalents for meter and assonance, the prose version seems to resist students' sensibilities because of its heavily rhetorical construction. Where the verse "L'Invitation" is swift and elegant, the prose version may seem ponderous, in part because of its reliance on repetition ("to many the sign of a dull mind" [Metzidakis, *Repetition* 1]). Where the verse seems concentrated, the prose poem "is an example of perfect, unmitigated expansion" (Riffaterre 124). I have already pointed to conservative aspects of Baudelaire's poetic: the strictness of versification (relative to Victor Hugo), the influence of Jacques-Bénigne Bossuet and Agrippa d'Aubigné. The oft-noted culinary comparisons can still shock students now as much as they once did Suzanne Bernard; so can the deliberately banal or commonplace elements of the prose "L'Invitation." In some cases, Baudelaire has transposed a poetic element into its prosaic opposite: thus "une vieille amie" 'a familiar confidante' is far from being a correlative to "mon enfant, ma sœur" 'my child, my sister' (Sandras 131; *Parisian Prowler* 37). Students are rarely satisfied with the explanation that these aspects can be seen as an ironic corrective to the code or medium of poetry (Johnson, "Poetry"); surely, in writing the prose version, Baudelaire's point or purpose was more than merely providing us with a chance for deconstructive criticism.

At this point, reference to media theory and intermediality can help clinch the argument for the prose poem's paradoxical autonomy. In an essay on Baudelaire's invention of the prose poem as a historical crisis in nineteenth-century poetics, Roger Shattuck has argued that the third chapter, "De la couleur," of the *Salon de 1846* is "a word tableau which we could call the first impressionist painting" and "a prose poem straining to transform itself into an impressionist painting" (27, 29). Again, we must be careful to keep genres distinct here, for all their Romantic overlapping: as already noted, the prose poems are not simply copying painting as Baudelaire's art criticism may have. Yet Shattuck's point brings us back again to the intermediality at work here. The visual quality of Baudelaire's writing is not merely an ekphrasis and does not reside only in a list of concrete details; rather, it depends on the atmospheric evocation of nearly immaterial media such as "un bel espace de nature," atmosphere, "vibration," the sea, air, color, all conceived of as part of a "universal analogy" including the viewer (27). The reader is exhorted to see these as part of a "single principle that will embrace all the elements of his [sic] experience" (30). Is the prose "L'Invitation," in relying on analogy and imperative, not doing the same thing? The paradox of the prose "L'Invitation" lies in the seemingly material and concrete description of something that does not exist except through analogy and evocation. Its rhetorical devices may be seen as means to evoke this immaterial vision (at times, through the suggestion of other media) and suggest its illusory reality. The challenge for the reader lies in the tension between the banal, everyday particularity of certain details and the unifying primacy of the poetic imagination. It might be pointed out to the students that the line "comme une magnifique batterie de cuisine" 'a magnificent array of kitchen utensils' (*Œuvres complètes* 1: 302; *Parisian Prowler* 38) already anticipates the shock of surrealism. The length of the prose poem and its use of repetition can thus be seen as means to envelop the reader, just as "le merveilleux nous enveloppe et nous abreuve comme l'atmosphère" 'the marvelous envelops and saturates us like the atmosphere'(*Œuvres complètes* 2: 496; *Selected Writings* [Charvet 1972] 107). This intermedial suggestion of the visual can be backed up historically with the association between the prose poem and print making (etching or lithograph) (Beaujour 46). Time permitting, we may also look at illustrations for "L'Invitation" to see how others have visualized the poem.

When we finally come to translating the prose poem, some of the problems will already have been encountered with verse. A central difficulty is one of semantics, and one must watch out for *faux amis* ("false cognates"), or worse, in the prose version. Baudelaire's "pays superbe" (*Spleen* [Pichois] 335) is better rendered by Edward Kaplan's "magnificent land" (*Parisian Prowler* 37) than Martin Sorrell's "superb country" (*Paris Spleen* [Sorrell] 33) or even Louise Varèse's "wonderful country" (*Paris Spleen* [Varèse] 32). So, too, the poise and tone of the original is more finely echoed in Kaplan's "familiar confidante" (for "vieille amie") than in Sorrell's "lady long dear" or Varèse's "old love." "Familiar," of course, has the virtue of resonating with another poem, "Correspondances," with its uncanny "regards familiers" (*Fleurs* [Pichois] 11). I suggest to the class that they might try to get something of the ironic self-mocking tone of a charlatan traveling salesman or circus barker into their translation, to catch some of Baudelaire's awareness of the relation between art and commodity aesthetics.

The central point of the class is to expand the interpretative and pedagogical tools at our disposal for teaching and understanding Baudelaire—a logical move, given diverse backgrounds, levels, and training of the students in our upper-level literature courses. The perspectives of creative writing fiction students differ from those of poetry students. Students who are themselves school teachers may draw useful lessons for their own teaching. Historicizing the concept of intermediality by way of Baudelaire's poetics, and taking interpretative care to locate figures transposed between poetry and prose, keeps the discussion from becoming shapeless.

NOTES

My thanks go to Marcus Myers, for allowing me to quote his translation ("We would see drowsy ships . . . "), and to Professor Michelle Boisseau, my team-teacher from the English department, who brought in a poet's view of Baudelaire.

[1] "All art constantly aspires to the condition of music," in the oft-quoted phrase of Walter Pater (qtd. in Hill 106, 111).

[2] Theodor Adorno saw surrealism as having anticipated the bombs of World War II (102); for Friedrich Kittler, German Romantic literature provided an entire code of inwardness with which to educate the bourgeoisie (*Discourse*), and Friedrich Nietzsche anticipated many of the media effects of the twentieth century.

Translation Studies and the Prose Poems

Peter Connor

The author of *Le Spleen de Paris* is known in France not only as a poet and literary critic but also as the translator of the tales of Edgar Allan Poe. Baudelaire first came across Poe's writings in January 1847, when the Fourierist newspaper *La Démocratie pacifique* ("Peaceful Democracy")[1] published "The Black Cat" in a translation by Isabelle Meunier. His own first translation of a Poe story, "Révélation magnétique" ("Mesmeric Revelation"), appeared in July 1848. But it was not until 1851, when he managed to borrow some volumes of the *Southern Literary Messenger* (of which Poe had been editor from 1834 to 1838) that Baudelaire was able to embark in earnest on the immense translation project that was to occupy him for most of the remainder of his life. The Poe translations, commercially more successful than any of his own literary efforts (Kopp, *Spleen* 259), were collected and published in three volumes by Michel Lévy: *Histoires extraordinaires* ("Extraordinary Tales"), prefaced by Baudelaire's essay "Edgar Poe, sa vie et ses ouvrages" ("Edgar Poe, His Life and His Works"), appeared in 1856; *Nouvelles histoires extraordinaires* ("New Extraordinary Tales"), preceded by his "Notes nouvelles sur Edgar Poe" ("New Notes on Edgar Poe"), appeared in 1857; and *Histoires grotesques et sérieuses* ("Grotesque and Serious Tales") appeared in 1865. To the forty-six tales contained in these volumes we can add the *Aventures d'Arthur Gordon Pym* (1858; "Adventures of Arthur Gordon Pym") and *Eurêka* (subtitled "A Prose Poem" [1863]). While these volumes do not represent the entirety of Poe's tales—there are some twenty-six stories that Baudelaire did not translate—they demonstrate the depth of Baudelaire's attachment to an author he refers to in devotional terms—"Faire tous les matins ma prière à Dieu . . . à mon père, à Mariette et à Poe, comme intercesseurs" 'To pray every morning to God . . . to my father, to Mariette and to Poe, as intercessors' (*Œuvres complètes* 1: 673)—as well as an extraordinary commitment to the practice of translation, which, more than a mere source of income, played a formative role in his artistic evolution, especially in the design and realization of the prose poems collected in *Spleen*.

This essay examines how Baudelaire's experience as a translator, which predates the Poe translations and does not end with the *Histoires grotesques et sérieuses*, contributed to his own methods of composition and shows how a fuller understanding of his theory and practice of translation can shed light on questions concerning the genesis, form, and subject matter of *Spleen*. My remarks are based on my experience teaching *Spleen* in two undergraduate courses—one a survey of nineteenth-century French literature, taught in French, the other a workshop in translation, taught in English and offered through the Program in Comparative Literature. In both courses I emphasize the scope and variety of Baudelaire's translation projects, focusing on the translations of Poe but considering also *Le Jeune Enchanteur* (1846; *The Young Enchanter* [*Œuvres complètes* 1: 523–45]) and referencing briefly two other translations of direct relevance to *Spleen*: Baudelaire's renderings of parts of Henry Wadsworth Longfellow's *Hiawatha* (where we find Baudelaire experimenting with both prose and poetic versions of a single source, as he would do with some of his own poems [*Œuvres complètes* 1: 243–68]) and his final translation, dictated to Arthur Stevens in 1865, based on Thomas Hood's "Bridge of Sighs" (a poem that he first read in Poe's essay "The Poetic Principle" and that provides the title for "Anywhere out of the world" [*Œuvres complètes* 1: 269–71]). The purpose of this overview is to show that Baudelaire's aesthetics are informed by his practice of translation and, in particular, by his conception of the poet as a kind of translator, an idea expressed in broad terms in his essay on Victor Hugo: "Or, qu'est-ce qu'un poète . . . si ce n'est un traducteur, un déchiffreur?" 'Now what is a poet . . . if not a translator, a decipherer?' (*Œuvres complètes* 2: 133). A secondary goal of mine is to demonstrate, through the example of Baudelaire, but referencing also François-René de Chateaubriand, Gérard de Nerval, Alfred de Vigny, and Prosper Mérimée, that translating for many writers in nineteenth-century France, far from constituting a practice separate from or parallel to their primary literary production, was integral to their poetic practice and played a crucial role in introducing new forms of literary expression, including the prose poem (Chevrel, D'Hulst, and Lombez). In both my courses, we then proceed to analyze the prose poems, and we closely examine English translations of selected poems. In the workshop, I assign readings in the theory of translation in order to provide students with the conceptual vocabulary they need to evaluate Baudelaire's translating "project," "position," and "horizon" (Berman 58–66).

The Young Enchanter

Of Baudelaire's pre-Poe translations—leaving aside his renderings of a few English music hall songs ("M'aimez-vous, dit Fanny, l'autre jour . . ." 'Do you love me, said Fanny, the other day . . .')—*Le Jeune Enchanteur*, which appeared in *L'Esprit public* in 1846, is the most intriguing. Considered for over a century to be an original composition by Baudelaire, it was revealed in 1950 (by W. T. Bandy ["Baudelaire et Croly"]) to be a translation of *The Young Enchanter—from a Papyrus of Herculaneum*, a novella included in an English keepsake dating from 1836 (*Œuvres complètes* 1: 1405). The mistaken attribution is understandable: the work was published under Baudelaire's name (*The Young Enchanter* had appeared anonymously; we now know it to be the work of a certain Reverend George Croly), and Baudelaire refers to it in two letters to his mother as a work of his own hand (*Correspondance* 1: 133, 134). The presence of a translation hidden in Baudelaire's oeuvre immediately raises interesting issues of authorship, originality, and literary property—issues that are central to translation studies and especially relevant to an understanding of Baudelaire's modernist aesthetics, which is highly dependent on forms of transnational borrowing—he would on occasion be accused of plagiarizing Poe (see Salines ch. 4; Jamison ch. 3; Grava 3–5). What logic underlies the decision to publish this work under Baudelaire's name? Was it Baudelaire's idea, a Roman-style annexation of a translated text (Friedrich Nietzsche, in *The Gay Science*, reminds us that in Roman times, when "to translate meant to conquer," it was common to delete the name of the author and insert the translator's name in its place [83])? What does this decision say about publishing practices and the status of translated texts (and translators) in the mid–nineteenth century? It interests students to know that the outright appropriation of foreign texts was common in Baudelaire's time: the first French translation of a Poe story, "La Lettre volée," mentions neither Poe's name nor that of the translator. As Bandy writes, "stealing from a fellow countryman was a crime, but stealing from a foreigner was permissible" (qtd. in Salines 135).

That Baudelaire was able to pass off a translated text as native French prose suggests that he favored an adaptive translation strategy, one that values idiomatic fluency and adherence to the linguistic norms of the target culture. Such a judgment is complicated, however, by the presence of some surprising lexical choices. That Baudelaire's translation of certain words occasionally departs from standard, dictionary-sanctioned equivalents has been read by scholars in different ways, and it is instructive for students to consider how the perception of deviation in translation has changed over time. An earlier generation of scholars explains such anomalies through recourse to biography: since at the time of the publication of *Le Jeune Enchanteur* Baudelaire's knowledge of English was less than perfect, what we have here are simply errors. F. W. J. Hemmings considers *Le Jeune Enchanteur* as nothing more than a "translation exercise" taken on by Baudelaire to improve his English (105), while Claude Pichois notes "des erreurs fort ingénues" 'Some very naive errors' and "des bévues de débutant" 'beginner's blunders' (he cites Baudelaire's translation of *actual* and *actually* as *actuel* and *actuellement* [*Œuvres complètes* 1: 1405]). Emily Salines, on the other hand, writing more recently and as a translation scholar, detects a pattern of "incursions of English-inspired elements in the French text" (24), lexical and syntactical anglicisms such as "accointance," "désappointé," or (pace Pichois) "actuellement," which she takes to be deliberate "modifications" (25) of the original rather than simple mistranslations.

Still, what strikes the reader of *Le Jeune Enchanteur* are the stylistic fluency and naturalness of Baudelaire's prose. The translation is notable for its overall closeness to the original; Baudelaire's approach, literal, aims for accuracy. Baudelaire expresses this goal explicitly in his renderings of Poe, in which he seeks "une exactitude minutieuse dans les plus petits détails" 'meticulous exactness in the smallest details' (*Correspondance* 2: 373). Such fidelity might appear surprising: since no one could know that the work was a translation, Baudelaire was free to take every kind of creative license with his (invisible) source text. In only one instance does he radically alter Croly's original: at the end of the story, Baudelaire adds, almost as though he were appending his signature, a short passage of his own invention, followed by a translation into alexandrines of Horace's *Ode to Thaliarch*. This interpolation is of interest in that it anticipates a practice of textual appropriation that will become increasingly prominent in Baudelaire's subsequent writings. It gestures, for example, toward the complex textual montage of *Un Mangeur d'opium* (1860; "An Opium Eater"). At once a translation, an adaptation, and an analysis of *Confessions of an English Opium Eater* by Thomas De Quincey, *Un Mangeur* mixes various modes of rewriting with original reflexion in what Baudelaire calls an "amalgam": "il s'agissait de fondre mes sensations personnelles avec les opinions de l'auteur et d'en faire un amalgame dont les parties fussent indiscernables" 'it was a matter of blending my own sensations with the opinions of the author so as to make an amalgam in which the parts would be indiscernible' (*Correspondance* 1: 669; see also *Œuvres complètes* 1: 519). The technique is in evidence also in Baudelaire's essays on Poe, especially "Edgar Poe, sa vie et ses ouvrages," which draws heavily, in the form of summary and disguised translation, on an obituary of Poe by John Reuben Thompson and an overview of Poe's works by John Moncure Daniel (*Œuvres complètes* 2: 249–88).

Learning the circumstances surrounding the publication of *Le Jeune Enchanteur* and learning the notion of amalgam presaged in the work prepare students to recognize the intricate enfolding of intertexts—the network of allusions, borrowings, and translations—they will encounter in the prose poems, for example, the "indiscernible" amalgam of "Les Foules" ("Crowds"), endebted both to Poe's "The Man of the Crowd" and to De Quincey, whose vivid description of London crowds inspires the expression "bain de multitude" (*Œuvres complètes* 1: 468]). It is important that students begin thinking about the significance of translation in Baudelaire's evolution as a writer and about translation as a creative rather than a reproductive act. The debate around his knowledge of English and his use of anglicisms gives students a feel for his signature or thumbprint as a translator and sensitizes them to a key issue in translation studies, that of "foreignizing" versus domesticating translation strategies (Venuti, *Translator's Invisibility* 15–20). The importation of original and extraneous material foreshadows a practice of appropriation and textual hybridization that becomes increasingly central to Baudelaire's method of composition and reveals that practice to be facilitated by his early experiment with translation.

Le Spleen de Paris *as/and Translation*

Equipped with a rudimentary sense of how to read and analyze a translation, students are impatient to examine one or two of Baudelaire's versions of Poe. Baudelaire presents himself, notably in the prefatory note to "Révélation magnétique," as a literalizing translator who does not shy away from deforming his native French in the interest of representing the "truth" of the source text: "Il faut bien s'attacher à suivre le texte *littéral*. . . . J'ai préféré faire du français pénible et parfois baroque et donner dans toute sa vérité la technie philosophique d'Edgar Poe" 'One must endeavor to follow the text *literally*. . . . I have preferred to create a labored and sometimes baroque French and to present Edgar Poe's philosophical technics in all its truth' (*Œuvres complètes* 2: 249). I invite students to evaluate the accuracy of this theoretical statement through close stylistic analysis of any one of the stories translated by Baudelaire and to entertain the idea of a relation between the "français pénible et parfois baroque" and the *prose poétique* that Baudelaire forged in *Spleen*.

Students are quick to hear echoes of Baudelaire's American counterpart in the prose poems. Obvious pairings of readings to illustrate resemblances with Poe are "The Man of the Crowd" with "Les Foules" and "The Imp of the Perverse" with "Le Mauvais Vitrier." These alone suffice to expose the "triad of qualities"—lucidity, strangeness, and perversity—that in Jonathan Culler's account Baudelaire carried over from Poe ("Baudelaire and Poe" 69). At the level of form, the textual economy of the *poème en prose* owes more to Poe's particular refashioning of the tale than to anything in Aloysius Bertrand's *Gaspard de la nuit*. Baudelaire himself remarks on the tautness and compression of Poe's style: "serré et concaténé" 'taut and concatenated,' it "supprime les accessoires" 'suppresses accessories' (*Œuvres complètes* 2: 283, 282), rhetorical features that apply equally well to the lean, flexed prose of *Spleen*. The guiding question here is: Given the thematic, stylistic, and formal resemblances between Poe's writings and *Spleen*, can we legitimately consider some of Baudelaire's prose poems to be prolongations of, or supplements to, the direct translations of Poe published by Lévy? In order to speak coherently about translation, understood now in the wider sense of literary transposition, some theory can be usefully introduced. Baudelaire's suggestive notion of an amalgam can be set in relation to theoretical and applied readings that foreground translation as rewriting, refraction, manipulation, recuperation, reframing, and so on (see Caws; Jamison; Johnson, "Poetry"; Lefevere; Derrida, "Des Tours"; Wallaert).

Baudelaire thought of *Spleen* as a "pendant" 'counterpart' to *Les Fleurs du Mal* (*Œuvres complètes* 2: 1299); his ambition was to produce a hundred prose poems to mirror the count in the first edition of the earlier book. "[C]'est encore *Les Fleurs du Mal*, mais avec beaucoup plus de liberté, de détail, et de raillerie" 'It's *Les Fleurs du Mal* again, but with much more freedom, detail, and mockery' (1: 1298), he wrote. While it would be rash to argue on the basis of this assertion that *Spleen* is simply a sort of free translation of *Les Fleurs du Mal*, the language of sameness ("encore") and difference ("mais") suggests that Baudelaire conceived of the relation between the two volumes according to a broadly translational logic. Some of the prose poems of course exist in verse form; these doublets deserve to be studied as acts of self-translation. In addition to bearing witness to Baudelaire's reliance on translation as a creative resource, they reveal the complex operation of revision and rewriting—what Barbara Johnson calls "the work of mutilation and correction" ("Poetry" 61)—underlying his method of composition in *Spleen*.

Viewing *Spleen* through the lens of translation studies allows a nuanced reassessment of Poe's influence on Baudelaire and on the poems in *Spleen*, a vexed issue that remains a formidable pedagogical challenge. Overly suggestive of a unidirectional, linear model of literary production, the theory of influence seems inadequate to account for the oddly specular, and rather fantastic, relation that Baudelaire himself imagines. "Savez-vous pourquoi j'ai si patiemment traduit

Poe?" 'Do you know why I have so patiently translated Poe?,' he wrote to Théophile Thoré in 1864. "Parce qu'il me ressemblait. La première fois que j'ai ouvert un livre de lui, j'ai vu, avec épouvante et ravissement, non seulement des sujets rêvés par moi, mais des PHRASES pensées par moi, et écrites par lui vingt ans auparavant" 'Because he resembled me. The first time I opened a book by him, I saw, with horror and delight, not only subjects dreamed of by me, but SENTENCES thought by me, and written by him twenty years before' (*Correspondance* 2: 386). This statement scrambles a host of consecrated notions about writing, confounding the distinction between original and translation (e.g., the idea that when Baudelaire was translating Poe, he was in fact translating himself back into the original), challenging simplistic notions of authorship (with his translations of Poe, Baudelaire felt that he was presenting to the French public "une partie de moi-même" 'a part of myself' (*Œuvres complètes* 2: 348) and scuttling the facile hypothesis of Poe as a literary antecedent. It is not surprising that critics have been wary of using the word *influence* to describe the Poe-Baudelaire relationship. The proliferation of terms they do use attests to the complexity of this highly idiosyncratic case of intertextuality and to an uncertainty as to how to theorize it. Baudelaire himself speaks in terms of resemblance and mathematical parallelism, Charles Asselineau of "possession" (39), Louis Seylaz of creative imitation (qtd. in Grava 4). Others envisage the relationship in terms of "affinity" (Grava 1–26), "elective affinity" (Hemmings 102–116), "échange" 'exchange' and "interpénétration" 'interpenetration' (Lemonnier 53), discipleship (see Brix), identification, and so on. Still others contest the idea that Baudelaire was influenced by Poe at all: Henri Lemaître finds Poe's theory of "l'insolite" 'the unusual' already articulated in *Le Salon de 1859*, before Baudelaire had ever heard of Poe (*Petits Poèmes* [Lemaître] xxiii); Enid Starkie asserts that Baudelaire "drew nothing from Poe that was not already in himself" (218), et cetera. The intricacy of the Poe-Baudelaire affiliation (several critics speak of "Poedelaire" [Gutbrodt]) mirrors the relation of mutual implication and indebtedness between translation and original as it is theorized in the writings of Jacques Derrida, whose sustained reflection on translation and translatability, which touches on the Baudelaire of the prose poems, suggests productive ways to think about the complex operation of literary transfer at work here (*Given Time*).

Translating Baudelaire

"Baudelaire had translated Poe, but no one as good had come along to translate Baudelaire," muses Robert, the protagonist of Ernest Hemingway's "A Room on the Garden Side," an unpublished short story set in Paris (Shakespeare 241). That there is no canonical English version of Baudelaire, neither of *Les Fleurs du Mal* nor of *Spleen*, is arguably a desirable state of affairs: instead of having one dominant English-language version of Baudelaire, we have an entire shelf of different renderings, each of which has merit or at least is of interest.

While scholars have affirmed the pedagogical rewards of studying translations of *Les Fleurs du Mal* (Hubert; Culler, "Teaching Baudelaire"; C. Scott), much less attention has been paid to translations of *Spleen*. This lack of attention might be due to the perception that translating prose is more straightforward than translating poetry (Michael Hamburger suggests as much in the introduction to his own translation [3]). Georges Blin, contemplating the relative absence of stylization in *Spleen* as compared with *Les Fleurs du Mal*, calls attention to Baudelaire's deliberate use of "les adjectifs les plus plats: *joli, charmant, superbe, magnifique . . .*" 'the dullest adjectives: *pretty, charming, superb, magnificent*' (Introduction 26), terms for which lexical equivalents in English are readily available. Issues of rhyme and meter are less prominent in the prose poems, and the modernity of theme and language, so close to our own experience, might seem to facilitate the task of the translator. But Baudelaire knew that what he had to avoid at all costs was "d'avoir l'air de montrer le plan d'une chose à mettre en vers" 'to appear to be giving the plan for something to be put into verse' (*Correspondance* 2: 207). As Blin writes, the rhythmic prose of *Spleen* in fact is "une concurrence directe avec la strophe et le vers" 'in open competition with stanza and verse' (21): the lyricism of Baudelaire's "prose poétique" is often marked ("Les Bienfaits de la lune," "Un Hémisphere dans une chevelure," "Enivrez-vous," etc.) and never absent. The poetic devices and techniques to which Baudelaire has recourse in *Spleen*—the enervated lyricism ("un lyrisme de l'asthénie" 'the lyricism of asthenia,' as John E. Jackson calls it [*Baudelaire* (2001) 166]), the detached narrative voice, the frequent tonal shifts, the suggestive wordplay (the pun on *fosse/fausse* 'tomb/false' in "Laquelle est la vraie?"), the pervasive irony—present daunting challenges for translators, which is one reason *Spleen* is repeatedly retranslated.

Close examination of translations of *Spleen* can be an effective way to access the nuances of Baudelaire's prose. By comparing sometimes radically divergent English language versions, students refine their sense of the ambiguity, the polysemy, and the highly elusive tone of the original. Somewhat paradoxically, a questionable translation, a willfully subjective translation, or even a mistranslation can lead to a more productive discussion than a translation that is apparently more accurate (Hubert 72). For this reason, I focus on translations by accomplished poets, who give themselves license to depart from the literal in order to reach a more felicitous poetic effect. I work primarily with the English-language versions by Arthur Symons, Hamburger, Louise Varèse, Edward K. Kaplan, Keith Waldrop, and Francis Scarfe, in combinations I vary from year to year (offering no more than three versions per poem).

"Enivrez-vous," first published in 1864, has several advantages. It is brief, allowing for attention to detail, and revolves around central Baudelairean motifs such as time, escapism, intoxication, spleen, and the ideal, which connect it not only to other poems in the volume (e.g., "La Chambre double," "Anywhere out of the world") but also to *Les Fleurs du Mal* (the section "Le Vin") and to *Les Paradis artificiels* ("Du vin et du haschisch"). In this poem, the oscillation between prosaic experience ("la morne solitude de votre chambre") and poetic ideal (the ecstasy of drunkenness) is inscribed stylistically in the copresence of "rugged" ("heurté," to take up the language of "À Arsène Houssaye") statement ("Il faut être toujours ivre") alongside "ondulations de la rêverie" (the *envolée* "Et si quelquefois . . ."). Analysis of this beautifully lyrical sentence ("Et si . . .") can lead us back to Poe (if we can still legitimately say "back to Poe"), who, exactly "vingt ans auparavant," (*Correspondance* 2: 386) published a story that describes the effect of opium ("A Tale of the Ragged Mountains") and in which we find the following sentence:

> In the quivering of a leaf—in the hue of a blade of grass—in the shape of a trefoil—in the humming of a bee—in the gleaming of a dew-drop—in the breathing of the wind—in the faint odors that came from the forest—there came a whole universe of suggestion—a gay and motley train of rhapsodical and unmethodical thought.
>
> (Poe, *Complete Edgar Allan Poe Tales* 397)

Baudelaire remarked this sentence in "Le Poème du haschich," where it serves him as a point of departure for a reflexion on the rhapsodic (*Œuvres complètes* 1: 428); the similarities of Poe's structure and rhythm with "Enivrez-vous" are striking. It is an interesting example of prosodic borrowing in which Baudelaire seems to transpose the rhapsodic élan of Poe's sentence into his own poetic prose.

There is something ludic in the exercise of comparing different versions of a single poem. Debate, often argument, begins with the titles—for example, "Get Drunk," "Get Drunk!," "Get High," "Be Drunk," "Trinck!" Is "Get High" (Kaplan) already dated? Is it accurate? Does "Trinck!" (Scarfe) reveal a translator's desire for novelty, a need to translate against earlier interpretations? Students are quick to notice—and often to censure—the slightest departure from literalism. Why does Varèse capitalize "Time" (*heure*) in "'It is Time to get drunk'"? Should she have sought some alternative to the word "Time" to render "l'heure [de s'enivrer]," to mark a distinction with "le Temps," which appears twice in the poem? My students, who are fearless, believe they can do better. I let them try; it would be perverse to deny them the pleasure of such a challenge. Critics from Valéry Larbaud to Gayatri Spivak have acknowledged that translating a poem is very different from reading one, in terms of the level of understanding and intimacy each act presupposes. "No amount of tough talk can get around the fact that translation is the most intimate act of reading," writes Spivak (315). One cannot translate what one doesn't understand, even if that understanding is provisional, questionable, or faulty. Translating a poem plunges students headlong into what George Steiner calls "the hermeneutic motion," bringing them face to face with the thrill, the despair, and the violence of translation—"this charming and somewhat dangerous pastime," as Friedrich Schleiermacher terms it (61).

NOTE

[1] All translations are mine, unless otherwise indicated.

The Poet as Journalist: Teaching Baudelaire's Prose Poems with the History of the Press

Catherine Nesci

> . . . these are horrors and monstrosities that would make
> your pregnant women readers abort.
>
> — Baudelaire[1]

In this age of *Google* searches, social media, computer games, multiple video streams, and around-the-clock wireless connectivity, students and professors carry into the classroom new reading habits and an evolving remapping of time and space mediated by data-rich devices. Such devices cannot fail to inflect students' and professors' perceptual and social experiences. Digital humanities and pedagogical online environments have turned electronic and audiovisual tools into vital media for teaching and appreciating literary works that belong, for most, to an era of data-poor communication networks. In the last decade of the twentieth century, I started teaching Baudelaire's prose poems by using both print and digital formats for advanced courses on nineteenth-century French and comparative literature in which students explored the writer's immersion in the new visual and print media environment of his time. Such courses include undergraduate offerings—Reading Paris (1830–1890), taught in French; Time Off in Paris, taught in English—and graduate seminars such as Modernity and the City, taught in French or English. Whether Baudelaire's prose poems are anthologized in print or posted online, when students read them today, they are sharing in many ways a type of interaction with the written word that nineteenth-century readers knew.

The term *media* encompasses more generally the material structure and objects mediating the storage, dissemination, and transmission of experience (Mark Hansen 172). I use the term *print media* in this essay to refer to the French (and mainly Parisian) daily or periodical press of the nineteenth century. There poetry and fiction started to appear regularly in the late 1830s, often in the lower section of the newspaper, which was dedicated to the entertaining or educational feuilleton. *Feuilleton* refers to columns of literary, dramatic, and artistic criticism and, starting in 1836, to serialized novels.[2] Thanks to the digitization of numerous dailies and reviews, which now provide a rich archive of electronic research and teaching tools, our students can share the visual and reading experience of the readers of the prose poems when the poems first appeared in the daily press and in magazines devoted to literature and the arts. Equipped with images of the original publishing platform, students can better understand how modern print media shaped Baudelaire's new poetic language in the 1850s and 1860s; they thus gain an awareness that helps them engage in fruitful close readings.

Le Spleen de Paris has long catalyzed students' recognition of a sense of alienation, fragmentation, and contingency, but studying this collection of fifty prose poems in the context of a now readily accessible history of print media helps students better see the modernity of Baudelaire's hybrid poetic language and its close connection to the material infrastructure of a nineteenth-century periodical press, a connection that may at first appear to be distant from current reading culture.[3] They are invited to delve into a parallel media universe of the nineteenth century. Recent research on Baudelaire as a journalist provides a useful framework for this exploration of *Spleen.* Baudelaire published, with very few exceptions, his poetry; literary, artistic, and philosophical essays; and pieces of translation and fiction in the dailies, reviews, and other press media of his time. Most poems of *Spleen* appeared in the periodical press before their posthumous publication in the fourth volume of the writer's complete works in 1869. Alain Vaillant, Marie-Ève Thérenty, and Silvia Disegni, among other scholars, have shown that several features of Baudelaire's literature resulted from its inclusion in the daily or periodical press (Vaillant, "Presse"; Disegni, "Poètes"). Such features include a plurality of voices, an impersonal style, triviality of tone and topic, a distanced irony, and an inscription of the transitory quality of each issue in which a work appeared. Such characteristics—certainly familiar to Internet surfers and online readers—inform Baudelaire's prose poems and the theorization of the new urban genre in his dedication letter to Arsène Houssaye, which was published before nine prose poems in the daily *La Presse* on 26 August 1862.

In this essay, I begin by setting the historical framework linked to the new civilization of the media that developed in the 1830s. The periodical press offered a new publishing matrix to literature, which affected poetry as well as fiction. I then focus on the first prose poems that were published in the daily *La Presse* in the later summer of 1862 and show how Baudelaire instills self-reflexivity and ironic reversal in the midst of the informational flow, thus disrupting the conformity and moral codes that are reinforced at the highly censored top of the newspaper.

Poetry and the Press: The Shock of Two Cultures

The widespread notion of a poet prostituting his high art in the lowly journalistic medium often hides essential aspects of the relation between poetry and the press in the nineteenth century. Although his correspondence testifies to a relentless need for money and a use of the periodical press to pay his growing debts, Baudelaire, unlike most of his contemporaries, never depended on the press as a main source of income. In his introduction to *Baudelaire journaliste* ("Baudelaire as Journalist"), Vaillant reminds us that Baudelaire, according to Jean Ziegler and Claude Pichois, earned a little over ten percent of his income (an estimated 8,320 francs) for his work as a journalist, whereas he received a total of 58,000 francs out of his paternal inheritance and close to 20,000 francs as a loan from his mother (Introduction 10–11).[4] Vaillant shows convincingly that, following the demise of the elitist publication of poems in separate volumes and "the cultural disqualification of poetry" ("Baudelaire, artiste moderne" 44), the so-called *petits romantiques* as well as writers such as Théophile Gautier, Gérard de Nerval, and Théodore de Banville published their works in the periodical press.[5] Such a format for the dissemination and consumption of poetry better fitted new cultural behaviors and changed the orientation of the form as well as thematic content of these poets' works (Disegni, "Poètes"; Vaillant, "Baudelaire, artiste moderne" 45; Vincent-Munnia, "Naissance"). Vaillant studies Baudelaire's transformation from his initial persona as bohemian poet publishing in the literary and the daily press of the 1840s to his contribution to more established artistic periodicals in the early 1850s and his recognition, in the late 1850s, as a journalist, great poet, and opponent of the Second Empire's moral and political authority.[6]

   The various periodical media where Baudelaire's verse poems were first printed mixed poetry with the news and polemics featured on the front page and in the top columns of newspapers, the lead article of which was termed the *Premier-Paris*.[7] Using figurative language and allegory, poetry could also say things that censored news could not (Vaillant, "Baudelaire, artiste moderne" 45).[8] In addition, the "mediatic matrix"—to use the apt expression forged by Thérenty (47–120)—forced the poet to experience the impersonality and polyphony of journalistic writing. As a result, the words of the glorious poet resonated in the chaotic and dissonant concert of the press media. In the mediatic matrix, sublime and intimate lyricism mingled with the banality and triviality of the press content, notably the *faits divers* ("news in brief") of the political daily, and with the jokes, hoaxes, and derision found in the *petite presse* (Disegni, "Poètes" 86–89). For the poet of "Correspondances," who sought the reunification of sensory flux through synesthesia, the journalistic medium could only portend dystopia.

   The mediatic matrix not only influenced the dissemination and reception of Baudelaire's prose poems but also shaped his aesthetic creation of them. The texts display short narrative or descriptive paragraphs that mingle or juxtapose the anecdotal realism typical of everyday urban life and the prose of the daily press with a contemplative, self-reflective, and enigmatic reverie on the temporal flux, the alienated self and soul, and, more generally, precarious human life.[9] Their first publication started only four days after the author of *Les Fleurs du Mal* was convicted of "outrage à la morale publique et religieuse et aux bonnes mœurs" ("offense to public and religious morality and good morals") by the sixth district court on 20 August 1857 (see Leclerc). In its edition of 24 August 1857, the short-lived weekly literary and artistic review *Le Présent* (later *Revue européenne*) published six prose poems: "L'Horloge" ("The Clock"), "Un Hémisphère dans une chevelure" ("A Hemisphere in Tresses"), "L'Invitation au voyage" ("Invitation to the Voyage"), "Le Crépuscule du soir" ("Twilight"), "La Solitude" ("Solitude"), and "Les Projets" ("Plans").[10]

An account of Baudelaire's career as a journalist up to 1857 sheds light on some of the material conditions in which the project of *Le Spleen de Paris* took shape in the early 1860s, a time when the writer, now famous, started to publish more and more prose poems in specialized artistic reviews and well-known Parisian dailies. The same texts appeared repeatedly in both kinds of print media, the format and ideological lines of which were often quite dissimilar. Such multiple and contrasting publications occurred for the most well-known poems ("Les Foules" ["Crowds"], "Les Veuves" ["Widows"], "Le Joujou du pauvre" ["The Pauper's Toy"], and "Les Yeux des pauvres" ["The Eyes of the Poor"]); for the lesser studied (e.g., "Les Bons Chiens" ["The Good Dogs"]); and for the more disturbing (e.g., "La Corde" ["The Rope"]).[11] That in late summer and early fall 1862 Baudelaire published the first twenty prose poems in *La Presse* (close to half the texts in the posthumous edition) and his dedication to Houssaye (then director of the artistic and literary review *L'Artiste* as well as editor-in-chief of *La Presse*) shows that the poet did not hesitate to publish a large selection of his book in progress in the feuilleton of the daily press—that is to say, in the columns devoted to serialized novels, entertainment, and cultural life. Baudelaire immersed his new poetic works in newspaper discourse, thus interlacing the pursuit of beauty and the exhibition of triviality. Though the poems actually blurred in an explicit manner the "line separating artistic text and social world" (Terdiman 309), to what extent can we say that Baudelaire's prose poems instilled a form of subversion into the journalistic medium?

The Prose Poems in the Journalistic Matrix

Reading the letter to Houssaye and then the nine prose poems as they first appeared—in the bottom section of *La Presse* (below the bolded, continuous line) and printed over the six columns and first two pages in the edition of 26 August 1862—provides numerous interpretive clues.[12] Visually, the boldfaced type and the uppercase and lowercase letters of *"Petits Poèmes en prose"* underscore the incongruity and hybridity of the feuilleton du jour. Taking the place of what usually tags a serialized novel (fiction) or a piece of criticism (nonfiction), the large title of the collection of little texts names a new literary genre, thus attracting the interest of readers and creating a scoop. On the one hand, the typographic form and content of the title blend grandeur (visually represented by the large font uppercase bolded letters and underscoring the elevated category of poetry) with inconsequence ("petits," the small or insignificant prose, the merely prosaic). On the other hand, the notions of grandeur and triviality are melded, aurally and vocally, by the triple alliteration of the p and the triple occurrence of a two-syllable rhythm: pe/tits/ po/èm/e(s) en/ prose. Looking at the full pages of the newspaper and not only at the bottom columns of the feuilleton, one notes how typography supports both prose fiction and prosaic topics. That the titles of each prose poem below the line and the headings for the diverse rubrics above the line on page 2 are both in boldface confuses categories of discourse.

Jean-Pierre Bertrand points out that the titles of the prose poems mimic titles for chapters of a novel, an effect reinforced by the final mention of "la suite à demain" ("the rest of the story for tomorrow") under the signature block of the author, which appears in large capital letters (331). The twenty poems published in the three editions of the daily *La Presse* are numbered in a continuous manner, in roman numerals, with the mention, after the twentieth poem and the signature block, in the edition of 24 September 1862, of "La suite prochainement" ("The rest of the story soon"), although there was no continuation.[13] Such numbering enhances the narrative effect of the collection.

In addition to the typography and narrative markings, the tops and bottoms of the pages are linked by news content that appears above and below the lines, which were then called the top floor and the *rez-de-chaussée* ("ground floor or street level"). At the top of page 1 of the 24 August 1862 edition, the *Premier-Paris* section reports on the desperate situation of the Republican revolution led by Giuseppe Garibaldi in Italy. The news of the insurrection is followed by Garibaldi's call to the Hungarian people to rebel against the Austro-Hungarian Empire. Then follow various other news of foreign policy originating from other newspapers or correspondents. At the top of page 2, a long, tedious commercial bulletin is followed by the exciting results of horse races ("The Dieppe steeple chase"), the announcement of "Actes Officiels" (government awards, such as the Legion of Honor), and, finally, three full columns of "Faits Divers," a miscellany of local or colonial events, including accidents, petty crimes, and homicides — listed in no particular order.

Warfare, violence, and incongruity spread to the bottom of the feuilleton, which displays stories parodying the narrative mode of *faits divers*, including their shock and violence. According to Bertrand, "Ce qu'ajoute le poème, c'est une dimension réflexive et poétique à une réalité plus vraie que nature quoiqu'inventée de toutes pièces, comme si, au fond, la matière même de l'actualité, quelle qu'elle soit, pouvait se transformer en prétexte poétique . . . " 'What the poem adds is a self-reflective and poetic dimension to a reality that is truer than nature, although totally made up, as if the news material, whatever its content, could become an opportunity for poetry . . .' (331). In the 26 August 1862 edition of *La Presse*, the top section of the daily portrays Garibaldi with empathy, as an "adventurous captain" who finds himself in desperate circumstances; other news of the day include murders and wreckage. Similarly, the prose poems at the bottom of the page bring a series of disturbing news and desperate characters (*Petits Poèmes. La Presse*). One of the most disturbing is an anguished woman, marginalized by her age and decrepitude, whose wrinkled face frightens a child ("Le Désespoir de la vieille" ["The Old Woman's Despair"]). Like the colorful character sketches (in French, *physionomies* and *physiologies*) then popular in the mass media, an assortment of eccentric, marginal people populate the series of poems-chapters: their lead figure is a stranger or foreigner who claims his absolute detachment from the social world in an enigmatic reported dialogue ("L'Étranger" ["The Stranger"]). Dreamers carry "écrasantes Chimères" ("overwhelming Chimeras") ("Chacun la sienne" ["To Each his Own"], which is the original title of "Chacun sa chimère" ["To Each His Chimera"]). The poet multiplies first-person narratives, which function as self-portraits: by a dejected idealist in the shorter piece "Le *Confiteor* de l'Artiste" ("The Artist's *Confiteor*"); by an addict (in the first long piece, "La Chambre double" ["The Double Room"]); by a sadistic man and damned soul abusing a poor glazier (in the second long piece, "Le Mauvais Vitrier" ["The Bad Glazier"]). Despite the varying length of the prose poems, they are all organized by the same condensation of effects and fragmentation into small paragraphs. Shock, surprise, and antagonism are common as these texts explore both internal and external conflicts.

Transposing the News: Split Subjects and Class Divisions

In the first-person narrative "The Double Room," the shock comes in the form of "un coup terrible, lourd . . . à la porte . . ." 'an awful, heavy knock . . . on the door . . .' and the entrance of a "Specter," who precipitates the loss of the oneiric mental vision, the source of which loss is revealed in the second section of the poem: "la fiole de laudanum . . ." ("the vial of laudanum . . . "). The Specter dispels the dream image of the enchanted bedroom, and mundane time returns, as does the sordid reality of the poet's repulsive, soiled room. Two passages deride the modern obsession of the news and the material underpinnings of the journalistic world, which shape the readers' disenchanted experience of mediated time as the advent of exciting, groundbreaking information. The first passage pertains to the Specter's third and final incarnation as "le saute-ruisseau d'un directeur de journal qui réclame la suite du manuscrit" 'a newspaper editor's errand boy calling for the manuscript's next installment' (7). The second appears when the poet evokes human finitude with irony by reminding readers of "une Seconde dans la vie humaine qui [a] mission d'annoncer une bonne nouvelle, la *bonne nouvelle* qui cause à chacun une inexplicable peur" 'the one Second in human life whose mission it is to announce *good news*, the good news that causes everyone such inexplicable fear' (8). From the simulated, drug-induced paradise (and its "éternité de délices!" 'eternity of delights!') to the urban hell (and its "éternel ennui" 'eternal ennui' [7]), the fall into a petty material reality echoes the reality that is narrated at the top of the newspaper page.

The bitter awareness of the present, miserable moment also points to the time of expressive work and poetic transposition. The relation to work is conflicted, especially when the subject underscores his final failure to recover his idealized vision by staging himself in bondage: "Sue donc, esclave! Vis donc, damné!" 'So sweat, slave! So live, damned one!' (8). The poetic transposition of the hallucinatory experience opposes an impersonal reverie to the poet immersed in a hideous, trivial world and obliged to face responsibilities. The responsibilities are represented by three successive spectral visitors: the bailiff summons the poet to pay his debts, the concubine begs for money, and the newspaper editor requests the next installment of the poet's feuilleton. Additional references to the poet's literary work show the travails of the writing process and the dictatorship of newspaper or magazine editors who impose increasingly tight deadlines: "les manuscrits, raturés ou incomplets; l'almanach où le crayon a marqué les dates sinistres!" 'the manuscripts, scratched up or unfinished; the calendar where the menacing dates are marked in pencil!' The image of "les tristes fenêtres où la pluie a tracé des sillons dans la poussière" 'the dreary windows where rain has traced furrows in the dust' may allude to the writing process and its associated tears and "douleurs" 'sorrows.' The knock on the door and the reappearance of triviality are felt by the poet as a violent blow: "un coup de pioche dans l'estomac" 'I felt a pickax strike me in the stomach' (7).[14]

Before we turn to "Le Mauvais Vitrier" ("The Bad Glazier") and "Le Chien et le flacon" ("The Dog and the Scent-Bottle"), it is worth reading the top of the newspaper, the *faits divers* bric-a-brac, which includes short narratives of France's military expeditions and colonial conquests in North Africa, Asia, and Central America. The large network of British, French, and colonial newspapers, serving as sources of news, exhibits the web of information that traverses the world and reaches the readers of metropolitan centers. Several stories are of homicides, wounded soldiers and sailors, lost ships, and drastic alterations to the grid of Parisian streets. In one of the *faits divers*, reported from *L'Echo de Sétif*, a young Jewish man kills an Arab for drinking out of his water-can; "indigné d'une pareille audace" 'outraged by such audacity, the "Israélite" 'Israelite' grabbed a shovel and dealt the Arab a violent blow on the head. Mortally wounded, the native (in French, "*l'indigène*") fell and met an instantaneous death. A French character embodies the law when a judge comes to the scene of the crime and has the young Jewish man arrested for the murder. Justice will be served in the French colony!

Although Baudelaire did not know ahead of time this *fait divers* pitting an Arab against a Jew in the colonial Algerian context, one can read it alongside "The Bad Glazier"—the fable of a dandy narrator torturing a working-class character—as well as "The Dog and the Scent-Bottle" on the same page. In "Dog," the poet's dog barks at his master for making him breathe the most delicate perfume and stands ready to sniff "avec délices" 'with delight' a "paquet d'excréments" 'a lump of excrements.' Talking to his dog, the poet makes a daring comparison: "vous ressemblez au public, à qui il ne faut jamais présenter des parfums délicats qui l'exaspèrent, mais des ordures méticuleusement choisies" 'you resemble the public, which must never be offered delicate perfumes that exasperate them, but only meticulously selected garbage' (12) — an open reference to the sensational, gruesome, and trivial stories of the *faits divers*.

In the first-person narrative "Le Mauvais Vitrier," Baudelaire practices sensationalism with a vengeance. The poem shows class divisions and also pits the pleasure principle against the reality principle. Reality triumphs at the top of the page in rubrics ostensibly praising Europe's conquering spirit and, as it came to be known, civilizing mission. Often read as an ironic remake of Houssaye's staging of class fraternity and bourgeois guilt in the 1857 prose poem "La Chanson du vitrier" ("The Song of the Glazier"), it offers the readers of the newspaper a new kind of petty crime. Baudelaire gives what could be a simple urban incident the durable form of a *conte cruel* ("a cruel tale"); he delivers a moral, religious, and psychological reflection on an immoral, absurd act of malice that generates "l'infini de la jouissance" 'the infinity of delight' in the offender oblivious of "l'éternité de la damnation" 'an eternity of damnation' (15).[15] In paragraph 11, the narrator-moralist and soon wrongdoer talks directly to his imagined readers before introducing the last, and personal, example illuminating the psychological laws he has exposed in paragraphs 1 and 6. Before recounting his aggression of a windowpane salesman out of selfish enjoyment, he opposes his own state as one "fatigué d'oisiveté" 'worn out with idleness' to the working glazier, "dont le cri perçant, discordant, monta jusqu'à [lui] à travers la lourde et sale atmosphère parisienne" 'whose piercing, discordant cry reached [him] through the heavy and dirty Parisian atmosphere' (14). The tension culminates in climax when the dandy attacks the glazier with "un petit pot de fleurs" 'a little pot of flowers' (his "engin de guerre" 'engine of war'): "et le choc le renversant, il acheva de briser sous son dos toute sa pauvre fortune ambulatoire, qui rendit le bruit éclatant d'un palais de cristal crevé par la foudre" 'The shock knocked him over, and he ended by breaking his entire poor itinerant fortune under his back, which produced the brilliant sound of a crystal palace smashed by lightning' (15). If one remembers that, in his letter-envoi to *La Presse*'s editor (printed on page 1 of the daily), Baudelaire had given as an example of urban lyric prose Houssaye's translation "en une chanson [du] cri strident du *Vitrier* . . ." '[of the] Glazier's strident cry into a song . . .' we may interpret the final shattering noise as a biting, discordant replay of Houssaye's "song" as well as a mad, gratuitous gesture generating a fleeting beauty out of crime and cruelty.

Visualizing Baudelaire's prose poems in their original journalistic matrix offers twenty-first-century students opportunities to understand the material infrastructure of a poetic text, something that, not so long ago, was reserved for specialized researchers. By being able to recontextualize *Le Spleen de Paris* in this way, students can forge their own perceptions of the relation between the "artistic text" and the discordant discourse of the newspaper, which purports to represent the "social world," to use Terdiman's categories (309). Better informed about the close interactions between literature and the periodical press, students can thus better grasp mid-nineteenth-century modernity as an aesthetic concept linked to ceaseless cycles of media innovation and obsolescence, the cult of the new and the news, and the corollary rejection of outmoded goods and news items. These cycles, cult, and rejection in turn torment the poet's wounded, unstable self and lead the poet to choose opacity, allegory, and horror as the predominant modes of his poetry.

In our age of ubiquitous computing, split-screen displays, elaborate (digital) editing, and mingling of graphic and text, reading such works as Baudelaire's *Spleen de Paris* in its seemingly odd press appearance brings us back to a process of the past that is not so far removed from browsing pages on the Internet, moving through flows of information, and engaging in cyberflânerie. If we wish to make sense of our environment, we need to achieve a consciousness and critical appraisal of the mediated nature of contemporary human experience, a task that the interpretation of poetic setting and "ethical irony" (Kaplan, "Baudelairean Ethics" 89) in the labyrinthine mosaic of the daily press invites us to discover.

NOTES

[1] All translations are mine, unless otherwise indicated. In French: ". . . ce sont des horreurs et des monstruosités qui feraient avorter vos lectrices enceintes." Baudelaire was referring to his *Prose Poems* in a letter to Louis Marcelin (*Correspondance* 2: 465 [15 Feb. 1865]). In 1862, Marcelin launched the elegant magazine *La Vie parisienne*, in which Baudelaire published two prose poems, "Les Yeux des pauvres" ("The Eyes of the Poor") and "Les Projets" ("Plans"), in 1864; these were republished at the end of 1862 in the new incarnation of an older literary magazine, the *Revue de Paris*.

[2] On the feuilleton, see Queffélec; Dumasy-Queffélec; and Thérenty and Vaillant, *1836: L'An I de l'ère médiatique* 230–47.

[3] I teach Baudelaire and the history of print media in advanced literary courses taught in French and in general education courses in translation. Both types of courses are interdisciplinary and include architectural and urban history as well as literary and visual materials.

[4] Vaillant refers to the work of Pichois and Ziegler 481–97 (Introduction 11). According to Graham Robb, Baudelaire became a journalist once he lost the right to spend his father's inheritance as he wished. The cliché equating journalism with prostitution does not hold against the actual practices of poets as *feuilletonistes* (Robb, *Poésie* 314–21).

[5] The term *petits romantiques* refers to the marginalized, bohemian, and eccentric young Romanticists of the 1830s–40s (writers such as Aloysius Bertrand, Alphonse Rabbe, Petrus Borel, and Xavier Forneret), but the notion and grouping is now quite contested (see Steinmetz). On their invention of prose poems in the 1820s–40s, see Vincent-Munnia (*Premiers Poèmes* and "Naissance"); Vincent-Munnia, Bernard-Griffiths, and Pickering.

[6] The daily press included the major press (*grande presse*), which focused on polemics and political content (and had to pay a *cautionnement*), and the *petite presse* or lowly press, which did not deal with political events and adopted a satirical and ironical tone throughout. Baudelaire published in the daily *Le Corsaire* and in *Le Satan*, which merged as *Le Corsaire-Satan* in the 1840s (Robb, *Corsaire-Satan* 7–15). *La Civilisation du journal* helps navigate the complex features and protean embodiments of the new print media of nineteenth-century France (Kalifa, Régnier, Thérenty, and Vaillant).

[7] On the *Premier-Paris*, see Thérenty 208–35; Vaillant, "Article."

[8] An example of this role is the three long poems that Baudelaire dedicated to Victor Hugo and the liminal poem of the new Parisian section of the 1861 edition of *Les Fleurs du Mal*. "Rêve Parisien" ("Parisian Dream") was first published on 15 November 1857 in *Le Présent*; "Les Petites Vieilles" ("The Old Women") and "Les Sept Vieillards" ("The Seven Old Men") were first published under the title of "Fantômes parisiens" ("Parisian Ghosts") in the *Revue contemporaine* on 15 September 1859, and "Le Cygne" ("The Swan") was first published in *La Causerie* on 22 January 1860. Vaillant proposes a fascinating political reading of all four poems (Vaillant, "Baudelaire, artiste moderne" 56–57).

[9] For the history of prose poems published in the press before Baudelaire's use of the new genre, see Vincent-Munia, "Naissance"; Disegni, "Poètes."

[10] "Le Crépuscule du soir" and "La Solitude" were first published in book format in 1855 (in a volume of homage to Claude-François Denecourt, who pioneered natural tourism and turned the Fontainebleau forest into a hiking site) and were republished many times. They also appeared in the *Revue Fantaisiste* in 1861; the *Figaro* and the *Nouvelle Revue de Paris* in 1864, thus in a biweekly periodical (the *Figaro* at that time); and in literary reviews, as if the poems fitted different audiences.

[11] Only five prose poems were not prepublished in the press: "Le Galant Tireur" ("The Gallant Marksman"), "La Soupe et les nuages" ("The Soup and the Clouds"), "Perte d'auréole" ("Loss of Halo"), "Mademoiselle Bistouri" ("Miss Scalpel"), and "Assommons les pauvres" ("Let's Beat the Poor").

[12] The order and numbering of the twenty prose poems as they were first published in August and September 1862 in *La Presse* have been preserved in the posthumous translation *Paris Spleen* and in most current English editions. For digitized versions of the poems, which I both project in class and circulate in hard copy to students, I use the digital archives of the French National Library, *Gallica* (see *Petits Poèmes en prose. La Presse*).

[13] The previous publication of some prose poems in *Le Présent* generated troubles with Houssaye, who suppressed the publication of additional prose poems in *La Presse*'s feuilleton of early October 1862. See Baudelaire's letter to Houssaye on that topic (*Correspondance* 2: 263–64 [8 Oct. 1862]).

[14] For a more elaborate reading of this well-studied poem and its relation to Samuel Taylor Coleridge's 1797 "In Xanadu did Kubla Khan . . ." and Edgar Allan Poe's "Philosophy of Composition," see Murphy, *Logiques* 89–112; Spadon.

[15] The comparison between Baudelaire's poem and Houssaye's has been made by numerous critics. See, for example, Murphy, *Logiques* 325–92.

Le Spleen de Paris and the *Cyberflâneur*

Cheryl Krueger

Why study Second Empire French prose poems in twenty-first-century anglo-phone universities? The question may seem ill placed or oddly timed here, on the pages of a North American volume dedicated to teaching Baudelaire's *Le Spleen de Paris.* Yet given the current crisis in the humanities—not the first such crisis, to be sure, but a new incarnation that is ours to face—it seems important to acknowledge this shadow of doubt when organizing courses that may be deemed superfluous.

The ongoing national (and international) dialogue on the relevance and utility of the humanities was indeed on my mind when I launched a recent undergraduate seminar called The Flâneur. The goal of this course was to study *Le Spleen de Paris* in relation to the iconic, often sentimentalized figure of the Second Empire street roamer. I wanted to emphasize the elusive and ever-shifting definition of the flâneur in nineteenth-century texts and images. At the same time, I hoped to trace how he or she resurfaces in twenty-first-century iterations. I posited that the prose poems offer a type of flâneur poetics and that this poetics has much in common with the cognitive processes of a generation raised on digital media, surrounded and jostled not by crowded streets but by information highways. Like the flâneur navigating a city throng, the Net-generation reader may appear to be a distracted, overstimulated, and underfocused wanderer. Don Tapscott maintains that the Internet and easily accessible digital resources have changed (even enhanced) the way students encounter, process, and manipulate information. It is difficult to assess the cognitive fallout of digital technology and social media: daily weigh-ins from the popular press and academic forums show that in the time it takes to analyze a new digital phenomenon, it will have evolved, changed its format, or become obsolete. But for better or worse (see Sherry Turkle's sobering *Alone Together*), students in classrooms today, students who will shape generations to come, are already immersed body and mind in digital experience; they already traverse real and virtual spaces.

In my flâneur course, I encouraged modes of interaction and participation that students already knew, while guiding them to be more aware of practices they performed automatically. Instead of telling them that Baudelaire's work mattered, I found ways for them to show me how and why they read; how they reflected on their personal and academic connections, or approaches, to reading (contemplating, interacting with, writing about) *Le Spleen de Paris.*

I recognize that the description of my course could veer perilously close to proselytizing. In fact, indoctrinating students about the lessons of the prose poems themselves, or the value of certain learning tools, or the significance of literature is anathema to my experiment. In the closing essay of *Approaches to Teaching Baudelaire's* Flowers of Evil (ed. Porter), Ross Chambers explores the inexorable paradox of "teaching about life," particularly when dealing with Baudelaire, a poet who "considered poetry and teaching to be absolutely incompatible" and for whom "poetry that teaches was a contradiction in terms" ("Classroom" 171; see Claire Chi-ah Lyu's discussion, in this volume, of Chambers's essay). The acceleration of urban life evoked in the prose poems highlights ethical dilemmas brought about by a rapidly changing social, spatial, and temporal environment. Yet, in prose as in verse, Baudelaire "implicitly dissociates ethics from aesthetics" (Porter, Preface 1). His idiosyncratic and tormented portrayal of right and wrong, virtue and vice, good and evil may challenge the reader to examine his or her own beliefs about social responsibility and moral relativism. But the prose poems do not teach a moral lesson any more than they claim the utility of poetry.

I share Chambers's desire to see poetry as a vehicle for understanding modern, everyday life without making the convergence of literature and real life didactic. Chambers advocates "a pedagogy of transportation" and calls deviation "the only destination one may have" ("Classroom" 181). Baudelaire himself admitted that his prose poems did not turn out to be what he had planned (*Spleen* [Pichois] 276 ["À Arsène Houssaye"]; *Parisian Prowler* 128 ["Letter to Arsène Houssaye").[1] My approach to teaching Baudelaire's prose poems is an attempt at one such deviation, one of many possible pedagogies of transportation, a way to replace a hermeneutics of suspicion—a term more often identified with reading practices but applicable, I think, to paradigms of planning and steering courses—with a hermeneutics of chance and discovery.

In this essay I first summarize my understanding of flâneur poetics in relation to Baudelaire's prose poems and essays. I emphasize textual features and reader dynamics that situate his prose poems at the crossroads of literary analysis, cultural studies, and twenty-first-century approaches to learning. I then outline the pedagogical experiment that brought together twenty-first-century digital rovers and nineteenth-century urban strollers in the space of the classroom and beyond.

Flâneur Poetics

Flânerie—walking, strolling, loitering, meandering, sauntering—has been theorized in the nineteenth century, then in subsequent literary theory and social histories, as a symptom of modernity and urban expansion (see Benjamin, *The Arcades Project*; Boutin, "Rethinking"; Chambers, *Loiterature*; D'Souza and McDonough; Lauster; Nesci; Ferguson 80–114; Rignall; Tester; White). The term *flâneur* predates Baudelaire and the modern era. By the early nineteenth century, flâneurs appeared on the pages of illustrated *physiologies* and *tableaux,* what Benjamin would later call panoramic literature (*Writer of Modern Life* 66–70)—for example, Léon Curmer's *Les Français peints par eux-mêmes* [3: 65–72; "The French Depicted by Themselves"]), Louis Huart's 1841 *Physiologie du flâneur* ("Physiology of the Flâneur"), Victor Fournel's 1858 *Ce qu'on voit dans les rues de Paris* (267–359; "What One Sees on the Streets of Paris"). They also appeared in essays and novels (Honoré de Balzac's 1829 *Physiologie du mariage* and 1835 *Le Père Goriot*, for example). Yet the privileged artist-flâneur as most know him today derives from the essay "Le Peintre de la vie moderne" (1859 and 1863; "The Painter of Modern Life"), in which Baudelaire identifies both the painter Constantin Guys and the convalescent narrator of Edgar Allan Poe's short story "The Man of the Crowd" (1840) as flâneurs.

Poe's "Man of the Crowd" is in fact about two men. The first, a nameless convalescent protagonist, gazes through a café window, then stealthily follows an inscrutable stranger through a London throng. The convalescent shows an unbridled, irresistible, perhaps fatal curiosity and impulse toward observation that is fundamental to the *physiologie* of the Baudelairean flâneur-painter of modern life. Like the narrator who secretly watches others in Baudelaire's prose poem "Les Fenêtres" ("Windows"), he never meets the man he follows, the man for whom the essay is named. Yet Poe's convalescent is left with a defining feature of the flâneur experience: a story to tell.

The first and last sentences of Poe's "Man of the Crowd" include the words "er lasst sich nicht lesen" 'it is unreadable' ("Man" 232, 239). The first time, "er" clearly refers to a book, but the second time, the pronoun could designate the book or the man, neither of which can be read. In both "The Man of the Crowd" and Baudelaire's "Windows," the observing flâneur, confronted with the impossibility of reading the strangers he sees, resolves his desire to know, or to penetrate, others by writing them: "j'ai refait l'histoire de cette femme, ou plutôt sa légende, et quelquefois je me la raconte à moi-même en pleurant. Si c'eût été un pauvre vieux homme, j'aurais refait la sienne tout aussi aisément." 'I have refashioned that woman's history, or rather legend, and sometimes I tell it to myself weeping. If it had been a poor man, I would have just as easily refashioned his as well' (*Spleen* [Pichois] 339; 93).

In a similar way, the understanding or reading of the Baudelairean flâneur itself shifts each time one retells or rewrites its legend. Baudelaire reads Poe's privileged, articulate, self-aware convalescent as a kindred spirit of the world traveler Guys. However, Benjamin reads Baudelaire's essay "Painter of Modern Life" as a commentary on Poe's second flâneur, the man in the crowd followed by the curious, window-watching reader of faces (*Writer* 66–96 [see the "Flâneur" portion of "The Paris of the Second Empire in Baudelaire"]). All these subjective and sometimes inaccurate readings within readings combine to create the portrait and the story of Baudelaire's seemingly obvious yet elusive flâneur.[2] The notion of a single, definable Second Empire flâneur is in many ways a Baudelairean urban legend.

Benjamin's analysis of "Painter" and Poe's "Man of the Crowd" established the figure of the flâneur as an individual in the throng, subjected to sensory overload, navigating the daily shock and alienation of fast-paced urban life. The focus on phantasmagoria, panorama, and the specular nature of commodification has led to the conceptualization of *flânerie* as a practice linked to vision, mobility, and progress. However, as I argued in a recent article ("Flâneur Smellscapes"), Baudelaire's version of *flânerie* extends beyond the iconic act of strolling, public elbow rubbing, and observation to a more complex, nonlinear process comprising thought, decision making, social interaction, multisensorial perception, silence, artistic production, and a type of world travel that I call worldwide, global *flânerie* or *flânerie mondiale*.

Like Poe's convalescent, Guys is a keen observer, but, more than that (and this important aspect is largely missing from the mythology of the Baudelairean flâneur), he is a great traveler, a cosmopolitan (*Œuvres complètes* 2: 689), and a man of the world:

> La foule est son domaine. . . . Sa passion et sa profession, c'est d'*épouser la foule*. Pour le parfait flâneur, pour l'observateur passionné, c'est une immense jouissance que d'élire domicile dans le nombre, dans l'ondoyant, dans le mouvement, dans le fugitif et l'infini. Être hors de chez soi, et pourtant se sentir partout chez soi; voir le monde, être au centre du monde et rester caché au monde. . . .

> The crowd is his domain. . . . His passion, his profession is to *espouse the crowd*. For the perfect flâneur, for the passionate observer, it is an immense pleasure to take up residence in masses, in undulation, in movement, in the fugitive and the infinite. To be out away from home and nevertheless to feel at home everywhere; to see the world, to be at the center of the world and to remain hidden from the world. . . .   (2: 691–92; my trans.)

This privileged lover of the throng reappears in the prose poem "Les Foules" 'Crowds': "Il n'est pas donné à chacun de prendre un bain de multitude: jouir de la foule est un art. . . . Le poète jouit de cette incomparable privilège, qu'il peut à sa guise être lui-même et autrui. . . . Le promeneur solitaire et pensif tire une singulière ivresse de cette universelle communion" 'Not everyone is capable of taking a bath in the multitude: enjoying crowds is an art. . . . The poet enjoys the incomparable privilege of being able, at will, to be himself and an other. . . . The solitary and thoughtful stroller derives a unique intoxication from this universal communion' (*Spleen* [Pichois] 291; 21). Like Guys, this poet-flâneur feels "la passion du voyage" ([291]; translated as "a passion for travel" in Lloyd's *The Prose Poems* [44] and Sorrell's *Paris Spleen* [22], "a passion for traveling" in Kaplan's *Parisian Prowler* [21], "the passion for roaming" in Varèse's *Paris Spleen* [20], and "*wanderlust*" in Scarfe's *Paris Blues* [69]).

"Crowds" provides perhaps the most obvious example of flâneur motifs in the individual prose poems (for further examples, see Krueger, "Flâneur Smellscapes" 184–85). Similarly, the prose poems' mobile, shifting, and unnamed narrative persona recalls the "flâneur, or incognito stroller, sketched in [Baudelaire's] essay on Guys" (*Parisian Prowler* viii), an observer of modern life, compiling a quirky, textual panorama or fractured, Baudelairean *physiologie*. On the muddy streets of Paris, the flâneur encounters a host of fellow pedestrians: counterfeiters and gullible victims, seekers of luxury and hungry families, widows and prostitutes, marginalized immigrants, world travelers, even a flâneur dog. The theme of drifting into chance meetings is reinforced by the volume's unusual structural and narrative dynamics, which create an overall sense of nonlinear perambulation in the navigation from poem to poem—a sort of readers' *flânerie*. When Baudelaire invites the reader to impose arbitrary order on his fifty prose poems, to select points of entry and exit, to loiter or change direction on a whim, he is in a sense placing the reader in the role of an interactive, textual flâneur, whose interests will shape the interpretation of the texts. Nonlinearity, contingency, association, openness, flexibility, permeability—all belong to what I am calling a flâneur poetics, and all inspired me to seek a teaching approach that would allow students to experience Baudelaire's work in a similarly multifaceted, participatory way.

Baudelaire's depiction of the reader as a page surfer, dipping in at any point, starting and stopping at will, foreshadows the practice of browsing the Internet, a space that, like *Le Spleen de Paris*, has no beginning or end, since "tout, au contraire y est à la fois tête et queue, alternativement et réciproquement" 'everything in it is both tail and head, alternatively and reciprocally' (129 ["Letter to Arsène Houssaye"]). It was therefore not just the sociocultural, aesthetic theme (or problematic or paradigm) of *flânerie* that shaped my course, it was also the possibility that an individual yet interactive mode of living and learning today might have much in common with the mobile poetics of Baudelairean prose poems and *flânerie*. (On digital humanities and *Spleen*, see Catherine Nesci's essay in this volume). In fact, the examination of *cyberflânerie* provided a constant frame of reference throughout the semester.

Course Logistics

If any text binds readers to the thread of a plot, it is a course syllabus. Students therefore are readers who have particular difficulty following Baudelaire's advice to allow recalcitrant will, undulations of reverie, or the soul's lyrical movements to be their guide. By tradition and sheer logistical and bureaucratic necessity, they are usually bound to a reading list, a course schedule, theoretical frameworks, grading rubrics, and more.

My pedagogical experiment involved an alternative to the plotted course, insofar as such an alternative is possible at a time when straying from the syllabus is tantamount to breaking a legal contract. The class was conducted in French, with some readings in English. Students performed the sorts of tasks and projects I include in any advanced undergraduate course: a research paper (developed in stages, with peer review), a creative project, individual presentations, collaborative problem solving, online posting and discussion, regular reading, and reaction writing. Each component had its own posted criteria and rubrics for grading. Students were free to choose any edition of *Le Spleen de Paris*, paper or digital.

On the first day of class, after initial introductions, the students left all their belongings, including electronics, in the room with me in order to walk outdoors, unencumbered, for about ten minutes. I encouraged them to observe and sense the world around them and, above all, to avoid using the time to accomplish errands. As they trickled back into the classroom, they responded to the following prompt, projected in French on the screen: "Write about anything at all." We spent the rest of the class period discussing what they had written and how it felt to walk without the usual props and purposes. Some observed smells and sounds they had never noticed before. Some felt vulnerable without a means of communication; they didn't know where to look, where to put their hands. Some found themselves observing the gaze of others: people watching people, a child marveling at a construction site. Back in the quiet room, writing, some felt calm, focused, invigorated. Vows were made (some kept, some broken) to pair solitary strolling and thinking with thinking and writing on a regular basis.

Their preparation for the next class was to read any two prose poems from *Le Spleen de Paris,* as well as the online op-ed "Death of the Cyberflâneur," a title whose irony was not lost on the students, self-identified cyberflâneurs and cyberflâneuses. Were they, too, urban legends? In this piece, Evgeny Morozov, author of *The Net Delusion: The Dark Side of Internet Freedom*, warns that "the very practice of cyberflânerie seems at odds with the world of social media." He maintains that since 1998, when the rise of the cyberflâneur seemed to promise a bright future, digital roaming has devolved into a highly purposeful, market-driven, deceptively public practice. Morozov sees *Facebook* as the new Baron Haussmann, driving those with true flâneur sensibilities to metaphoric cork-lined rooms and making solitude, anonymity, curiosity, and chance amid the crowd nearly impossible for pounders of the virtual pavement. These initial reading assignments—the two randomly selected prose poems (not necessarily the same two for any given student) and the essay on *cyberflânerie*—opened nearly all the questions we would explore across the semester and served as touchstones in online and in-class discussions.

We spent the first several sessions on preselected flâneur readings (portions of "Physiologie du flâneur," Poe's "Man of the Crowd," Baudelaire's "The Painter of Modern Life," and selected essays by Benjamin collected in *The Writer of Modern Life*), but the rest of the reading syllabus was student-generated. Students sequenced their study of Baudelaire's prose poems and steered the selection of secondary readings and materials for the class on a biweekly basis. They led close readings and discussion for two to four prose poems per week; each student posted one reflective essay on the course blog; and all joined online discussions of the blog posts. Once each week, a student assigned, presented, and led discussion of a secondary article, one that the student had encountered in research for the final paper. We used an online syllabus and sign-up sheet, updated weekly to show which students would lead discussion and which was assigned. As a result, the syllabus that began with a skeletal list of due dates and placeholder TBAs now offers a snapshot of the unique trail blazed over fifteen weeks of individual and collaborative discovery, aided by digital archives (*Gallica*, *Project Gutenberg*, *HathiTrust*, and other databases), popular digital resources, and plenty of books and journals in print.

It was sometimes difficult for me to refrain from imposing certain readings. "L'Étranger," "Les Foules," and "Les Fenêtres" were chosen early, as were texts related directly to verse poems that many of the students already knew ("Un Hémisphère dans une chevelure" 'A Hemisphere in Tresses,' "L'Invitation au voyage" 'Invitation to the Voyage'). There was a long wait for the prose poem I see as a dramatization of the public-to-private dynamics of flânerie, "À une heure du matin" ("At One O'Clock in the Morning"). I feared the unsettling *flâneuse* of "Mademoiselle Bistouri" would pass unnoticed. Why weren't the art history students choosing "Le Désir de peindre" ("The Desire to Paint")? We never read "La Corde" ("The Rope").

One student reported that he closed his eyes to randomly select a prose poem, and some started at the beginning, but most immediately went for titles. They leaned toward words that seemed associated with *flânerie* and its discontents — "Les Vocations" ("Vocations"), "Les Projets " ("Plans") — or were drawn to dogs, fairies, toys, cake, soup, clouds, the moon. Often classroom conversation triggered interest in previously overlooked poems. Blog discussions showed that a few students were doing a good deal of reading on their own, beyond the course requirements. In class, most presented their close readings of individual prose poems using slides (*PowerPoint* or *Keynote*), often illustrated and with color-coded text for emphasis of reading axes, semantic fields, and other formal, linguistic, and thematic elements.

I encouraged students to use the secondary readings to carve out a research project. This could be a paper dealing with the prose poems or the theme of *flânerie* or an interdisciplinary topic involving fields represented by the many double majors in the class: anthropology, art history, English, music, pre-med, international studies, politics. We read everything from articles and book chapters on *flânerie* (Ferguson; Lauster; Nesci) to works on the prose poems (Carpenter's *Acts of Fiction*; Murphy's *Logiques du dernier Baudelaire*; M. Scott's *Baudelaire's Le Spleen de Paris*; Stephens's *Baudelaire's Prose Poems*; and many more) to studies of music, architecture, and performance art. Most students did not stray far from Baudelaire.

The final papers were carefully researched and compelling, but it was the creative projects that I found most memorable. Conceived to be a low-stress assignment, they allowed students to pursue — in as much or as little depth as they wished — an aspect of the course in relation to life outside class. The grading rubric did not reward talent or creativity per se (something I feel incapable of evaluating) but instead emphasized presentation, metacommentary (on how the project was chosen, the questions it raised, whether it was complete or ongoing, whether it could have been done differently, etc.), and engagement of class discussion. The results were a good number of films and performances: an in-class poetry slam with visual backup, a filmed improvisational ballet, a brief documentary, a filmed parody interview with Guys (who responds to Baudelaire's

"Le Peintre de la vie moderne"), and various filmed spin-offs of twenty- and twenty-first-century situationist art. Most projects had at least one digital component, and many involved writing: a pastiche of several prose poems in the form of a blog; original blogged poetry; a *Tumblr* site designed by chance with an Oulipian formula too complicated to describe here, but it showed all the roads leading to Baudelaire; a Baudelaire *Facebook* site. One student created an Acconci-inspired fabric sculpture; as in her earlier presentations, she eschewed technology in favor of three-by-five note cards.

Even within the increasingly impermeable boundaries of course design, The Flâneur seminar provided ways for students to explore sounds, images, and ideas that were first encountered in the modernity of *Le Spleen de Paris* and that resonate with what Baudelaire might still call *"une* vie moderne," that is, *one* particular [and not the only] modern life (*Spleen* [Pichois] 275). By the end of the semester, students had read more individual prose poems than in any undergraduate course I had offered before, and they had connected these works to a variety of ideas and cultural practices. At the same time, and without my coercion, they showed sustained interest in the texts themselves and what the texts had to say about a different time, place, and perspective.

What I did not anticipate was the appeal for students of evasive literary forms and figures or, more accurately, the appeal of evasiveness itself. Students debated the taxonomy of the self-defining, self-negating *poèmes en prose* but did not strive to pin down the genre. They were drawn to the very word *flâneur*, which, like *Spleen de Paris*, cannot be neatly translated into English. *Flânerie* and *Spleen de Paris*, by name and by nature, offer travel without a compass, a voyage that is "about departing (or deviating)" and a "plunge into the Unknown," as Chambers said of Baudelaire's verse "Voyage" ("Classroom" 182). Students were not necessarily seeking reflections of themselves in the nineteenth-century literature. The lure of the strange and unknown that had drawn them to words like *flâneur* and *Spleen* in the course description motivated their reading of the texts throughout the semester.

The seed of interest in global *flânerie* that I had planted in students sparked much debate. Students also introduced topics I had not anticipated. For example, they frequently raised the question of *flânerie à deux*. Above all, their identification with *flânerie* revealed a deep nostalgia I would not have expected in readers their age: nostalgia for past travels (usually, though not exclusively, in Paris); nostalgia for other courses (many of the students were soon to graduate); and that strange nostalgia one feels for something one has never in fact lived, something just out of reach—in this case, nineteenth-century France. The feeling of nostalgia that permeated the course led me to think about the nostalgic features of Baudelaire's "Le Peintre de la vie moderne" and related prose poems, a subject that in my research I will further explore in relation to exoticism and *flânerie mondiale*.

The Baudelaire works studied in The Flâneur prompted discussions of the environment, urban planning, poverty, foreignness, immigration, psychology, consumer culture, cultural history, identity, mind-body connection and disconnection, literary theory, the history of print media, and much more. Students examined the moral ambiguities inherent in the new experience of accelerated urban expansion in Baudelaire's time, along with similar quandaries in our own time arising from the exponential growth of the digital universe: cyberbullying, stalking, eavesdropping, threats to privacy. We considered the difficulties and the stakes of navigating the realms of mass communication, social networking, and cyberspace without an ethical compass. In other words, the prose poems proved relevant to students' experiences in countless ways. Yet I was pleasantly surprised when students sought out, even seemed to want to preserve, what was different about *Le Spleen de Paris*, its author, and its era.

The course I have described was not so much an attempt to solve or respond to the humanities crisis as evidence of my grappling with it. I still hang on to the conviction that the humanities need not justify their importance solely in terms of practicality, applicability, market value, or immediate relevance to the life and times of a given reader; that documentation of the human condition in various forms of expression—whether immediately comprehensible and relatable or challenging, disconcerting, idiosyncratic, complicated, spare, resistant to easy interpretation—has intrinsic worth. I anticipated that the course's intersections of literature, culture, time, space, and media would facilitate deeply focused reading while sparking broader interdisciplinary connections, self-reflection, even mindfulness. I tried to promote intellectual curiosity, active learning, and collaboration by fostering the experience of digression, discovery, surprises, and breakthroughs available through scholarly *flânerie*. Of course, none of this happened all the time, nor for all the students. But there were moments when the new paths opened by Baudelaire's unique texts led to intense engagement with reading, writing, contemplation, as well as thoughtful consideration of how literary studies can shock and puzzle readers but also resonate with everyday life and social interactions, online or on the street.

NOTES

[1] All translations from Baudelaire's *Le Spleen de Paris* are taken from Edward Kaplan's translation, *The Parisian Prowler*, unless otherwise indicated.

[2] Martina Lauster discusses Benjamin's "flawed" reading of Baudelaire and Poe, arguing that Benjamin's "idea of the *flâneur* is not only of limited value for an understanding of nineteenth-century urban experience, but can be seen positively to hamper it" (139). We returned often to this topic in my course.

NOTES ON CONTRIBUTORS

Joseph Acquisto, professor of French at the University of Vermont, is the author of *French Symbolist Poetry and the Idea of Music*; *Crusoes and Other Castaways in Modern French Literature*; and *The Fall Out of Redemption: Writing and Thinking Beyond Salvation in Baudelaire, Cioran, Fondane, Agamben, and Nancy*. He is also the editor of *Thinking Poetry: Philosophical Approaches to Nineteenth-Century French Poetry*.

Heather Willis Allen is associate professor of French at the University of Wisconsin-Madison. Her publications include *Alliages culturels: La Société française en transformation* (with Sébastien Dubreil); *Educating the Future Foreign Language Professoriate for the Twenty-First Century* (with Hiram H. Maxim); and *A Multiliteracies Framework for Collegiate Foreign Language Teaching* (with Kate Paesani and Beatrice Dupuy).

Aimée Boutin is professor of French at Florida State University. She is the author of *Maternal Echoes: The Poetry of Marceline Desbordes-Valmore and Alphonse de Lamartine* and *City of Noise: Sound and Nineteenth-Century Paris*. She has also published articles on Baudelaire and Romantic women poets as well as on Sand and Balzac.

Scott Carpenter is professor of French at Carleton College. His publications on literary studies include *Aesthetics of Fraudulence in Nineteenth-Century France: Frauds, Hoaxes, and Counterfeits*; *Reading Lessons: An Introduction to Theory*; and *Acts of Fiction: Resistance and Resolution from Sade to Baudelaire*. He is also the author of a novel, *Theory of Remainders*, and a volume of short stories, *This Jealous Earth*.

Peter Connor, professor of French and comparative literature at Barnard College, is the author of *Georges Bataille and the Mysticism of Sin* and the translator of *The Tears of Eros*, by Georges Bataille, and *The Inoperative Community*, by Jean-Luc Nancy.

Edward K. Kaplan, Kevy and Hortense Kaiserman Professor in the Humanities Emeritus, taught French and comparative literature and religious studies at Brandeis University from 1978 to 2015. He has published books on Jules Michelet and the Jewish philosopher Abraham Joshua Heschel. His works on Baudelaire include a book, *Baudelaire's Prose Poems: The Esthetic, the Ethical, and the Religious in* The Parisian Prowler (also translated into French); a translation of the poems, *The Parisian Prowler*, awarded the Lewis Galantière Prize of the American Translators Association; a translation of *La Fanfarlo*; and a classroom edition of *Les Fleurs du Mal*. He has also published articles on Michelet, Baudelaire, Hugo, Nerval, Rimbaud, Desbordes-Valmore, Bachelard, Jabès, and Bonnefoy, as well on Thomas Merton and Howard Thurman.

Cheryl Krueger is associate professor of French at the University of Virginia. She is the author of *The Art of Procrastination: Baudelaire's Poetry in Prose* and coauthor of *Tâches d'encre* and *Mise-en-scène: Cinéma et lecture*. Her articles on French literature, film, and cultural studies have appeared in a variety of journals. Her current book project treats the culture and poetics of olfaction and perfume in nineteenth-century France.

Françoise Lionnet is Professor of French, Comparative Literature and African and African American studies in Residence at Harvard University. Her books include *Writing Women and Critical Dialogues: Subjectivity, Gender and Irony* and *The Known and the*

Uncertain: Creole Cosmopolitics of the Indian Ocean, both published in Mauritius; and *Minor Transnationalism* and *The Creolization of Theory*, edited with Shu-mei Shih. She is also Distinguished Professor of French and Comparative Literature at UCLA.

Claire Chi-ah Lyu is associate professor of French at the University of Virginia. She is the author of *A Sun within a Sun: The Power and Elegance of Poetry*. Her articles have appeared in a number of journals including *L'Esprit Créateur*, *French Forum*, and *Nineteenth-Century French Studies*. Her current project seeks to propose a new paradigm of reading in literary studies: contemplative rather than suspicious reading.

Stamos Metzidakis is professor of French at Washington University in Saint Louis. His publications include *Difference Unbound: The Rise of Pluralism in Literature and Criticism*; *Understanding French Poetry: Essays for a New Millennium*; and *Repetition and Semiotics: Interpreting Prose Poems*. His teaching and research focus on modern literature and theory. His forthcoming books are "Des lignes et des lettres: Essais néo-formalistes" and "Recollecting French America: A Personal Chronology."

Catherine Nesci is professor of French and comparative literature at the University of California, Santa Barbara. Her books include *La Femme mode d'emploi: Balzac, de* La Physiologie du mariage *à* La Comédie humaine; *Le Flâneur et les flâneuses: Les Femmes et la ville à l'époque romantique*; and *Écriture, performance et théâtralité dans l'œuvre de George Sand* (edited with Olivier Bara). She is currently expanding her reflection on *flânerie* in women writers and artists, including Colette, Agnès Varda, and Régine Robin.

Kate Paesani is director of the Center for Advanced Research on Language Acquisition (CARLA) at the University of Minnesota. Her research interests include literacy-based foreign language curriculum and instruction, literature across the curriculum, and foreign language teacher development. She is the author of *A Multiliteracies Framework for Collegiate Foreign Language Teaching* (with Heather Willis Allen and Beatrice Dupuy).

Laurence M. Porter is currently an Oberlin College Affiliate Scholar in Comparative Literature. He edited the MLA Approaches to Teaching volumes on Baudelaire's *Les Fleurs du Mal* and Flaubert's *Madame Bovary*. His monographs include *The Crisis of French Symbolism*; *Women's Vision in Western Literature*; and others on Freud, Hugo, *Madame Bovary*, and modes of the Romantic lyric.

Larson Powell is professor of German at the University of Missouri, Kansas City. He is the author of *The Technological Unconscious in German Modernist Literature: Rilke, Benn, Brecht, and Doeblin* and *The Differentiation of Modernism: Postwar German Media Arts*. He has published and lectured in German, French, and English, on German film and literature as well as on musicology, psychoanalysis, systems theory, and philosophical aesthetics.

Scott M. Powers, associate professor of French at the University of Mary Washington, has contributed to two volumes in the MLA Approaches to Teaching series. He is the editor of *Evil in Contemporary French and Francophone Literature* and the author of *Confronting Evil: the Psychology of Secularization in Modern French Literature*. He is currently pursuing a study of secularization in the novels of Michel Tremblay.

Debarati Sanyal is professor of French at the University of California, Berkeley. She is the author of *Memory and Complicity: Migrations of Holocaust Remembrance* and *The Violence of Modernity: Baudelaire, Irony, and the Politics of Form* and the coeditor of

Noeuds de mémoire: Multidirectional Memory in Postwar French and Francophone Culture, a special issue of *Yale French Studies*. Her current project investigates the poetics of political asylum.

Beryl Schlossman is professor of comparative literature at the University of California, Irvine. Her publications include *Joyce's Catholic Comedy of Language*; *The Orient of Style: Modernist Allegories of Conversion*; and *Objects of Desire: The Madonnas of Modernism*. Other refereed publications include a volume of poetry, *Angelus Novus*, and a novella, *Left Bank Dream*. Current work includes a book on Baudelaire and Benjamin.

Maria Scott is lecturer in French at the University of Exeter. Her publications include *Baudelaire's* Le Spleen de Paris*: Shifting Perspectives* and *Stendhal's Less-Loved Heroines: Fiction, Freedom, and the Female*, which was published in French translation as *Stendhal, la liberté et les héroïnes mal aimées*. She is working on a book about fictional strangers and the question of empathy.

SURVEY RESPONDENTS

The following scholars and teachers generously agreed to participate in the survey of approaches to teaching Baudelaire's prose poems that preceded and informed preparation of this volume. Without their assistance, this volume would not have been possible.

Joseph Acquisto, *University of Vermont*
Robert Barsky, *Vanderbilt University*
Martine Benjamin, *Princeton University*
Jerry Blanton, *Miami-Dade College*
Maria da Glória Bordini, *Universidade Federal do Rio Grande do Sul*
Sara Steinert Borella, *Franklin College*
Suzanne Braswell, *University of Miami*
Christine M. Cano, *Case Western Reserve University*
Scott Carpenter, *Carleton College*
Peter Connor, *Barnard College*
F. Elizabeth Dahab, *California State University, Long Beach*
Michael Demson, *Sam Houston State University*
Thérèse De Raedt, *University of Utah*
Brooke Donaldson Di Lauro, *University of Mary Washington*
Sébastien Doubinsky, *Aarhus University, Denmark*
David R. Ellison, *University of Miami*
Jean-François Fournier, *University of Notre Dame*
Sima Godfrey, *University of British Columbia*
John Hicks, *Cornell University*
Edward K. Kaplan, *Brandeis University*
Elizabeth M. Knutson, *United States Naval Academy*
Francoise Lionnet, *University of California, Los Angeles*
Rosemary Lloyd, *Indiana University, Bloomington*
Claire Chi-ah Lyu, *University of Virginia*
Lori Martindale, *Whatcom Community College, WA*
Gloria Melgarejo, *Saint Cloud State University*
Stamos Metzidakis, *Washington University in Saint Louis*
Jean-Jacques Poucel, *Yale University / Southern Connecticut State University*
David A. Powell, *Hofstra University*
Larson Powell, *University of Missouri, Kansas City*
Scott Powers, *University of Mary Washington*
Vaheed Ramazani, *Tulane University*
Timothy Raser, *University of Georgia*
Marilyn Gaddis Rose, *Binghamton University, State University of New York*
Adam Rosenthal, *Emory University*
Beryl Schlossman, *University of California, Irvine*
Bendi Benson Schrambach, *Whitworth University*
Maria Scott, *University of Exeter*
Richard Stein, *University of Oregon*

Kelle Truby, *University of California, Riverside*
Teresa Villa-Ignacio, *Harvard University*
Anne F. Walker, *University of California, Merced*
Christophe Wall-Romana, *University of Minnesota, Twin Cities*
Nancy Watanabe, *University of Oklahoma Libraries*
Joyce Wu, *Duke University*
Keri Yousif, *Indiana State University*
Melvin Zimmerman, *York University*

WORKS CITED

Works by Baudelaire

Editions of Baudelaire's Prose Poems

Baudelaire: Le Spleen de Paris: Petits Poèmes en prose. Ed. Jean-Luc Steinmetz. Paris: Le Livre de Poche, 2003. Print.

La Fanfarlo [and] Le Spleen de Paris: Petits Poèmes en prose. Ed. Barbara Wright and David Scott. Paris: Flammarion, 1987. Print.

Petits Poëmes en prose. *La Presse* 26 Aug. 1862: 1–2. *Gallica*. Web. 5 Oct. 2013. <http://gallica.bnf.fr/ark:/12148/bpt6k479531x/f1.image>.

Petits Poëmes en prose. Ed. Robert Kopp. Paris: Corti, 1969. Print.

Petits Poèmes en prose. Ed. Philippe Lehu. Paris: Larousse, 2008. Print.

Petits Poèmes en prose (Le Spleen de Paris). Ed. Henri Lemaître. Paris: Garnier, 1962. Print.

Le Spleen de Paris. Ed. Claude Pichois. Baudelaire, *Œuvres complètes* 1: 275–363.

Le Spleen de Paris (Petits Poèmes en prose): Suivi d'une anthologie sur le poème en prose. Ed. Alain Couprie and Johan Faerber. Paris: Hatier, 2013. Print. Classiques and CIE Lycée.

Le Spleen de Paris: Petits Poèmes en prose. Ed. Robert Kopp. Paris: Gallimard, 2006. Print. Classiques.

Translations of Baudelaire's Prose Poems

Baudelaire in English. Ed. Carol Clark and Robert Sykes. London: Penguin, 1997. Print. Penguin Classics: Poets in Translation.

Paris Blues: Le Spleen de Paris. Trans. Francis Scarfe. London: Anvil, 2012. Print.

The Parisian Prowler: Le Spleen de Paris. Petits Poèmes en prose. Trans. Edward Kaplan. Athens: U of Georgia P, 1997. Print.

Paris Spleen. Trans. Martin Sorrell. Richmond: One World Classics, 2010. Print.

Paris Spleen. Trans. Louise Varèse. New York: New Directions, 1970. Print.

Paris Spleen: Little Poems in Prose. Trans. Keith Waldrop. Middletown: Wesleyan UP, 2009. Print.

———. *The Poems and Prose Poems of Charles Baudelaire*. Trans. James Huneker. New York: Brentano's, 1919. Web. *Project Gutenberg*. 1 Aug. 2012.

———. *Poems in Prose from Charles Baudelaire*. Trans. Arthur Symons. London: Mathews, 1905. Print.

———. *The Prose Poems and* La Fanfarlo. Trans. Rosemary Lloyd. Oxford: Oxford UP, 1991. Print.

———. *Twenty Prose Poems*. Trans. Michael Hamburger. San Francisco: City Lights, 2001. Print.

Editions and Translations of Baudelaire's Other Works

Art in Paris: Salons and Other Exhibitions. London: Phaidon, 1965. Print.

L'Art romantique. Paris: Garnier, 1931. Print.

Baudelaire journaliste: Articles et chroniques. Ed. Alain Vaillant. Paris: Flammarion, 2011. Print.

Complete Poems. Trans. Walter Martin. Exeter: Carcanet, 2006. Print.

Correspondance. Ed. Claude Pichois. 2 vols. Paris: Gallimard, 1973. Print.

"La Double Vie par Charles Asselineau." Pichois, *Oeuvres complètes* 1: 87–102.

Exposition Universelle, 1855. Ed. Claude Pichois. Baudelaire, *Œuvres complètes* 2: 577–78. Print.

Fanfarlo. Trans. Edward K. Kaplan. Brooklyn: Melville, 2012. Print.

Les Fleurs du Mal. Trans. Richard Howard. Boston: Godine, 1982. Print.

Les Fleurs du Mal. Ed. Edward K. Kaplan. Newark: Molière: 2010. Print. French Classics.

Les Fleurs du Mal. Ed. Claude Pichois. Baudelaire, *Œuvres complètes* 1: 1–145.

The Flowers of Evil. Trans. James McGowan. Oxford: Oxford UP, 1993. Print. Oxford World Classics.

The Flowers of Evil. Trans. Keith Waldrop. Middletown: Wesleyan UP, 2006. Print.

Intimate Journals. Trans. Christopher Isherwood. New York: Dover, 2006. Print.

Œuvres complètes. Ed. Claude Pichois. 2 vols. Paris: Gallimard, 1975. Print. Bibliothèque de la Pléiade 1.7.

"The Painter of Modern Life" and Other Essays. Trans. and ed. Jonathan Mayne. London: Phaidon, 1995. Print.

Le Peintre de la vie moderne. Ed. Claude Pichois. *Œuvres complètes* 2: 683–725.

Les Poèmes mascarins de Charles Baudelaire. Ed. and trans. Emmanuel Richon and Vimala Rungasamy. Paris: L'Harmattan, 1993. Print.

"Projets de préface." Ed. Claude Pichois. Baudelaire, *Œuvres complètes* 1: 181–86.

Salon de 1859. Ed. Claude Pichois. Baudelaire. *Œuvres complètes* 2: 608–82.

Selected Letters of Charles Baudelaire. Ed. and trans. Rosemary Lloyd. Chicago: U of Chicago P, 2006. Print.

Selected Poems from Flowers of Evil. Trans. Wallace Fowlie. Ontario: Bantam, 1963. Print.

Selected Writings on Art and Artists. Trans. P. E. Charvet. Harmondsworth: Penguin, 1972.

Selected Writings on Art and Artists. Trans. P. E. Charvet. Cambridge: Cambridge UP, 1981. Print.

Pichois, Claude. *Album Baudelaire: Iconographie réunie et commentée par Claude Pichois*. Paris: Gallimard, 1974. Print. Bibliothèque de la Pléiade.

Primary and Critical Works by Others

Acquisto, Joseph. *Crusoes and Other Castaways in Modern French Literature: Solitary Adventures*. Newark: U of Delaware P, 2012. Print.

———. *The Fall out of Redemption: Writing and Thinking beyond Salvation in Baudelaire, Cioran, Fondane, Agamben, and Nancy*. New York: Bloomsbury, 2015. Print.

———. *French Symbolist Poetry and the Idea of Music*. London: Ashgate, 2006. Print.

Adorno, Theodor. "Rückblickend auf den Sürrealismus." *Noten zur Literatur*. Frankfurt: Suhrkamp, 1997. Print. Vol. 11 of *Gesammelte Schriften*.

Aggeler, William F., comp. *Baudelaire Judged by Spanish Critics, 1857–1957*. Athens: U of Georgia P, 1971. Print.

Ahearn, Edward J. "Femme, ville, empire: 'Les Foules,' 'Le Cygne,' 'La Belle Dorothée.'" Guyaux and Scepi 11–15.

Alexis, Jacques Stephen. *Les Arbres musiciens*. Paris: Gallimard, 1957. Print.

Allen, Heather W. "A Multiple Literacies Approach to the Advanced French Writing Course." *French Review* 83.2 (2009): 368–87. Print.

Allen, Heather W., and Kate Paesani. "Exploring the Feasibility of a Pedagogy of Multiliteracies in Introductory Foreign Language Courses." *L2 Journal* 2.1 (2010): 119–42. Print.

Ampère, Jean-Jacques. "De l'Histoire de la littérature française." *Revue des deux-mondes* 3.1 (1834): 406–25. Print.

Asselineau, Charles. *Charles Baudelaire: Sa vie et son œuvre*. 1869. Cognac: Le Temps qu'Il Fait, 1990. Print.

"Attacks Called Great Art." *The New York Times*. New York Times, 19 Sept. 2001. Web. 6 Nov. 2015. <http://www.nytimes.com/2001/09/19/arts/attacks-called-great-art.html>.

Aynesworth, Donald. "Humanity and Monstrosity in *Le Spleen de Paris*." *Romanic Review* 73.2 (1982): 209–21. Print.

Baguley, David, ed. *A Critical Bibliography of French Literature: The Nineteenth Century*. 2 vols. Syracuse: Syracuse UP, 1994. Print.

Bakhtin, Mikhail M. *The Dialogic Imagination*. Trans. Caryl Emerson and Michael Holquist. Ed. Holquist. Austin: U of Texas P, 1981. Print.

Balzac, Honoré de. *Le Père Goriot*. Paris: Flammarion, 2006. Print.

Bandy, W. T. *Baudelaire devant ses contemporains*. 3rd ed. Paris: Klincksieck, 1995. Print.

———. "Baudelaire et Croly—La Vérité sur *Le Jeune Enchanteur*." *Mercure de France* 1 Feb. 1950: 230–47. Print.

———. *Baudelaire Judged by His Contemporaries (1845–1867)*. New York: Columbia UP, 1933. Print.

Barthes, Roland. "Theory of the Text." *Untying the Text: A Post-structuralist Reader*. Ed. Robert Young. London: Routledge, 1981. 31–47. Print.

Beaujour, Michel. "Short Epiphanies: Two Contextual Approaches to the French Prose Poem." Caws and Riffaterre 39–59.

Beauverd, Jacques. "Avez-vous compris 'L'Invitation au voyage'?" *Hommages à Jacques Petit*. Paris: Belles Lettres, 1985. 743–51. Print.

Belcher, Wendy Laura. *Writing Your Journal Article in Twelve Weeks*. Thousand Oaks: Sage, 2009. Print.

Benjamin, Walter. *The Arcades Project*. Trans. Howard Eiland and Kevin McLaughlin. Cambridge: Belknap, 1999. Print.

———. *Baudelaire*. Ed. Giorgio Agamben, Barbara Chitussi, and Clemens-Carl Härle. Paris: La Fabrique, 2013. Print.

———. *Charles Baudelaire, un poète lyrique à l'apogée du capitalisme*. Trans. Jean Lacoste. Paris: Payot, 1980. Print.

———. *Das Passagenwerk*. Frankfurt: Suhrkamp, 1983. Print.

———. "The Storyteller." *Illuminations: Essays and Reflections*. New York: Schocken, 1968. 83–109. Print.

———. "The Task of the Translator." Biguenet and Schulte 71–83.

———. *"The Work of Art in the Age of Its Technological Reproducibility" and Other Writings on Media*. Cambridge: Harvard UP, 2008. Print.

———. *The Writer of Modern Life: Essays on Charles Baudelaire*. Ed. Michael W. Jennings et al. Cambridge: Harvard UP, 2006. Print.

Berman, Antoine. *Toward a Translation Criticism: John Donne*. Trans. Françoise Massardier-Kenney. Kent: Kent State UP, 2009. Print.

Bernard, Suzanne. *Le Poème en prose de Baudelaire jusqu'à nos jours*. Paris: Nizet, 1959. Print.

Bernhardt, Elizabeth. "Progress and Procrastination in Second Language Reading." *Annual Review of Applied Linguistics* 25 (2005): 133–50. Print.

Bersani, Leo. *The Culture of Redemption*. Cambridge: Harvard UP, 1990. Print.

Bertrand, Aloysius. *Gaspard de la nuit: Fantaisies à la manière de Rembrandt et de Callot*. Ed. Max Milner. Paris: Gallimard, 1980. Print.

Bertrand, Jean-Pierre. "Une Lecture médiatique du *Spleen de Paris*." Thérenty and Vaillant, *Presse* 329–37.

Bien, Gloria. *Baudelaire in China: A Study in Literary Reception*. Newark: U of Delaware P, 2013. Print.

Biguenet, John, and Rainer Schulte, eds. *Theories of Translation*. Chicago: U of Chicago P, 1992. Print.

Blin, Georges. Introduction. Baudelaire, *Spleen* [Kopp] 7–41.

———. *Le Sadisme de Baudelaire*. Paris: Corti, 1948. Print.

Bloom, Harold, ed. *Charles Baudelaire.* New York: Chelsea House, 1987. Print.

Bonenfant, Luc. *Les Avatars romantiques du genre: Transferts génériques dans l'œuvre d'Aloysius Bertrand.* Québec: Nota Bene, 2002. Print.

Boucher, Gwenaëlle, ed. *Poètes créoles du XVIIIᵉ siècle: Parny, Bertin, Léonard.* Vol 1. Paris: L'Harmattan, 2009. Print.

Bourdieu, Pierre. *Les Règles de l'art.* Paris: Seuil, 1992. Print.

Boutin, Aimée. *City of Noise: Sound and Nineteenth-Century Paris.* Urbana: U of Illinois P, 2015.

———. "Rethinking the Flâneur: Flânerie and the Senses." *Dix-Neuf: Journal of the Society of Dix-Neuviémistes* 16.2 (2012): 124–32. Web. 15 Sept. 2012.

Breton, André. *Manifestoes of Surrealism.* Trans. Richard Seaver and Helen R. Lane. Ann Arbor: U of Michigan P, 1969. Print.

Brix Michel. "Baudelaire, 'disciple' d'Edgar Poe?" *Romantisme* 122 (2003): 55–69. Print.

Brooks, Peter. *Reading for the Plot.* New York: Knopf, 1984. Print.

Broome, Peter. *Baudelaire's Poetic Patterns: The Secret Language of* Les Fleurs du Mal. Amsterdam: Rodopi, 1999. Print.

Burnshaw, Stanley, ed. *The Poem Itself.* Fayetteville: U of Arkansas P, 1995. Print.

Burton, Richard D. E. *Baudelaire and the Second Empire.* Oxford: Clarendon, 1991. Print.

———. *Baudelaire in 1859: A Study in the Sources of Poetic Creativity.* Cambridge: Cambridge UP, 2009. Print.

———. "Bonding and Breaking in Baudelaire's *Petits Poèmes en prose.*" *Modern Language Review* 88.1 (1993): 58–73. Print.

———. "Destruction as Creation: 'Le Mauvais Vitrier' and the Poetics and Politics of Violence." *Romantic Review* 83.3 (1992): 297–322. Print.

———. *The Flâneur and His City: Patterns of Daily Life in Paris, 1815–1851.* Durham: Durham Mod. Langs., 2010. Print.

Butor, Michel. *Histoire extraordinaire: Essai sur un rêve de Baudelaire.* Paris: Gallimard, 1961. Print.

Byrnes, Heidi, Hiram H. Maxim, and John Norris. "Realizing Advanced Foreign Language Writing Development in Collegiate Education: Curricular Design, Pedagogy, Assessment." *Modern Language Journal* 94, supp. (2010): 1–221. Print.

Calinescu, Matei. *Five Faces of Modernity.* Durham: Duke UP, 1987. Print.

Calvino, Italo. *Six Memos for the Next Millennium.* New York: Vintage, 1988. Print. The Charles Eliot Norton Lectures, 1985–86.

Carpenter, Scott. *Acts of Fiction: Resistance and Revolution from Sade to Baudelaire.* University Park: Pennsylvania State UP, 1966. Print.

———. *Aesthetics of Fraudulence in Nineteenth-Century France: Fraud, Hoaxes, and Counterfeits.* Farnham: Ashgate, 2009. Print.

Caws, Mary Ann. "Insertion in an Oval Frame: Poe Circumscribed by Baudelaire." Bloom 101–23.

Caws, Mary Ann, and Hermine Riffaterre, eds. *The Prose Poem in France: Theory and Practice.* New York: Columbia UP, 1983. Print.

Chambers, Ross. *An Atmospherics of the City: Baudelaire and the Poetics of Noise*. New York: Fordham, 2015. Print.

———. "Baudelaire's Dedicatory Practice." *SubStance* 56 (1988): 5–17. Print.

———. "Baudelaire's Street Poetry." *Nineteenth-Century French Studies* 13.4 (1985): 244–59. Print.

———. "The Classroom versus Poetry; or, Teaching Transportation." Porter, *Approaches* 170–82.

———. *Loiterature*. Lincoln: U of Nebraska P, 1999. Print.

———. *Mélancolie et opposition*. Paris: Corti, 1987. Print.

———. "Modern Beauty: Baudelaire, the Everyday Cultural Studies." *Romance Studies* 26.3 (2008): 249–70. Print.

Chesters, Graham. *Baudelaire and the Poetics of Craft*. Cambridge: Cambridge UP, 1988. Print.

Chevrel, Yves, Lieven D'Hulst, and Christine Lombez, eds. *Histoire des traductions en langue française: XIXᵉ siècle 1815–1914*. Lagrasse: Verdier, 2012. Print.

Citton, Yves. *Lire, interpréter, actualiser: Pourquoi les études littéraires?* Paris: Amsterdam, 2007. Print.

Cohen, Emily-Jane. "Mud into Gold: Baudelaire and the Alchemy of Public Hygiene." *Romanic Review* 87.2 (1996): 239–55. Print.

Cohn, Robert Greer. "A Poetry-Prose Cross." Caws and Riffaterre 135–62.

Compagnon, Antoine. *Les Antimodernes*. Paris: Gallimard, 2005. Print.

———. *Five Paradoxes of Modernity*. New York: Columbia UP, 1994. Print.

Cope, Bill, and Mary Kalantzis. "'Multiliteracies': New Literacies, New Learning." *Pedagogies: An International Journal* 4.3 (2009): 164–95. Print.

Cowan, Michael. "Imagining Modernity through the Ear: Rilke's *Aufzeichnungen des Malte Laurids Brigge* and the Noise of Modern Life." *Arcadia* 46.1 (2006): 124–46. Print.

Culler, Jonathan D. "Baudelaire and Poe." *Zeitschrift für französische Sprache und Literatur* 100 (1990): 61–73. Print.

———. "Baudelaire's Destruction." *Modern Language Notes* 127.4 (2012): 699–711. Print.

———. "Teaching Baudelaire, Teaching Translation." *Profession* (2010): 91–98. Print.

———. "Teaching the Devil." Porter, *Approaches to Teaching* 139–46.

Curmer, Léon, ed. *Les Français peints par eux-mêmes: Encyclopédie morale du XIXᵉ siècle*. 1840–42. Preface and notes by Pierre Bouttier. 2 vols. Paris: Omnibus, 2003. Print.

———, ed. *Les Francais peints par eux-mêmes: Encyclopédie morale du XIXᵉ siècle*. 10 vols. 1840–42. Paris: Phillipart, 1861. Print. *Gallica*. Web. <http://gallica.bnf.fr/ark:/12148/bpt6k207984c>

D'Amelio, Nadia, ed. *Les Traductions extraordinaires d'Edgar Poe*. Mons: CIPA, 2010. Print.

De George, Fernande. "The Structure of Baudelaire's *Petits Poèmes en prose*." *L'Esprit Créateur* 13 (1973): 144–53. Print.

de Jonge, Alex. *Baudelaire, Prince of Clouds: A Biography*. New York: Paddington, 1976. Print.

Delerm, Philippe. *La Première Gorgée de bière et autres plaisirs minuscules*. Paris: Gallimard, 1997. Print.

Deleuze, Gilles. *Spinoza: Practical Philosophy*. Trans. Robert Hurley. San Francisco: City Lights, 1988. Print.

de Man, Paul. *Blindness and Insight*. Minneapolis: U of Minnesota P, 1983. Print.

———. *The Rhetoric of Romanticism*. New York: Columbia UP, 1984. Print.

Derrida, Jacques. "Des Tours de Babel." Graham 218–27.

———. *Donner le temps I: La Fausse Monnaie*. Paris: Seuil, 1992. Print.

———. *Given Time: I. Counterfeit Money*. Trans. Peggy Kamuf. Chicago: U of Chicago P, 1992. Print.

———. *La Vérité en peinture*. Paris: Flammarion, 1978. Print.

———. "What Is a 'Relevant' Translation?" Venuti, *Translation* [2012] 365–88.

Devi, Ananda. "La Cathédrale." *Solstices*. Port-Louis: Le Printemps, 1976. Print.

"Devoir." *Le Grand Dictionnaire universel du XIXᵉ siècle*. Ed. Pierre Larousse. Vol. 6. Paris: Administration du grand dictionnaire universel, 1866–77. 671–75. Print.

Dienstag, Joshua. *Pessimism: Philosophy, Ethic, Spirit*. Princeton: Princeton UP, 2006. Print.

Disegni, Silvia, ed. *Poésie et journalisme au XIXᵉ siècle en France et en Italie*. Spec. issue of *Recherches et travaux* 65 (2004): 5–185. Print.

———. "Les Poètes journalistes au temps de Baudelaire." Disegni, *Poésie* 83–98.

Donato, Richard, and Frank B. Brooks. "Literary Discussions and Advanced Speaking Functions: Researching the (Dis)Connection." *Foreign Language Annals* 37.2 (2004): 183–199. Print.

D'Souza, Aruna, and Tom McDonough. *The Invisible* Flâneuse? *Gender, Public Space, and Visual Culture in Nineteenth-Century Paris*. Manchester: Manchester UP: 2006. Print.

Dumasy-Queffélec, Lise. "Le Feuilleton." Kalifa, Régnier, Thérenty, and Vaillant 925–36.

Edmundson, Mark. *Why Read?* New York: Bloomsbury, 2004. Print.

Eitner, Lorenz. "The Open Window and the Storm-Tossed Boat: An Essay in the Iconography of Romanticism." *Art Bulletin* 37.4 (1955): 281–90. Print.

Ensemble Clément Janequin, perf. *L'Écrit du cri*. Harmonia Mundi, 2009. CD.

Ernaux, Annie. *Journal du dehors*. Paris: Gallimard, 1995. Print.

Evans, Margery. *Baudelaire and Intertextuality: Poetry at the Crossroads*. Cambridge: Cambridge UP, 1993. Print.

Felski, Rita. *Uses of Literature.* Blackwell: Malden, 2008. Print.

Ferguson, Priscilla Parkhurst. *Paris as Revolution: Writing the Nineteenth Century-City.* Berkeley: U of California P, 1997. Print.

Fight Club. Dir. David Fincher. Twentieth Century Fox, 1999. Film.

"Fight Club—Homework Scene." *Vimeo*. Vimeo, 31 May 2012. Web. 9 Nov. 2015. <http://vimeo.com/43177217>.

"Fight Club Ikea Catalogue Scene." *Critical Commons*. Critical Commons, n.d. Web. 9 Nov. 2015. <http://criticalcommons.org/Members/adiab/clips/FF_Fincher FightClub-possum.mp4/view>.

Flower, Linda. "Introduction: Studying Cognition in Context." *Reading-to-Write: Exploring a Cognitive and Social Process*. Ed. Flower, Victoria Stein, John Ackerman, Margaret J. Kantz, Kathleen McCormick, and Wayne C. Peck. New York: Oxford UP, 1990. 3–32. Print.

Fondane, Benjamin. *Baudelaire et l'expérience du gouffre*. Paris: Seghers, 1972. Print.

Fournel, Victor. *Ce qu'on voit dans les rues de Paris*. Paris: Dentu, 1867. Print.

———. *Les Cris de Paris: Types et physionomies d'autrefois. 1887*. Paris: Editions de Paris, 2003. Print.

Fraser, Ryan. "Traduction et le texte interprétatif: Deux interprétations de Baudelaire." *Métamorphoses: Réflexions critiques sur la littérature, la langue et le cinéma*. Toronto: Paratexte, 2002. 107–21. Print.

Gautier, David. "L'Invitation au voyage." *YouTube.com*. YouTube, 10 Apr. 2007. Web. 21 July 2011. <http://www.youtube.com/watch?v=jDRpmM9ttMI&feature =related>.

Gautier, Théophile. *Baudelaire*.1868. Paris: Le Castor Astral, 1991. Print.

Gauvin, Lise, and Cécile van den Avenne, eds. *Parodies, pastiches, réécritures: La Question des modèles dans les littératures francophones*. Lyon: ENS, 2013. Print.

Gavalda, Anna. *Je voudrais que quelqu'un m'attende quelque part*. Paris: Le Dilettante, 1999. Print.

Genette, Gérard. *Figures III*. Paris: Seuil, 1972. Print.

Gerrard, Lisa, Barbara Rusterholz, and Sheri S. Long. *En train d'écrire: A Process Approach to French Composition*. New York: McGraw, 1993.

Giroux, Henry, and Imre Szeman. "Ikea Boy Fights Back: *Fight Club*, Consumerism, and the Political Limits of Nineties Cinema." Lewis 96–104.

Glissant, Édouard. *La Lézarde*. Paris: Seuil, 1958. Print.

———. *Poétique de la relation*. Paris: Gallimard, 1990. Print.

Godfrey, Sima. "Baudelaire's Windows." *L'Esprit Créateur* 22.4 (1982): 83–100. Print.

———. "The Dandy as Ironic Figure." *SubStance* 36 (1981–82): 21–32. Print.

Graham, Joseph, ed. *Difference in Translation*. Ithaca: Cornell UP, 1985. Print.

Grava, Arnolds. *L'Aspect métaphysique du mal dans l'œuvre littéraire de Charles Baudelaire et d'Edgar Allan Poe*. Lincoln: U of Nebraska P, 1956. Print.

Guerlac, Suzanne. *The Impersonal Sublime: Hugo, Baudelaire, Lautréamont*. Stanford: Stanford UP, 1990. Print.

Gutbrodt, Fritz. "Poedelaire: Translation and the Volatility of the Letter." *Diacritics* 22.3–4 (1992): 49–68. Print.

Guyaux, André, and Henri Scepi, eds. *Lire* Le Spleen de Paris. Paris: P de U Paris, Sorbonne, 2014. Print.

Hadot, Pierre. *Éloge de Socrate*. Paris: Allia, 1998. Print.

Hall, Joan Kelly. *Methods for Teaching Foreign Languages: Creating a Community of Learners in the Classroom*. Upper Saddle River: Prentice-Hall, 2001. Print.

Handwerk, Gary J. *Irony and Ethics in Narrative.* New Haven: Yale UP, 1985. Print.

Hansen, Mark B. N. "New Media." Mitchell and Hansen 172–85.

Hansen, Miriam Bratu. *Cinema and Experience: S. Kracauer, W. Benjamin, and T. W. Adorno.* Berkeley: U of California P, 2012. Print.

Hanssen, Beatrice. *Critique of Violence: Between Poststructuralism and Critical Theory.* London: Routledge, 2000. Print.

Hargreaves, Alec, Charles Forsdick, and David Murphy, eds. *Transnational French Studies: Postcolonialism and* Littérature-monde. Liverpool: Liverpool UP, 2010. Print.

Harrington, Karen. "L'Invitation au Voyage." Thompson 109–21.

Hemmings, F. W. J. *Baudelaire the Damned: A Biography.* London: Scribner's, 1982. Print.

Hiddleston, J. A. *Baudelaire and* Le Spleen de Paris. Oxford: Oxford UP, 1987. Print.

Hill, Donald L., ed. *The Renaissance: Studies in Art and Poetry.* Berkeley: U of California P, 1980.

Hilton, Frank. *Baudelaire in Chains: Portrait of the Artist as a Drug Addict.* London: Owen, 2004. Print.

Horney, Karen. *Neurosis and Human Growth: The Struggle toward Self-Realization.* New York: Norton, 1950. Print.

———. *Our Inner Conflicts.* New York: Norton, 1945. Print.

Houssaye, Arsène. "La Chanson du vitrier." *Œuvres complètes.* Ed. Claude Pichois. Vol. 1. Paris: Gallimard, 1976. 1309–11. Print.

———. *Œuvres poétiques complètes: L'Amour, l'art, la vie; Histoire d'Arsène Houssaye.* Paris: Hachette, 1857. Print.

Huart, Louis. *Physiologie du flâneur.* Paris: Aubert, 1841. *Gallica.* Web. 15 Sept. 2012. *Gallica.* Web. <http://gallica.bnf.fr/ark:12148/bpt6k62352r>

Hubert, Judd. "Using Translation in Explicating *Les Fleurs du Mal*: 'La Cloche fêlée.'" Porter, *Approaches* 72–77.

Hugo, Victor. *Les Contemplations.* Ed. Léon Cellier. Paris: Garnier, 1969. Print.

———. *Cromwell.* Ed. Anne Ubersfeld. Paris: Garnier-Flammarion, 1968. Print.

Jackson, John E., ed. *Baudelaire.* Paris: Livre de Poche, 2001. Print.

Jahraus, Oliver. *Literatur als Medium: Sinnkonstitution und Subjekterfahrung zwischen Bewusstsein und Kommunikation.* Weilerswist: Velbrück, 2003. Print.

Jakobson, Roman. "On Linguistic Aspects of Translation." Biguenet and Schulte 144–51.

Jameson, Fredric. *The Modernist Papers.* London: Verso, 2007. Print.

Jamison, Anne. *Poetics en Passant: Redefining the Relationship between Victorian and Modern Poetry.* New York: Palgrave, 2012. Print.

Jankélévitch, Vladimir. *L'Ironie.* Paris: Flammarion, 1964. Print.

Johnson, Barbara. *Défigurations du langage poétique: La Seconde Révolution baudelairienne.* Paris: Flammarion, 1979. Print.

———. "Poetry and Its Double: Two 'Invitations au Voyage.'" Bloom 35–62.

Kalifa, Dominique, Philippe Régnier, Marie-Ève Thérenty, and Alain Vaillant, eds. *La Civilisation du journal. Histoire culturelle et littéraire de la presse française au XIXe siècle.* Paris: Nouveau Monde, 2011. Print.

Kaplan, Edward K. "Baudelaire and the Battle with Finitude: 'La Mort,' Conclusion of *Les Fleurs du Mal.*" *French Forum* 4.3 (1979): 219–31. Print.

———. "Baudelairean Ethics." Lloyd, *Cambridge Companion* 87–100.

———. *Baudelaire's Prose Poems: The Esthetic, the Ethical, and the Religious in* The Parisian Prowler. Athens: U of Georgia P, 1990. Print.

———. "Poetry, Truth, and Human Sanctity: Baudelaire's Experimental Genre." *L'Esprit Créateur* 39.1: 15–25. Print.

———. Preface. Baudelaire, *Parisian Prowler* vii–xii.

———. "Teaching the Ethical Baudelaire." Porter, *Approaches* 147–53.

Katz, Stacey. "Teaching Literary Texts at the Intermediate Level: A Structured Input Approach." *SLA and the Literature Classroom: Fostering Dialogues. Issues in Language Program Direction: A Series of Annual Volumes* (2001): 155–71. Print.

Kern, Richard. *Literacy and Language Teaching*. Oxford: Oxford UP, 2000. Print.

———. "Reconciling the Language-Literature Split through Literacy." *ADFL Bulletin* 33.3 (2002): 20–24. Print.

Kern, Richard, and Jean Marie Schultz. "Beyond Orality: Investigating Literacy and the Literary in Second and Foreign Language Instruction." *Modern Language Journal* 89.3 (2005): 381–92. Print.

Kierkegaard, Søren. Fear and Trembling *and* The Sickness unto Death. Trans. Walter Lowrie. Princeton: Princeton UP, 1968. Print.

King, Russell S. "Syntactic Compensations in the Two Versions of Baudelaire's 'L'Invitation au voyage.'" *Nottingham French Studies* 12 (1973): 22–32. Print.

Kittler, Friedrich. *Discourse Networks 1800/1900*. Trans. Michael Metteer. Stanford: Stanford UP, 1990. Print.

Kristeva, Julia. "Bakthine, le mot, le dialogue et le roman." *Critique* 239 (1967): 438–65. Print.

Krueger, Cheryl. *The Art of Procrastination: Baudelaire's Poetry in Prose*. Newark: U of Delaware P, 2007. Print.

———. "Flâneur Smellscapes in *Le Spleen de Paris.*" *Dix-neuf* 16.2 (2012): 181–92. Web. 19 Aug. 2012.

———. "Form, Content and Critical Distance." *Foreign Language Annals* 34.1 (2001): 18–27. Print.

———. "Telling Stories in Baudelaire's *Spleen de Paris.*" *Nineteenth-Century French Studies* 30.3 (2002): 281–99. Print.

Labarthe, Patrick. Petits Poèmes en prose *de Charles Baudelaire: Commentaires.* Paris: Gallimard, 2000. Print.

Larbaud, Valéry. *Sous l'invocation de Saint Jérôme*. Paris: Gallimard, 1986. Print.

Lauster, Martina. "Walter Benjamin's Myth of the Flâneur." *Modern Language Review* 102.1 (2006): 139–56. Print.

Lawler, James R. *Poetry and Moral Dialectic: Baudelaire's Secret Architecture*. Madison: Fairleigh Dickinson UP, 1997. Print.

Leclerc, Yvan. *Crimes écrits: La Littérature en procès au XIXe siècle.* Paris: Plon, 1991. 223–81. Print.

Le Dantec, Y.-G., ed. *Œuvres en prose d'Edgar Allan Poe*. Paris: La Pléiade, 1951. Print.

Lefevere, André. *Translating Literature*. New York: MLA, 1992. Print.

Lemonnier, Léon. *Edgar Poe et les poètes français*. Paris: Nouvelle Revue Critique, 1932. Print.

Leroy, Christian. *La Poésie en prose française du XVIIe siècle à nos jours: Histoire d'un genre*. Paris: Champion, 2001. Print.

Lewis, Jon, ed. *The End of Cinema As We Know It: American Film in the Nineties*. New York: New York UP, 2001. Print.

Lionnet, Françoise. "Critical Conventions, Literary Landscapes, and Postcolonial Eco-criticism." McDonald and Suleiman 127–44.

———. "'The Indies': Baudelaire's Colonial World." *PMLA* 123.3 (2008): 723–36. Print.

———. Introduction. *Francophone Studies: New Landscapes*. Ed. Lionnet and Dominic Thomas. *MLN* 118.4 (2003): 783–86. Print.

———. *The Known and the Uncertain: Creole Cosmopolitics of the Indian Ocean*. Mauritius: L'Atelier d'Écriture, 2012. Print.

———. "Littérature-monde, francophonie et ironie: Modèles de violence et violence des modèles." *Parodies, pastiches, réécritures: La Question des modèles dans les littératures francophones*. Ed. Lise Gauvin and Cécile van den Avenne. Lyon: ENS, 2013. 80–94. Print.

———. "'New World' Exiles and Ironists from Evariste Parny to Ananda Devi." *Post-colonial Poetics*. Ed. Patrick Crowley and Jane Hiddleston. Liverpool: Liverpool UP, 2011. 13–34. Print.

———. "Reframing Baudelaire: Literary History, Biography, Postcolonial Theory, and Vernacular Languages." *Diacritics* 28.3 (1998): 63–85. Print.

———. "Universalisms and Francophonies." *International Journal of Francophone Studies* 12.2–3 (2009): 203–21. Print.

Llorca, Iris, and Valérie Thévenon. "L'Arabesque des éléments construisant la répétition entre *Les Fleurs du Mal* et *Le Spleen de Paris* de Charles Baudelaire." Vegliante 17–34.

Lloyd, Rosemary, ed. *Baudelaire's World*. Ithaca: Cornell UP, 2002. Print.

———, ed. *The Cambridge Companion to Baudelaire*. Cambridge: Cambridge UP, 2006. Print.

———. *Charles Baudelaire*. London: Reaktion, 2008. Print.

Loriot-Raymer, Gisèle, Michèle Vialet, and Judith Muyskens. *À vous d'écrire: Atelier de français*. New York: McGraw-Hill, 1996. Print.

Lowell, Robert. *Imitations*. New York: Farrar, 1961. Print.

Luhmann, Niklas. *Art as a Social System*. Trans. Eva Knodt. Stanford: Stanford UP, 2000. Print.

Lyu, Claire Chi-ah. *A Sun within a Sun: The Power and Elegance of Poetry*. Pittsburgh: U of Pittsburgh P, 2007. Print.

Maclean, Marie. *Narrative as Performance: The Baudelairean Experiment*. London: Routledge, 1988. Print.

Mainzer, Joseph. "Le Vitrier-Peintre." Curmer 2: 300–04.

Marion, Jean-Luc. *Prolegomena to Charity*. Trans. Stephen E. Lewis. New York: Fordham UP, 2002. Print.

Martin, Laurey K. "Breaking the Sounds of Silence: Promoting Discussion of Literary Texts in Intermediate Courses." *French Review* 6.4 (1993): 549–56. Print.

Marx, Karl. *The Eighteenth Brumaire of Louis Bonaparte*. 1852. *Marxists Internet Archive*. Web. 3 Sept. 2014. <https://www.marxists.org/archive/marx/works/1852/18th-brumaire/ch05.htm.>

———. "The Eighteenth Brumaire of Louis Bonaparte." *Karl Marx, Frederick Engels Collected Works*. Trans. Richard Dixon et al. Vol. 11. New York: Intl., 1979. 99–197. Print.

Marx, Karl, and Frederick Engels. *The Marx-Engels Reader*. Ed. Robert Tucker. New York: Norton, 1978. Print.

Mauron, Charles. *Le Dernier Baudelaire*. Paris: Corti, 1966. Print.

McDonald, Christie, and Susan Suleiman, eds. *French Global: A New Approach to Literary History*. New York: Columbia UP, 2010. Print.

McLees, Ainslie Armstrong. *Baudelaire's "Argot plastique": Poetic Caricature and Modernism*. Athens: U of Georgia P, 1989. Print.

Meitinger, Serge. "Les *Chansons madécasses* de Parny: Exotisme et libération de la forme poétique." *L'exotisme*. Ed. Alain Buisine and Norbert Dodille. Sainte Clotilde: Cahiers CRLH, 1988. 294–304. Print. CIRAOI 5.

Meltzer, Françoise. *Seeing Double: Baudelaire's Modernity*. Chicago: U of Chicago P, 2011. Print.

Metzidakis, Stamos. "Baudelaire et ses hypocrites lecteurs." *Orbis Litterarum* 44 (1989): 222–33. Print.

———. *Repetition and Semiotics: Interpreting Prose Poems.* Birmingham: Summa, 1986. Print.

Miller, J. Hillis. *The Ethics of Reading*. New York: Columbia UP, 1986. Print.

———. *The Linguistic Moment: From Wordsworth to Stevens*. Princeton: Princeton UP, 1987. Print.

Mills, Kathryn Oliver. *Formal Revolution in the Work of Baudelaire and Flaubert*. Newark: U of Delaware P, 2012. Print.

Mitchell, W. J. T., and Mark B. N. Hansen, eds. *Critical Terms for Media Studies*. Chicago: U of Chicago P, 2010. Print.

MLA Ad Hoc Committee on Foreign Languages. "Foreign Languages and Higher Education: New Structures for a Changed World." *Profession* (2007): 234–45. Print.

Monroe, Jonathan. *A Poverty of Objects: The Prose Poem and the Politics of Genre*. Ithaca: Cornell UP, 1987. Print.

Moore, Fabienne. *Prose Poems of the French Enlightenment: Delimiting Genre*. Farnham: Ashgate, 2009. Print.

Moretti, Franco. "Conjectures on World Literature." *New Left Review* 1 (2000): 54–68. Print.

Morozov, Evgeny. "Death of the Cyberflâneur." *The New York Times Sunday Review*. New York Times, 14 Feb. 2012. Web. 15 Sept. 2012. <http://www.nytimes.com/2012/02/05/opinion/sunday/the-death-of-the-cyberflaneur.html>

Murphy, Steve, ed. *Lectures de* Gaspard de la Nuit *de Louis ("Aloysius") Bertrand*. Rennes: PU de Rennes, 2010. Print.

———, ed. *Lectures du* Spleen de Paris. Rennes: PU de Rennes, 2014. Print.

———. *Logiques du dernier Baudelaire: Lectures du* Spleen de Paris. Paris: Champion, 2003. Print.

———. "*Le Mauvais Vitrier* ou la Crise du verre." *Romanic Review* 82.3 (1990): 339–49. Print.

Nadar. *Charles Baudelaire intime: Le Poète vierge*. 1911. Neuchâtel: Ides, 1994. Print.

Nakaji, Yoshikazu, and Keiji Suzuki, eds. *Baudelaire au Japon: Hommage à Yoshio Abé*. Paris: Champion, 2011. Print. L'Année Baudelaire 13–14.

Nancy, Jean-Luc. *La Création du monde ou la mondialisation*. Paris: Galilée, 2002. Print.

Nesci, Catherine. *Le Flâneur et les flâneuses: Les Femmes et la ville à l'époque romantique*. Grenoble: Ellug, 2007. Print.

New London Group. "A Pedagogy of Multiliteracies: Designing Social Futures." *Harvard Educational Review* 66.1 (1996): 60–92. Print.

Newmark, Kevin. "Traumatic Poetry: Charles Baudelaire and the Shock of Laughter." *Trauma: Explorations in Memory*. Ed. Cathy Caruth. Baltimore: Johns Hopkins UP, 1995. 236–55. Print.

Nietzsche, Friedrich. *The Gay Science*. Trans. Josefine Nauckhoff. Cambridge: Cambridge UP, 2001. Print.

Nünning, Ansgar, and Vera Nünning. *An Introduction to the Study of English and American Literature*. Trans. Jane Dewhurst. Stuttgart: Klett, 2004. Print.

Nussbaum, Martha. *Not for Profit: Why Democracy Needs the Humanities*. Princeton: Princeton UP, 2012. Print.

Ockenden, Alexander. "Baudelaire, Lacaussade and the Historical Identities of 'La Belle Dorothée.'" *French Studies Bulletin* 64.8 (2014): 64–68. Print.

Oehler, Dolf. *Le Spleen contre l'oubli: Baudelaire, Flaubert, Heine, Herzen*. Trans. Guy Petitdemange. Paris: Payot, 1996. Print.

Ortega, Lourdes, and Heidi Byrnes, eds. *The Longitudinal Study of Advanced L2 Capacities*. New York: Routledge, 2008. Print.

Oukada, Larbi, Didier Bertrand, and Janet L. Solberg. *Controverses*. 2nd ed. Boston: Heinle, 2011. Print.

Paesani, Kate. "Using Literature to Develop Foreign Language Proficiency: Toward an Interactive Classroom." *Nineteenth- and Twentieth-Century French Literary Studies: Pedagogical Strategies*. Ed. Charles J. Stivale. New York: MLA, 2004. 13–25. Print.

Paris, Bernard J. *Karen Horney: A Psychoanalyst's Search for Self-Understanding*. New Haven: Yale UP, 1994. Print.

Parny, Évariste de. *Œuvres de Parny: Elégies et poésies diverses*. Paris: Garnier, 1862. Print.

Pichois, Claude, and Jean Ziegler. *Baudelaire*. Paris: Julliard, 1987. Print.

———. *Baudelaire*. Trans. Graham Robb. London: Hamilton, 1989. Print.

———. *Baudelaire et l'Allemagne. L'Allemagne et Baudelaire*. Paris: Champion, 2004. Print. L'Année Baudelaire 8.

Pinson, Guillaume, and Maxime Prévost, eds. *Penser la littérature par la presse.* Spec. issue of *Études littéraires* 40.3 (2009): 7–171. Print.

Poe, Edgar Allan. *The Complete Edgar Allan Poe Tales.* New York: Avenel, 1981. Print.

———. *Histoires Extraordinaires.* Trans. Charles Baudelaire. Paris: Michel Lévy Frères, 1856. Print.

———. *Histoires Grotesques et Sérieuses.* Trans. Charles Baudelaire. Paris: Michel Lévy Frères, 1865. Print.

———. "The Man of the Crowd." *Selected Writings of Edgar Allan Poe.* Ed. G. R. Thompson. New York: Norton, 2004. 232–39. Print.

———. *Nouvelles Histoires Extraordinaires.* Trans. Charles Baudelaire. Paris: Michel Lévy Frères, 1869. Print.

Polio, Charlene, and Eve Zyzik. "Don Quixote Meets *Ser* and *Estar*: Multiple Perspectives on Language Learning in Spanish Literature Classes." *Modern Language Journal* 93.4 (2009): 550–69. Print.

Porter, Laurence M., ed. *Approaches to Teaching Baudelaire's* Flowers of Evil. New York: MLA, 2000. Print.

———. "Baudelaire and Walter Benjamin." *The Nineteenth Century.* Ed. David Baguley. Syracuse: Syracuse UP, 1994. 798–800. Print. Vol. 5, pt. 2 of *A Critical Bibliography of French Literature.*

———. *The Crisis of French Symbolism.* Ithaca: Cornell UP, 1990. Print.

———. Preface to the Volume. Porter, *Approaches to Teaching* 1–5.

Poulet, Georges. *Studies in Human Time.* Trans. Elliot Coleman. Baltimore: Johns Hopkins UP, 1956. Print.

Prendergast, Christopher. *Paris in the Nineteenth Century.* Cambridge: Blackwell, 1992. Print.

Queffélec, Lise. *Le Roman-feuilleton français au XIXe siècle.* Paris: PUF, 1989. Print.

Queneau, Raymond. *Exercices de style.* Paris: Gallimard, 1947. Print.

Racault, Jean-Michel. *Mémoires du Grand Océan: Des relations de voyage aux littératures francophones de l'océan Indien.* Paris: P de U Paris, Sorbonne, 2007. Print.

Richardson, Joanna. *Baudelaire: A Biography.* New York: St. Martin's, 1994. Print.

Ricoeur, Paul. *Fallible Man.* Trans. Charles Kelbley. Chicago: Regnery, 1965. Print.

Riffaterre, Michael. *Semiotics of Poetry.* Bloomington: Indiana UP, 1978. Print.

Rignall, John. *Realist Fiction and the Strolling Spectator.* London: Routledge, 1992. Print.

Robb, Graham. *La Poésie de Baudelaire et la poésie française 1832–1852.* Paris: Aubier, 1993. Print.

———, ed. *Le Corsaire-Satan en Silhouette: Le Milieu journalistique de la jeunesse de Baudelaire.* [By Auguste Vitu?]. Nashville: Vanderbilt UP, 1985. Print. Publications du Centre W. T. Bandy d'Études baudelairiennes 3.

Rousseau, Jean-Jacques. *Les Confessions.* Vol. 1. Paris: Flammarion, 1968. Print.

Runyon, Randolph Paul. *Intratextual Baudelaire: The Sequential Fabric of the* Fleurs du Mal *and* Spleen de Paris. Columbus: Ohio State UP, 2010. Print.

Ruprecht, Hans-George. "Aspects du baudelairisme mexicain." *Comparative Literature Studies* 11.2 (1974): 99–122. Print.

Said, Edward. *The World, the Text, the Critic.* Cambridge: Harvard UP, 1983. Print.

Salines, Emily. *Alchemy and Amalgam: Translation in the Works of Charles Baudelaire.* Amsterdam: Rodopi, 2004. Print.

Sandras, Michel. *Lire le poème en prose.* Paris: Dunod, 1995. Print.

Sanyal, Debarati. *The Violence of Modernity: Baudelaire, Irony, and the Poetics of Form.* Baltimore: Johns Hopkins UP, 2006. Print.

Sartre, Jean-Paul. *Baudelaire.* Paris: Gallimard, 1946. Print.

Schlegel, Friedrich. "Athenäums-Fragment No. 116." *Kritische Ausgabe.* Ed. Ernst Behler. Vol. 2. Paderborn: Schöningh, 1967. Print.

Schleiermacher, Friedrich. "On the Different Methods of Translating." Venuti, *Translation* [2012] 43–63.

Schlossman, Beryl. "Baudelaire l'extravagant." *(Res)sources de l'extravagance, Carnets, Revista Electrónica de Estudos Franceses* 4 (2012): 85–96. Print.

———. "Benjamin's *Ueber Einige Motive bei Baudelaire*: The Secret Architecture of 'Correspondances.'" *Modern Language Notes* 107.3 (1992): 548–79. Print.

———. "'Le Cygne'—Paris Downstream." *Critical Insights: The Poetry of Baudelaire.* Ed. Tom Hubbard. Amenia: Grey House; Salem, 2014. 106–25. Print.

———. "Images of the Aura: Some Motifs in French Modernism." *Actualities of Aura: Twelve Studies of Walter Benjamin.* Ed. Dag Petersson and Eric Steinskog. Göteborg: Nordicom, 2005. 281–95. Print.

———. "Les Métamorphoses Littéraires." *Carnets V, Revista Electrónica de Estudos Franceses.* Forthcoming.

———. *The Orient of Style: Allegories of Conversion.* Durham: Duke UP, 1991. Print.

———. "Review Essay on Walter Benjamin, *The Writer of Modern Life*: Essays on Charles Baudelaire." *H-France Review* 8 (2008): 87. Print.

Schlumpf, Erin. "Intermediality, Translation, Comparative Literature, and World Literature." *CLCWeb* 13.3 (2011): n. pag. Web. 14 Aug. 2014.

Schmidt, Siegfried J. *Why Literature Is Not Enough; or, Literary Studies as Media Studies.* Siegen: LUMIS, 1990. Print.

Schofer, Peter, and Donald B. Rice. *Autour de la littérature.* 3rd ed. Boston: Heinle, 2006. Print.

Schröter, Jens. "Discourses and Models of Intermediality." *CLCWeb* 13.3 (2011): n. pag. Web. 14 Aug. 2014.

Schultz, Jean Marie. "The Gordian Knot: Language, Literature, and Critical Thinking." Scott and Tucker 3–31.

Scott, Clive. *Translating Baudelaire.* Exeter: U of Exeter P, 2008. Print.

Scott, David. "Le Poème en prose comme symptôme de crise littéraire: Hétérogénéité et déconstruction dans *Le Spleen de Paris* de Baudelaire." *L'Esprit Créateur* 39.1 (1999): 5–14. Print.

Scott, Maria. *Baudelaire's* Le Spleen de Paris: *Shifting Perspectives.* Aldershot: Ashgate, 2005. Print.

———. *"La Belle Dorothée*, ou les taches aveugles du regard idéaliste-matérialiste." *Lectures du* Spleen de Paris. Ed. Steve Murphy. Rennes: PU Rennes, 2014. 237–50. Print.

———. "Intertextes et mystifications dans les poèmes en prose de Baudelaire." *Romantisme* 156.2 (2012): 63–73. Print.

Scott, Virginia, and Holly Tucker, eds. *SLA and the Literature Classroom: Fostering Dialogues.* Boston: Heinle, 2001. Print.

Seth, Catriona. "Les *Chansons madécasses* de Parny: Une Poésie des origines aux origines du poème en prose." Vincent-Munnia, Bernard-Griffiths, and Pickering 447–57.

Shakespeare, Alex. "Reading Hemingway's Baudelaire." *Literary Imagination* 14.2 (2012): 237–244. Print.

Shattuck, Roger. "Vibratory Organism: *Crise de prose*." Caws and Riffaterre 21–35.

Sheringham, Michael. *Everyday Life: Theories and Practices from Surrealism to the Present*. Oxford: Oxford UP, 2006. Print.

Simon, Jules. *Le Devoir*. Paris: Hachette, 1856. Print.

Siskin, H. Jay, Cheryl L. Krueger, and Maryse Fauvel. *Tâches d'encre: French Composition*. 3rd ed. Boston: Heinle, 2011. Print.

Sontag, Susan. *On Photography.* New York: Farrar, 1978. Print.

Spadon, Gino. *Scomposizione e analisi del poemetto baudelariano* La Chambre double. Venezia: Pistellato, 1983. Print.

Spivak, Gayatri. "The Politics of Translation." Venuti, *Translation* [2000] 397–416.

Starkie, Enid. *Baudelaire.* New York: New Directions, 1958. Print.

Starobinski, Jean. *La Mélancolie au miroir*. Paris: Julliard, 1989. Print.

Steiner, George. "The Hermeneutic Motion." Venuti, *Translation* [2012] 156–61.

Steinmetz, Jean-Luc. "Pour en finir avec les 'petits romantiques.'" *Revue d'histoire littéraire de la France* 105.4 (2005): 891–12. *Cairn*. Web. 20 Oct. 2012.

Stephens, Sonya. *Baudelaire's Prose Poems: The Practice and Politics of Irony*. Oxford: Oxford UP, 1999. Print.

———. "The Prose Poems." Lloyd, *Cambridge Companion* 69–87.

———. "Unfamiliarity and Defamiliarization: Teaching *Les Fleurs du Mal* with the *Petits Poèmes en prose*." Porter, *Approaches* 93–99.

Swaffar, Janet K., and Katherine M. Arens. *Remapping the Foreign Language Curriculum: An Approach through Multiple Literacies*. New York: MLA, 2005. Print.

Szarkowski, John. *Mirrors and Windows: American Photography since 1960*. New York: MOMA, 1978. Print.

Tapscott, Don. *Grown Up Digital*. New York: McGraw, 2009. Print.

Terdiman, Richard. *Discourse/Counter-discourse: The Theory and Practice of Symbolic Resistance in Nineteenth-Century France*. Ithaca: Cornell UP, 1985. Print.

Tester, Keith. *The Flâneur*. London: Routledge, 1994. Print.

Thérenty, Marie-Ève. *La Littérature au quotidien: Poétiques journalistiques au XIXe siècle*. Paris: Seuil, 2007. Print.

Thérenty, Marie-Ève, and Alain Vaillant. *1836: L'An I de l'ère médiatique: Analyse litté-raire et historique de* La Presse *de Girardin*. Paris: Nouveau Monde, 2001. Print.

———, eds. *Presse and Plumes. Journalisme et littérature au XIXᵉ siècle*. Paris: Nouveau Monde, 2004. Print.

Thompson, William J., ed. *Understanding* Les Fleurs du Mal*: Critical Readings*. Nashville: Vanderbilt UP, 1997. Print.

Trainor, James. "Walking the Walk*." Border Crossings* 88 (2008): 82–92. Web. 15 Sept. 2012.

Turkle, Sherry. *Alone Together: Why We Expect More from Technology and Less from Each Other*. New York: Basic, 2011. Print.

Vaillant, Alain. "L'Article de tête." Kalifa, Régnier, Thérenty, and Vaillant 893–905.

———. "Baudelaire, artiste moderne de la 'poésie-journal.'" Pinson and Prévost 43–60.

———. *Baudelaire, poète comique*. Rennes: PU de Rennes, 2007. Print.

———. "Charles Baudelaire (1821–1867)." Kalifa, Régnier, Thérenty, and Vaillant 1189–96.

———. Introduction. *Baudelaire journaliste* 7–33.

———. "La Presse littéraire." Kalifa, Régnier, Thérenty, and Vaillant 317–32.

———. "Le Vers à l'épreuve du journal." Disegni, *Poésie* 11–27.

Vegliante, Jean-Charles, ed. *De la prose au cœur de la poésie*. Paris: Sorbonne Nouvelle, 2007. Print.

Venuti, Lawrence, ed. *The Translation Studies Reader*. New York: Routledge, 2000. Print.

———, ed. *The Translation Studies Reader*. 3rd ed. New York: Routledge, 2012. Print.

———. *The Translator's Invisibility: A History of Translation*. 2nd ed. Abingdon: Routledge, 2008. Print.

Vincent-Munnia, Nathalie. "La Naissance du poème en prose français et la presse." Disegni, *Poésie* 29–41.

———. *Les Premiers Poèmes en prose: Généalogie d'un genre dans la première moitié du dix-neuvième siècle français*. Paris: Champion, 1996. Print.

Vincent-Munnia, Nathalie, Simone Bernard-Griffiths, and Robert Pickering, eds. *Aux origines du poème en prose français (1750–1850)*. Paris: Champion, 2003. Print.

Wallaert, Ineke. "Baudelaire's Rewriting of Poe's Fancy and Imagination." D'Amelio 81–99.

Wanner, Adrian. *Baudelaire in Russia*. Gainesville: U of Florida P, 1996. Print.

Weber, Samuel. *Benjamin's -abilities*. Cambridge: Harvard UP, 2008. Print.

———. *Inquiétantes singularités*. Paris: Hermann, 2014. Print.

———. *Mass Mediauras: Form, Technics, Media*. Stanford: Stanford UP, 1996. Print.

Weil, Simone. *Gravity and Grace*. Trans. Emma Crawford and Mario von der Ruhr. London: Routledge, 2002. Print.

White, Edmund. *The Flâneur: A Stroll through the Paradoxes of Paris*. New York: Bloomsbury, 2001. Print.

Wolf, Werner. "(Inter)Mediality and the Study of Literature." *CLCWeb* 13.3 (2011): n. pag. Web. 14 Aug. 2014.

Wordsworth, William. *Complete Poetical Works. Bartleby.com.* Bartleby.com, 1999. Web. 6 Nov. 2015.

Wright, Barbara, and David H. T. Scott. *Baudelaire:* La Fanfarlo *and* Le Spleen de Paris. London: Grant and Cutler, 1984. Print. Critical Guides to French Texts 30.

Yvan, Melchior-Honoré. *De France en Chine*. Paris: Bibliothèque des Chemins de Fer, 1855. Print.

INDEX OF NAMES